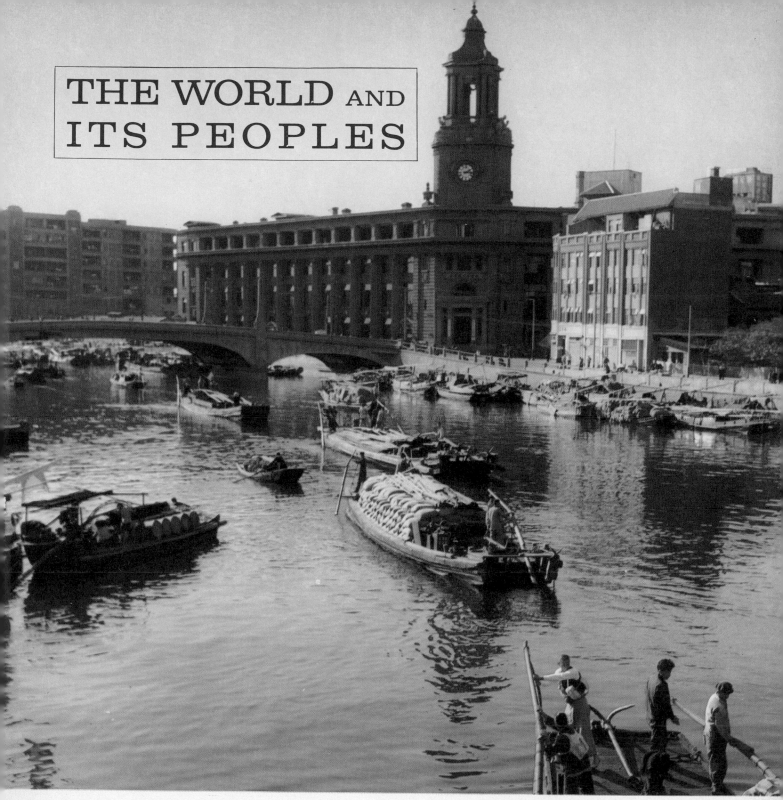

THE WORLD AND ITS PEOPLES

Merchant boats on the river at Shanghai.

CHINA

GREYSTONE PRESS/NEW YORK

Library of Congress Catalog Number: 65-10536

Cover and Book Designed by Harold Franklin

THE WORLD AND ITS PEOPLES—EDITORS AND CONTRIBUTORS

Table of Contents

PEOPLE'S REPUBLIC
OF CHINA

REPUBLIC OF
CHINA (TAIWAN)

MONGOLIA

A view of a well-preserved section of the Great Wall of China.

Peasants work terraced land in south-central China.

CHINA

a prologue

TODAY, THE COLOSSUS OF CHINA WITH ITS ESTIMATED 700 million people, occupying a land space nearly the size of Europe, stands menacingly poised under the direction of Communist rulers who aim to dictate from a position of strength the future course of world history—to choose between the road to international conflict or the highway to peace through co-existence with the non-Communist world.

The awakening of the sleeping giant—the emergence of the nation from the limbo of four milleniums of impotent languor—has occurred less than two decades since China, weak to the point of almost total collapse, emerged as one of the victorious powers at the close of World War II, in 1945.

For another five years, the long-suffering Chinese people faced the ravages of a civil war in which the Communist armies of Mao Tse-tung drove down from the former Japanese arsenals in Manchuria to sweep to exile, on the island fortress of Taiwan, Generalissimo Chiang Kai-shek and his Kuomintang (Nationalist) government.

From the ruins of the war against Japan, which began in 1937, and the devastation of the internecine strife that followed, there emerged the People's Republic of China, entrenched in absolute power within the massive city walls of ancient Peking.

Today, the People's Republic of China, stretching in an immense checker-board of towering mountain fastnesses, great river valleys and immense plains, from the sub-tropical borders of North Vietnam and Burma to the bleak, sub-zero harshness of Tibet and Russian Siberia, casts its imposing shadow over Southeast Asia and, indeed, over the divided post-war world.

China, bellicose, fanatically dedicated to the ruthless Communism of Marx, Lenin and Stalin, stands outside the councils of the United Nations; she is grimly determined to pursue, or so present-day portents would seem to indicate, a course of extending her type of totalitarianism, by subversion or force of arms, to her neighbors and even those countries outside the periphery of Southeast Asia, her sphere of greatest influence.

THE PEOPLE'S REPUBLIC OF CHINA TODAY IS, IN MOST respects, a vast land of regimentation and of puritanical dedication to the Communism of Mao Tse-tung and his cadres. Its 700 million people (many say that this is a conservative estimate of the population) have been conscripted, willingly or not, into the two forces that have been created to take the country, by great leaps forward, into a position of international strength: these forces are the military machine and the labor battalion of industry and agriculture.

China's army, which shocked the Free World by its mass-assault successes in its intervention in the Korean War and which now stands menacing India from the border of conquered Tibet, is believed to have a strength of about two million well-trained and well-equipped regulars. There are an estimated two million more in the provincial militia units, which are similar to America's National Guard or Britain's part-time Territorial Army.

The labor force, industrial and agricultural, consists of the remainder of the able-bodied population, both male and female.

To accomplish its great drive forward from the stagnation of the immediate post-war years, the directors of the Communist juggernaut in Peking have, amazingly in view of China's history, almost totally eradicated the age-old foundations of Chinese life, the Confucian precepts of filial devotion to family groups, the influence of religion, the inferior position of women, rigid class distinction and, most important of all, Chinese opposition to regimentation in any form.

The condition of China when the Communists came to power was pitiful. Large areas of the country had been devastated by civil war. The Kuomintang government, weakened by mass corruption and inefficiency, was powerless to halt the relentless tide of inflation which saw the national currency reduced to a pathetic travesty of its pre-war stability. Workers carried home millions of dollars each week as their wages; in actual value these were the equivalent of a very few American dollars. Food was scarce. Black markets flourished. Speculators cashed in. Millions of American dollars were made by racketeers in the former treaty ports of Shanghai, Tsingtao, Tientsin and the other large cities. Large amounts of grain, flour and other foodstuffs sent in by the United Nations Relief and Rehabilitation Agency, to stave off a threatened national famine, finished up in the warehouses of the speculators.

A man carrying his burden in the ancient way. The poster in the background displays modern machine parts and a lesson in reading.

Soldiers of Mao Tse-tung defend the Great Wall of China.

IN THE VAST HINTERLAND, THE PEASANTRY FACED starvation. In the coastal cities, many of them built and run by foreigners for nearly a century, the only change was that China was now absolute master of its own territory. In 1943, Britain, the United States and the other treaty powers had renounced their extraterritorial rights and Shanghai, Tientsin and the other little foreign enclaves were handed back to China.

Despite the appalling conditions in the interior, life was full of joy for the favored few everywhere. While hundreds of thousands of peasants flocked to the coast in search of work, the beautiful cabaret girls, the sing-song girls, the opium-den hostesses in Shanghai and the large cities catered to the high government officials, the wealthy businessmen and the opulent racketeers in well-known night-spots.

But all this Bacchanalian revelry had no place in the Communist scheme of things. By 1950, when the metropolis of Shanghai was firmly in Communist hands, the transformation was well under way.

Boatload after boatload of foreigners, many of whom had lived in China all their lives, now left. One after the other, the night-spots were closed.

Shanghailanders saw prostitutes, rounded up by Communist cadres, start rehabilitation courses with weeks of work at street-sweeping. Revelers were paraded in ridicule through the streets. Black-marketeers were arrested and sent to forced labor camps.

Above: *An oil refinery at Fushun, northeast China.*

Left: *Chinese children skillfully manipulate chopsticks.*

On a lake in hilly country, some Chinese children fish.

WITH ALMOST BARBARIC RUTHLESSNESS, THE COMMUNISTS turned to the task of shaping China into the enormous barracks it is today. The "capitalists" (shopkeepers, factory-owners, landlords and well-to-do peasantry), the Kuomintang government officials, the "foreign-influenced" professors, students and hundreds of other "anti-revolutionary elements" were hounded to suicide or dragged through streets crowded with jeering mobs to be executed.

Millions of others, who were considered unsuitable material for the "People's China," were sent on forced labor, building railroads, roads and bridges. Most of them, unused to such back-breaking toil, died.

Today, with years of experience behind them, the Communist cadres have relaxed their iron rule, and the life of the people, though grim by Western standards, is easier.

Women, for instance, are discarding the short crops, the cotton jackets and trousers and the workers' caps, which disguised their femininity and turned them into sexless robots working in offices, factories and other nationalized undertakings.

Today, in Peking, in Shanghai, almost everywhere, bright dresses, high-heeled shoes and make-up are re-appearing. But, compared with their sisters in the nearby British colony of Hong Kong, the Chinese women of the Communist revolution are drab and dowdy.

Shanghai, the great port and industrial center in Kiangsi province.

THE COMMUNISTS CONCENTRATED ON THE YOUTH OF China. Backed by the university students, most of whom were sympathetic, they began the task of destroying the foundations of family life, the influence of religion, capitalist structures, indeed, every aspect of the age-old Chinese way of life so long dominated by the principles of the sage Confucius.

There came the appalling sight of sons and daughters handing over "counter-revolutionary" fathers to the Communist "people's courts." In the countryside, peasants (long held in serfdom by landlords and money-lenders) took justice into their own hands and massacred their "exploiters."

Christian missionaries, priests and nuns, all of them devoted to the Chinese people, were walked in degrading processions through the crowds of Canton, Shanghai, Peking, Chungking and elsewhere for public trial. They were tortured, jailed and robbed.

Most of the foreign priests and nuns are now out of China, but some still linger on in the prisons of the land. The few remaining followers of Christian denominations are all "reformed" and have been forced to swear allegiance to the state and its leader.

Peasants gather the rice harvest. Rice is China's staple food crop.

Ironworks at Anshan on the Liaotung peninsula, northeast China.

IT WAS THE SAME WITH BUDDHISM, WITH TAOISM, WITH Confucianism. Believers toed the Communist line — or else.

By and large, the followers of the different religions on the China scene today are middle-aged or elderly. Their influence on the life of the Godless state is infinitesimal.

The youth of China has been indoctrinated. Young men and women, everywhere, are ardent Communists. The family system has been broken. The young attend the universities of the land, many of them founded by American or European Christians. They live in a communal world of hostels, of self-criticism meetings, of Five-Year Plans and anti-imperialist campaigns.

The women of China, traditionally "worthless creatures," have come into their own. Side by side with men, they drive tractors, fly airplanes, drop by parachute, play tough games and lose their femininity in hardened muscles and rough speech. Gone are the fragile "butterflies" of yesteryear whose only task was to brighten the life of Chinese males.

On the sports front, there is state support for every form of athletic activity. The Chinese shine at table-tennis, at weight-lifting, at soccer, at track and field.

In urban and agricultural centers there are weekly meetings; citizens are divided into district and village groups. At these meetings the latest government projects are debated, hygiene and cleanliness are taught and Communist cadres foster the causes of Peking.

For entertainment, there are films which are boring by Western standards; all are geared to the cause of Communism and the evils of capitalism or imperialism. There are traveling stage-shows, again bringing their lesson of Communistic happiness in serving the state. There are sports festivals. Dances (such as the Yangko) are permitted, but not the Twist or the rock and roll of the modern-day Free World.

All in all, life in China today is, judged by Western standards, a monotonous, dull, regimented existence.

The state runs its government stores. It dictates the entertainment habits of the people. Its efficient hand is everywhere. Its spies abound in every stratum of society, and distrust is a part of daily life.

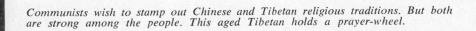

Communists wish to stamp out Chinese and Tibetan religious traditions. But both are strong among the people. This aged Tibetan holds a prayer-wheel.

WHAT HAS BEEN ACHIEVED SINCE THE EARLY 1950s? HAS China, with its clannish groupings, its countless dialects, its lack of patriotic fervor, been welded into a homogenous whole?

On the surface, success would appear to have been achieved. But when fear is the dominant feeling in so many walks of life, it might be regarded as only a paper success likely to collapse in any strong and determined confrontation of Peking by the outside world.

Nevertheless, with the youth of China behind it, the Communist government of Mao Tse-tung has made rapid strides in transforming the old lackadaisical "Middle Kingdom" into a bastion of strength.

Chinese scientists, aided at the start by the Russians, are on the way to making their country a nuclear power.

A typical primitive Chinese bridge spans the Sancha Ho in Kweichow.

The railway bridge over the Yangtze at Wuhan, Hupeh.

IN OCTOBER, 1964, IT WAS ANNOUNCED THAT CHINA HAD made successful nuclear test explosions. Soon China may rank alongside the U.S., the Soviet Union, Britain and France.

New railways have been built to open up the formerly inaccessible hinterland regions such as Szechwan, where the 400-mile Chungking-Chengtu line was completed in three years. Today, the rich mineral deposits of the southwest may travel quickly to the borders of the Soviet Union or to the coast by rail.

The Eastern Lanchow-Sinkiang Railway is nearing completion. This has converted Lanchow, terminus of the Lunghai Railway, into a central-China junction with the new line spreading out to Alma Ata, Soviet Central Asia, the Gobi desert and the vastness of remote Sinkiang.

Mao Tse-tung, Chairman of the Central Committee of the Chinese Party, proclaiming in a radio broadcast the establishment of the Chinese People's Republic in 1949.

LINES ARE CONNECTING THE VAST NEW STEEL CENTER AT Paotow with the Soviet Union and with the coastal ports.

Up to 1957, 6000 miles of new railroads were built. Backed by Soviet technical experts, over 200 major projects were started in inland China, away from the vulnerable coastline industrial belt.

The great Yellow River ("China's Sorrow," as it has been called) has been dammed to prevent floods. Rich silt is being gathered to aid agricultural programs instead of being carried out to sea.

Land-irrigation schemes have been started in the Yellow River and the Yangtse River basins. These mighty waterways have been harnessed to provide electrical power, and thus play their vital part in the plan to build a new and powerful society.

Right: *This Chinese classical actor portrays a military character, striking an enigmatical pose which expresses the uncertainty of China's place in relation to the modern world.*

Small children play in a tree-lined avenue in Kunming, Yunnan.

Nationalist (Kuomintang) troops march through Taipei, Taiwan.

TO ACCOMPLISH CHINA'S GOAL OF INDUSTRIAL AND agricultural strength (the final aim is parity with the United States in, perhaps, forty years' time) millions of peasants are being used as a never-ending labor force. And, with an enormous birth-rate, there is no danger of agriculture being side-tracked.

There has been a succession of agricultural failures, and famine conditions occur in many parts of the land. Even today, the agricultural picture is gloomy. Food, in huge quantities, must be imported, mainly from the Soviet Union and Eastern Europe.

China still has a long way to go to overcome the neglect of the past. But she has immense and rich mineral deposits within her reach. She could be, by the end of the century, self-sufficient in raw materials and, like the United States, independent to a major degree of the rest of the world.

So far, only a start has been made, but the results to date are phenomenal if the immense difficulties and the heritage of indolence left over by Chinese history are taken into account.

THE LAND

THE CHINESE REGION

Geographical Position and Contours

ON A MAP OF ASIA THE REGION OF China appears as a compact land mass shaped like a broad, irregular wedge. It stretches westward from the Pacific coast of Asia as far as the Pamir mountains in Central Asia and occupies the whole of central east Asia. Its boundaries extend from Moho in the Amur basin in the north down to Bastion Cape on the island of Hainan in the south, with its east-west extremities at the Amur-Ussuri confluence and the Pamir mountains respectively.

China is almost as large as Europe and nearly one-quarter the size of

Agricultural workers tending the young plants in the ricefields of east Kwangtung. The cultivation of rice, China's most important crop, involves a great deal of arduous and often delicate work, including planting, transplanting, thinning out shoots and keeping the roots of the plants clean.

The Potala, a palace, a monastery, a fortress and a shrine, is situated on the outskirts of Lhasa, the capital of Tibet. The building of the Potala complex was begun in 1641 and until the occupation of Tibet by soldiers of the Chinese People's Republic, it was the center of the Tibetan Buddhist faith. Prior to his flight to India, the Dalai Lama, spiritual ruler of Tibet, made the Potala his seat.

Asia, with an area of around 3,691,502 square miles. Its estimated population in 1963 was 716,000,000, or over 20 per cent of the total world population.

Few countries are as clearly defined geographically as China. The exact boundaries separating the country from its neighbors have for centuries been so clearly marked as to constitute an almost physical barrier, keeping China isolated from the rest of the world and giving a peculiar individuality to its civilization. Only in the present day, when the Chinese government has begun to make territorial demands from its neighbors, have certain of the country's boundaries become less well defined.

FRONTIER CHANGES

However, the frontiers of China have undergone wide changes during the course of its history. The first Chinese civilization grew up in the lower reaches of the Yellow River (Hwang Ho) in the time of the Hsia dynasty (2205-1766 B.C.); in the time of the Mongol dynasty (1280-1368 A.D.) its boundaries extended to the frontiers of Poland and the shores of the Aegean in the west, to the island of Sakhalin in the north, and

to Vietnam and Burma in the south. In the interval between these two territorial extremes, however, and in the past few centuries, the Sino-Mongolian race has generally remained within the accepted physical boundaries of China, and has progressively become consolidated there.

Some of China's physical boundaries are clearly defined, others are less clear. Among the well-defined boundaries are the eastern coastal border on the Pacific Ocean; the boundary formed by the watershed of the Himalayan and Karakoram ranges in the southwest and the Pamirs in the west; the Tien Shan range, the Altai mountains, the Kentei mountains and the Argun-Amur River in the north; and the Ussuri, Tumen and Yalu rivers in the northeast.

The less well-defined boundaries include the frontiers with Burma, Laos and Vietnam, the boundaries between Dzungaria and Soviet Kazakhstan and parts of the Mongolian-Siberian border. However, in areas with no clearly marked barriers of mountains or rivers, there are other factors which are equally effective as obstacles including the rugged country on the borders of Burma and Laos,

China's ocean frontier is divided into four principal sections. These are: (i) the Pohai (Po Sea) or Gulf of Chihli, enclosed by the two peninsulas of Liaotung and Shantung; (ii) the Hwang Hai, or Yellow Sea, extending southeastward from the two peninsulas as far as the mouth of the Yangtze River; (iii) the Tung Hai, or East China Sea, extending from the mouth of the Yangtze River to the island of Taiwan; (iv) the Nan Hai, or South China Sea, extending from south of the island of Taiwan to south of the Indochina peninsula.

OFFSHORE ISLANDS

There are numerous islands off the Chinese coast, the largest being Taiwan (Formosa) and Hainan. Smaller islands which are particularly numerous off the coasts of Chekiang, Fukien and Kwangtung provinces, include Quemoy, in the Bay of Amoy, the Chushan Archipelago, outside the Bay of Hangchow, and the Pescadores, or Penghu islands in Formosa Strait. In addition there are the coral atolls of the Nan Shan group in the extreme south of the South China Sea.

China is divided geographically into China Proper (which is bordered by the Pacific in the east and south, by the Great Wall in the north and approximately by the 100th Meridian East in the west) and other regions which, while Chinese territory, are geographically dissimilar to China Proper.

Geological Characteristics

The landscape of China varies considerably in its physical characteristics, with mountainous regions predominating. This is mainly due to the fact that the territory was one of the first land masses of the earth to assume a definite shape·and it has been the scene of a continuous and complex process of corrugation of the earth's crust. The strong seismic disturbances recorded in the first half of the 20th century in Kansu, northwest China, and Yunnan, southwest China, show that the phase of settlement is not yet complete.

Scientific research into the complexity of China's geological formations has only been going on for a few decades. The first national geological project was initiated in the 1930s, but it was not until after the formation of the People's Republic that research on a large scale was begun in the more remote regions.

Modern research has established that the territory of China is formed by three separate land masses, dating from the Pre-Cambrian, or Archaean Era. Chinese geologists have termed these three areas Tibetia, in the west, Gobia, in the north, and Cathaysia, in the southeast.

These masses, which are composed of crystalline and metamorphic rocks, such as gneiss, feldspar, granite, quartz and schists, have to a great extent withstood successive subsidences of the sea-bed and the upward movements of the earth's crust by which mountain ranges are created. They form the foundations of the major mountain and hill systems both in the areas of the Tibetan and Mongolian plateaus and in the eastern regions. In the latter region, the Pre-Cambrian formations are arranged in three massive belts, running parallel to each other from northeast to southwest.

The first belt forms the principal mountain massifs on the island of Hainan and in Kwangtung and Kiangsu-Fukien. The second forms the greater part of the mountains along the Sino-Korean frontier, the hills of the peninsulas of Shantung and Liaotung and the mountain massifs that divided China Proper into North and South China. The third belt forms the northernmost part of the Ta Khingan Shan, or Great Khingan range, and the parts of the Yin Shan range that separate North China from Mongolia.

The principal mountain ranges of central China, running from east to west, were formed in the Palaeozoic Era.

The Caledonian Era saw the formation of the great mountain system that traverses China from the Karakorams in the far west to the basin of the Yangtze River, including the Kunlun and Tsinling ranges and the parallel ranges of the Tien Shan and the Altai, and extending to the Shansi and Taiping mountains in the southeast of Szechwan.

The lower mountain massifs in the regions of Tsinghai, or Ch'ing-Hai, Chamdo, eastern Szechwan, Yunnan and Kwangsi, date from the Hercynian or mid-Upper Carboniferous period of folding.

The major coal basins of northern and central China were formed toward the end of the Palaeozoic Era.

During the Mesozoic Era, an extensive process of sedimentation took place in China. This silted up some of the largest basins of the country, among them those of northern Tibet, Szechwan and Shensi.

Comparatively few outcrops date from the Triassic period; among them are the tablelands of Kweichow-Kwangsi, the central part of Yunnan, and the outcrops in the Wushan, the mouth of the Yangtze River, and in the gorges enclosing the Yellow River which separates the provinces of Shansi and Shensi.

The period between the end of the Jurassic Era and the beginning of the Cretaceous period saw a greater amount of change in the formation of the earth's crust. As well as a continuation of the process of sedimentation, there was a certain amount of orogenic, or mountain producing, movement. This was responsible for

A section of the railroad line between Paoki, a commercial center in southwest Shensi, and Chengtu, a commercial center in the red basin of Szechwan. The line, constructed recently, is of considerable economic importance. Construction was made difficult by the nature of the terrain to be traversed, which included the outcrops of the Tsingling and Motien Ling mountains.

EASTERN ASIA

CHINA
Principal Cities

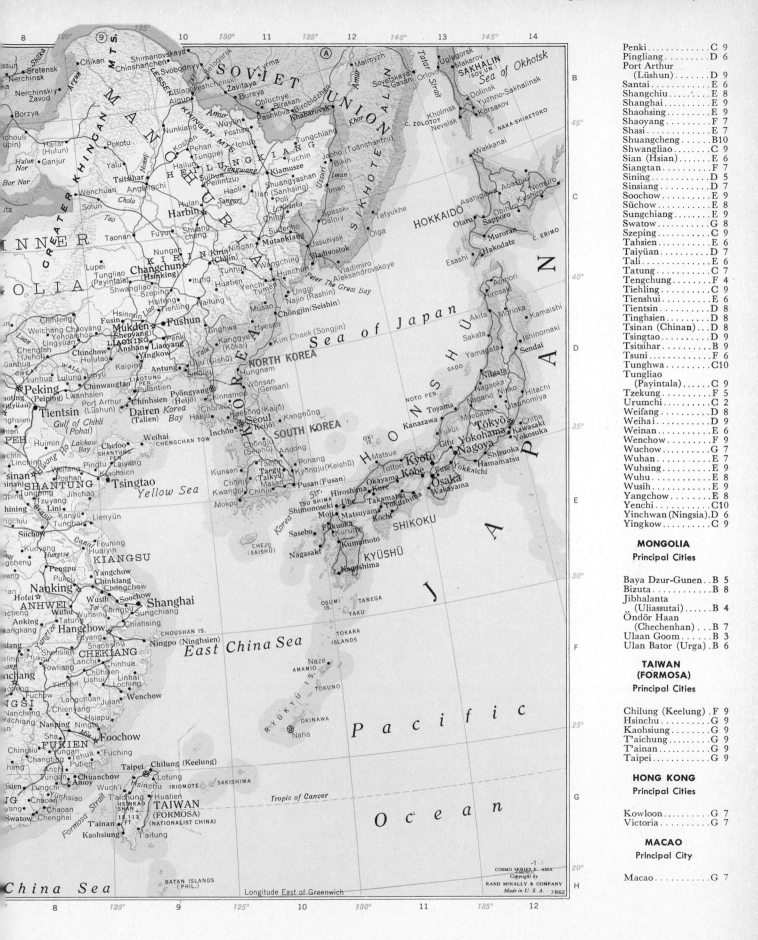

COSMO SERIES E. ASIA
Copyright by
RAND McNALLY & COMPANY
Made in U. S. A. 7R62

the formation of the Yin Shan range in the north of Hopeh-Shansi, the mountain massifs of Chekiang and Fukien, and the central and southern parts of the Great Khingan range.

Most of the changes in the earth's crust during the Tertiary period took place on the periphery of the territory. The Himalayan and Trans-Himalayan ranges, most of the island of Taiwan (Formosa), a great part of the Tsaidam basin, the Dzungaria basin, the Lesser Khingans and the shoulders of the Mongolian plateau were all formed during this period.

The Quaternary period saw a great deal of sedimentation due to the action of both wind and water. This was responsible for the formation of much of the Chinese plains, stretching from Manchuria to the lower reaches of the Yellow, Pai and Yangtze rivers and the Canton delta, to the desert basins of the Tarim, Dzungaria, eastern Tsaidam, Gobi, Alashan and Ordos.

A notable feature of the process of sedimentation caused by the action of winds was the formation of a bed of loess, or fine, yellowish loam. This bed of loess, varying in depth between 25 and 250 feet, covers a very large area in eastern Kansu, Shensi, Shansi and Honan. Alluvial deposits derived from the same loess, but mixed with other rock disintegration, form the bulk of the Yellow River plain. The loess was produced by wind erosion in the northwest deserts, particularly the Ordos, the windborne soil accumulating over the millennia on top of older geological formations.

During the Pleistocene period a very small amount of glaciation occurred in China. This is revealed in the "U-shaped" character of some valleys in the area of the middle reach of the Yangtze, and by the presence in Shansi and the Peking area of erratic masses, or rocks moved by a glacier from their original area and deposited in an area of a different geological character. Most geologists hold that the Chinese glacial period was very much shorter than that of Europe or North America.

Land Forms

The complex geological changes detailed above are responsible for the diverse characteristics of the mountains and hills of China. Three main characteristics may be noticed:

(i) The extremely mountainous nature of the whole country. Some 70 per cent of China may be described as mountainous or hilly. The altitude varies from 940 feet below sea level in the depression of Turfan in Sinkiang to a maximum of around 29,028 feet above sea level on Chomolungma, the Chinese name for Mt. Everest, on the Tibet-Nepal border.

(ii) The direction of the mountain ranges. Those in the western and central areas run mainly from east to west, and those in the east run almost at right angles to them. They are arranged in crescents which intersect to form major mountain groups.

(iii) The variety of shape of the country's various aspects. These include the rough alpine crests of the

Himalayas; the old, crumbling mountains of the Kunlun and Tien Shan; the undulating plateaus of Tibet, Shansi and Kweichow-Yunnan; the wide, flat inland basins of the Tarim and Tsaidam and the undulating basins of Szechwan; the wide, flat plain of North China and the undulating plain of Manchuria.

The most important of the mountain masses is the great Tibetan plateau, or Chang Tang. This extends northward from the Himalayas and Trans-Himalayas to the Kunlun and Bayan Kara mountains, and further north as far as the Altyn Tagh and the Nan Shan.

The Tibetan plateau is divided into three parts. These are:

(i) The highest and westernmost part, between the Kunlun mountains, the Trans-Himalayas and the Tanglha mountains, which forms a closed basin with an average altitude of about 12,000 feet.

(ii) The part formed by the valleys between the Himalayas and Trans-Himalayas in the south, and the valleys extending southward from the

east of the plateau.

(iii) The part formed by the Tsaidam swamp—Koko Nor, or Tsinghai basin, which is enclosed by the ranges of the Kunlun, the Altyn Tagh and the Nan Shan.

Three other basins, similar in formation to the Tsinghai, occur to the northwest of Tibet. They are the Tarim, the largest, which is surrounded by the Altyn Tagh, the Karakorams, the Pamirs and the Tien Shan; the Dzungaria basin, between the Tien Shan and the Altai mountains, which are both in Sinkiang; and the lake basin between the Altai mountains and the Tannu-Ola and Khangai mountains, in the western part of the Mongolian People's Republic.

To the east of the ranges which enclose these basins is the second great plateau of the Chinese region. This is the Mongolian plateau, which has an average altitude of 3000 to 4000 feet and extends northward from the Kansu corridor and the Great Wall as far as the Great Khingan in the east and the Kentei mountains in the north.

The third plateau of China is the one which, as has already been mentioned, is covered by a layer of loess. Shansi is the center of this plateau, which lies south of the Great Wall, on both sides of the south reach of the Yellow River and to the north of the Tsinling. Its altitude varies between 2500 and 5000 feet.

The last and highest of the Chinese plateaus is the Yunnan-Kweichow plateau, which varies in altitude between 2000 and 6000 feet. It lies to the south of the Szechwan basin, which is the richest and most important basin in the territory of China.

The mountain ranges, plateaus and basins described above make up about 70 per cent of China. The remaining 30 per cent is made up in almost equal proportions by the mountains, hills and plains of the northeast, the plains of the north and the mainly hilly area of the south. Manchuria is bordered by the low range of the Great Khingan in the west, the Lesser Khingan in the north and the Changpai mountains in the east.

The great alluvial plain of the north lies south of the Yin Shan and east of the Taihang and Funiu mountains. It is divided from the hilly zone of the south by a line of mountains which, although not of great

height, are of considerable geographic importance. They extend from the Tsinling and Funiu mountains southeastward along the Tapieh range, as far as the Tienmu mountains. Along this mountain line, there are very marked changes in soil, climate, vegetation, crops, anthropological characteristics and language.

THE LOW MOUNTAINS AND COASTS

Southern China is itself divided into two unequal sections by a second series of low mountains, the Nan Ling, and is bordered on the west by the plateau of Yunnan-Kweichow and on the east by the mountains of Fukien.

This disposition of mountain and hill systems in the Chinese region determines, to a great extent, the shape of its coastline. The coast is rocky around the two peninsulas of Liaotung and Shantung which enclose the Gulf of Chihli. The same characteristics occur around the mountainous provinces of the south, on the shores of the East China and South China seas, and in Chekiang, Fukien and Kwangtung. It is in these regions that most of the offshore islands are situated.

The rest of the coast has low, sandy beaches where the large rivers have piled up immense alluvial deposits, a process which still continues. Areas with these characteristics include the Gulf of Liaotung, the arc of land between Chinwangtao and the northern tip of the Shantung peninsula, the coast of Kiangsu province, the Canton delta and the areas around the estuaries of the many small rivers which join the sea between the bays of Hangchow and Canton.

Owing to the broad continental shelf which surrounds China, extending as far as Korea, the Kuril islands and the east side of Taiwan, the ocean is comparatively shallow. There are extensive sand banks on the east coast along the Gulf of Chihli, along the coast of Kiangsu and in the estuary of the Yangtze River.

Cold currents flow southward along the coast and warm currents flow northward from the South China Sea. They meet in the region of the Yangtze River estuary. The shallowness of the water, the mixing of currents of different temperatures and the organic substances carried down by the great river provide ideal conditions for marine life.

Peasants in Hopeh, eastern China, prepare their fields for sowing. The solidly-built carts are each pulled by a pair of small donkeys, the chief beasts of burden of the area. The main crops of Hopeh are cereals and cotton.

A scene on a calm day on the West Lake at Hangchow, Chekiang. The natural beauty of the area attracts many vacationers, and the luxurious appearance of the boats in the picture suggests that they may be pleasure craft. Hangchow and its environs are rich in historical remains such as monasteries, pagodas and shrines, and the city is famous as a cultural center.

Climate

As might be expected, in an area as large as China the climate varies a great deal. Few other regions of the world record in a single year such great extremes in wind direction and force, atmospheric pressure, volume of rainfall and range of temperature.

Atmospheric pressure and wind direction are regulated by a monsoonal cycle that causes the winds to change direction from winter to summer. In winter, cold, dry masses of continental air from the northwest flow down from the plateaus. In summer, warm, humid masses of oceanic air from the southeast flow inland over a great part of China.

The reasons for this are simple. Sea water is slow both to absorb the heat of the sun and to radiate it, while the rocky land masses absorb the sun's heat rapidly and lose it equally rapidly. This contrast is intensified in areas like China. Here the seas extend toward the south, where the intensity of the sun's rays is fairly constant, whereas in the north the sun's heat varies according to the season.

The alternation between the summer monsoon from the southeast and the winter monsoon from the northeast divides the Chinese year into two main seasons, summer and winter. The spring and fall seasons are much shorter and more variable in China than in other temperate zones.

PREVAILING WINDS

The force of the prevailing winds varies considerably. The winter winds, though sometimes very strong, do not exceed an average velocity of 25 miles per hour. The summer winds vary from the most moderate to the most destructive speeds. They are at their worst in the yearly typhoon season, which occurs usually between May and September. Typhoons from the region of the Marianas and Caroline Islands in the central Pacific bear down upon the Chinese coast around Taiwan, Kwangtung, Fukien, Chekiang and, sometimes, Shantung and Liaotung.

Owing to the sudden changes in atmospheric pressure, the speed of the winds and the violence of the rain, which produce heavy seas and floods, the typhoons possess great destructive powers.

The effect of the winds is considerably influenced by the high mountain massifs which form the eastern escarpment and by the lower hills which traverse the eastern plain from west to east. The mountainous escarpment in the extreme east constitutes more of an obstacle to the inward flow of humid oceanic winds from the southeast than it does to the dry continental winds blowing from the northwest toward the coast. Thus, the winter monsoon is generally more pronounced than the summer monsoon.

THE MOUNTAIN BARRIER

A more important obstacle to the dry, northwest winds is constituted by the mountain ranges running at right angles to the east coast, particularly the central chain running from the Tsinling to the Tienmu, which has already been mentioned as the barrier dividing China Proper into Northern and Southern China.

Temperature and rainfall are greatly influenced by the origin of the winds, either continental or oceanic, and by their direction, strength and humidity.

TEMPERATURE

The range of temperatures varies considerably between North and South China. The mean annual temperature of southern China is 68° - 77° F., while in northern Mongolia and Heilungkiang and Hsingan in the northeast it is 32° - 41° F.

The difference in temperature between north and south is less marked in summer, when the overall mean temperature varies from 68° F. in Hainan to about 86° F. in the northwest.

Daily variations in temperature,

which are mainly determined by the humidity of the air, are least marked near the coast, in lake districts and in areas affected by the west monsoon. Variations in daily temperature are greatest in the high, desert regions of the interior, where the air is dry and the radiation of the sun's heat from rocky surfaces is most intense.

The region with the most nearly equal distribution of the four seasons is the Yangtze valley, where winter and summer last four months each and spring and fall two months each. The Yunnan area has a short summer, but spring and fall last four months each. In the mountainous regions of central China winter lasts for about six months.

CLIMATIC REGIONS

China, which has both continental and maritime climates, can be roughly classified into a number of distinct climatic regions.

Northeast China has a cool, snow-forest climate. Northern China, or the lower Yellow River area, has a dry steppe climate north of the Yellow River, and a warm humid climate, characterized by dry winters and hot summers, in the south.

Central China, or the Yangtze valley, has a temperate, damp climate, with hot summers and dry winters. Southern China has similar conditions but is warmer and subtropical rather than temperate.

The Mongolian grassland has a dry steppe climate with cool summers. The Mongolian-Sinkiang mountain area, except at the higher elevations, has a cool, wet snow-forest climate. The Mongolian-Sinkiang desert area has a dry, desert climate.

Hainan and southwestern Taiwan are wet and tropical. Tibet is generally dry. The southwestern and Tsinling mountain ranges have a warm, humid climate with dry winters in the south.

The monsoons are the principal factors governing the cycle of rainfall. In almost all parts of China the wettest months are June, July, August and September, and the driest months are November, December, January and February. During the rainy season precipitation often is concentrated in different zones for short periods. When this concentration occurs over an extensive area in a single drainage basin, disastrous floods may result.

China's average annual rainfall varies from 60 to 80 inches in the southeast to less than 10 inches in the Gobi desert. There are, however, considerable differences in the volume of precipitation between one zone and another.

In general, northern China has hot, wet summers with a rainfall average of 25 to 30 inches. Southern China has a subtropical monsoon climate with an average precipitation of 80 inches.

Junks on the Yangtze near Chungking in southwest China. The Yangtze is joined at Chungking by the Kialing River and from this point onward it becomes an important transportation route. Chungking derives much of its importance as a commercial center from its position on the confluence of the two rivers.

The rainy season lasts from May through September in the south, from June through September in central China, and from July through August only in northern and southeastern China.

There is thus a clear distinction between the wet zones of the south and the dry zones of the north. However, the periodic concentration of rainfall in limited areas sometimes gives rise to serious droughts in other areas. Such droughts, although more frequent in the north, are not unknown in the south.

Hydrography

The distribution of rivers over the territory of China is determined by the country's topographical features and by its precipitation pattern. There are a large number of hydrographic basins, one of which, the Yangtze River basin, is among the largest in the world. Some three-fifths of these basins are traversed by rivers which flow into the sea, while less than two-fifths are enclosed basins. Of those which drain into the sea, the most important drain into the Pacific Ocean and the less important into the Indian Ocean.

The three largest Chinese rivers, the Yangtze River (3430 miles), the Hwang Ho, or Yellow River (2900 miles), and the Amur, or Heilung Chiang (2700 miles), all empty into the Pacitic Ocean.

THE YANGTSE AND YELLOW RIVERS

The Yangtze and the Yellow rivers rise in eastern Tibet, in the Tanglha and Bayan Kara mountains respectively. The Yangtze describes a broad arc to the south and the Yellow River to the north. Both then traverse the eastern half of China through two fundamentally differing zones. After about a third of their respective courses, the Yangtze enters a zone characterized by more abundant, better distributed rainfall, while the Yellow River enters a zone where rainfall is scanty and irregular.

The Yangtze is the major drainage basin of eastern Asia and has a number of large tributaries. Some of these are fed by melting snows, which help to supplement the water level. In addition the Yangtze receives water from several natural lakes, such as the Tungting and Poyang in the middle and lower reaches respectively.

The Yangtze flows through wooded valleys and, in the higher and middle reaches where the current is very rapid, the river's bed is carved out of hard rock. Thus, very little waste material is brought down by its water. The Yellow River, on the other hand, in its middle reaches flows through areas devoid of vegetation—either semi-desert or land composed of the sandy loess—and its waters accumulate a large amount of sediment.

Due to the general pattern of rainfall in China, the flow of the Yangtze

and Yellow rivers varies considerably, reaching a maximum in times of concentrated precipitation. In times of little rainfall, both rivers are reduced to meager streams.

In the case of the Yangtze, even in its lower reaches, the gradient of the river and the speed of its current are sufficient to transport the small amount of sediment in its water to the sea. Although the Yellow River has a steeper gradient, the amount of sediment in its waters is so great that in times of scanty rainfall vast quantities of sediment are deposited on the river bed.

It has been estimated that the Yellow River, in its lower reaches below the gorge of Sanmen, carries down about a billion tons of eroded soil and rock every year. Less than half of this reaches the sea, the rest being deposited on the river bed. As a result, from the point at which the Yellow River enters the plains the river bed begins to rise above the level of the land through which it flows.

During periods of concentrated rainfall the water level of the Yellow River at certain points rises to as much as 30 feet above the level of the surrounding plain. In Honan and Shantung men have struggled for three thousand years to raise the embankments of the river. So far, the level of the river bed has risen more quickly than the man-made embankments. Not only does the Yellow River burst its banks about every two years, but on numerous occasions it has completely changed its course and the position of its mouth. The latter has varied between points as far apart

A mountainous area in the province of Honan, eastern China. The terraced strips of cultivated land in the foreground are indicative of China's need to make use of every available piece of fertile ground. Landslides caused by water erosion are very common in this region, but this danger is being combatted by the planting of protective belts of forest and the construction of efficient drainage channels.

as Tientsin in the Gulf of Chihli to a point some 400 miles further south on the Kiangsu coast.

THE AMUR (HEILUNG CHIANG)

The third great river of China, the Amur or Heilung Chiang, rises in the Kentei mountains in Mongolia, where it is known as the Onon. Only after it joins with the Argun, which flows from the Great Khingan, does it take the Chinese name of Heilung Chiang and the Russian name of Amur.

The Amur flows through regions where rainfall is well distributed and precipitation is supplemented by water from melting snows. It has a rocky bed covered with vegetation and its volume of water is more constant than that of any other Chinese river. Thus, the amount of sediment carried down by the Amur is small.

THE LIAO, PAI HO AND HWAI

Among the important rivers that flow into the Gulf of Chihli are the Liao, which traverses southern Manchuria, and the Pai Ho, which forms a collective estuary for the various rivers which drain the basin north of the Yellow River.

The Hwai River flows into the Yellow Sea south of the Shantung Peninsula. The Hwai, like the Yellow River, is very irregular in the flow of its waters and carries a large amount of detritus. In the 14th century, the course of the Hwai was silted up by the Yellow River, which usurped its course for a time and deposited large amounts of sediment. As a result, the waters of the Hwai do not flow straight to the sea. Instead, the greater part of the Hwai's waters flow into a large lake called the Hungtse, about 125 miles from the coast. Here, some evaporation takes place and the residue joins the Grand Canal and is carried into the Yangtze. Only a part of the Hwai flows directly to the sea by means of underground watercourses and a recently constructed canal.

In the area to the south, the watercourses are short. This is due to the rock formation characteristic of the territories of Chekiang and Fukien.

The Canton River, or Chu Kiang (Pearl River), in the Canton delta, is 110 miles long. A number of the rivers of Kwangtung and Kwangsi flow into it, the most important being the Si Kiang, or West River.

The Canton delta is one of the most important on the Pacific coast. Its topographical features and distrib-

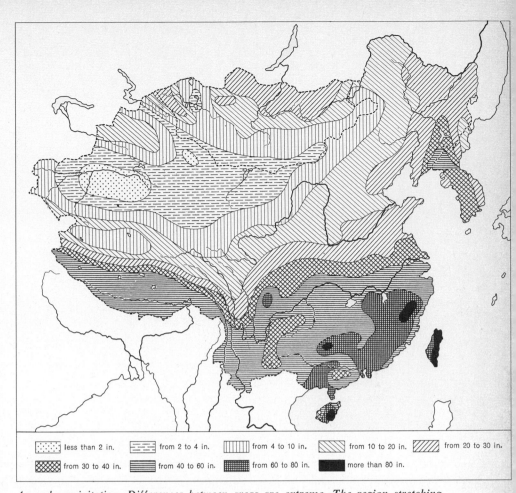

less than 2 in. | from 2 to 4 in. | from 4 to 10 in. | from 10 to 20 in. | from 20 to 30 in. | from 30 to 40 in. | from 40 to 60 in. | from 60 to 80 in. | more than 80 in.

Annual precipitation. Differences between areas are extreme. The region stretching from the Sinkiang Tarim basin and Tibetan plateau as far as the Gobi desert, has less than ten inches; precipitation increases gradually toward the southeast, reaching from 60 to 80 inches.

ution of rainfall are similar to those of the Yangtze.

THE TIBETAN RIVERS

Western Tibet is traversed by numerous rivers which flow southward through Yunnan. Some, like the Red River, the Black River and the Mekong, flow into the South China Sea. Others, like the Salween, or Salwin, flow into the Indian Ocean.

Another river which flows into the Indian Ocean is the Brahmaputra which, under the name of the Tsangpo, traverses the area between the Himalayas and Trans-Himalayas. It then turns abruptly to enter the plains of Assam. Its delta mingles with that of the Ganges.

A characteristic of the Tibetan rivers is their large and fairly regular volume of water, brought about by the water from the glaciers and snows, the steep gradient of their courses, and the depth and rocky characteristics of the canyons through which they flow. These factors make

the Tibetan river system one of the largest areas of hydroelectric potential in the world.

THE INLAND BASINS

As well as the river basins that drain into the sea, China has seven principal inland basins. These are the basins of Tibet, Tsaidam, Tarim, Dzungaria, the Lake District, Gobi and Kunlun Nor.

The basin of Tibet is formed by a number of short rivers and lakes. The largest of these lakes is the Nam Tso, or Tengri.

There are few rivers in the Tsaidam basin. There is, however, a large salt marsh and also the Tsinghai, or Koko Nor, which is one of the largest salt lakes in the Chinese territory.

The structure of the Tarim basin is more complicated. The Tarim River, at the foot of the Tien Shan, collects the huge volume of water that flows down from the glaciers and snowfields of the surrounding ranges, especially in the late spring. However,

Timber is prepared for transportation along a river in eastern Szechwan. The main forested areas in China are concentrated in the northeast and amount to about 360,000 square miles, a relatively low figure. Extensive reforestation schemes are now in progress. The provinces with the largest percentage of forested area are, in order, Szechwan, Heilungkiang, Kirin, Yunnan and Hunan.

evaporation and the loss of water by infiltration into sandy, desert soil, cause the Tarim to diminish gradually until its flow dies out in the large salt lake of Lop Nor. The position of the Lop Nor, a marshy depression, has been altered considerably within a few decades by the lower course of the Tarim.

Other short rivers and numerous lakes are found in the Dzungaria basin and in the Lake District north of the Altai range.

The most important river in the Gobi basin is the Etsin, which flows for 200 miles through the Ningsia area of Inner Mongolia and terminates in a small lake on the Mongolian Republic border. The Etsin shares the common features of the rivers of the inland basins; their torrential courses, the variations in the quality of their beds in the desert areas or steppes and frequent loss of water through evaporation or absorption.

Many of the Chinese lakes have already been mentioned. These include Lake Khanka, in the middle reach of the Ussuri; the Hungtze, into which the Hwai River flows; the Tungting and Poyang in the lower reach of the Yangtze; the Koko Nor in Tsinghai; the Nam Tso in Tibet; and the Lop Nor in Sinkiang. To these may be added the T'ai Hu, alongside the estuary of the Yangtze. Generally speaking, the lakes connected to rivers which flow through

basins draining into the sea contain fresh water. On the other hand, lakes constituting the end of rivers flowing through inland, enclosed basins are often salt, due to extensive evaporation.

The lakes connected with the Yangtze and Hwai rivers serve as an overflow system. Their level is extremely variable, depending on the seasonal flow of the rivers. They act as fluctuating reservoirs and are of some agricultural importance. As they recede, exposing large parts of their beds, ricefields are planted on the fertile alluvial soil.

In addition to the permanent lakes already mentioned, there are extensive areas in the lowlands of northern China which remain flooded for long periods during the rainy seasons. This is due both to poor natural drainage and to the breaching of the banks of the Yellow River. Considerable damage is caused by these floods.

Soil Types

The diversity of types of agricultural soil found in China is due to the combination of the various geological, topographic, climatic and hydrographic characteristics of the country.

There are a number of factors which affect both the nature of the soil itself and of the vegetable and animal life which it maintains. These include the friability, or likeliness to

crumble, of the soil; the organic substances mingled with it; its capacity for retaining humidity; the amount of sun it receives; and its temperature and that of the air above it.

With the exception of the northern and easternmost parts of Manchuria, soils with a high calcium content, varying in maturity and richness, predominate in China Proper, north of the Tsinling mountains. In general, the rainfall in these zones is fairly limited so that the humus, or decomposing organic matter, and the mineral salts dispersed in the upper layer of soil are not washed away or considerably diluted by rain. Instead, they remain near the surface encouraging the growth of vegetation which in its turn forms additional humus.

The thickness of vegetation in this area varies and the soil on which it grows also varies from light to dark brown in color, depending on rainfall, temperature and the strength of the winds. The best conditions are found in central Manchuria, where there is a zone of black, porous earth, eminently suitable for the cultivation of corn.

To the west of this zone, across the pastureland of eastern Mongolia and across Shensi, Ningsia, southern Mongolia, Kansu, Tsaidam and Sinkiang, the soil becomes gradually lighter. Its color changes from chestnut to light chestnut to gray, and finally to the yellow-gray of the desert and sand dunes of the Ordos, Gobi, Alashan and Taklamakan deserts.

In areas of low rainfall where subterranean layers of water occur, and where there are high temperatures and a consequently high rate of evaporation, the salts contained in the water are drawn to the surface, where they form a tightly-packed crust of extremely alkaline, sometimes saline, soil. This occurs in central Hopeh, northwestern Shantung and on the coast north of Kiangsu.

The soil in the alluvial plains of Liao, in the area watered by the tributaries of the Hai Ho and in the lower reaches of the Yellow River and the Hwai, is, like that of the mountains, rich in lime and calcium carbonate. The soil in these areas is generally in an immature state, and the continuous depositing of new materials by water and windborne sedimentation, together with intensive cultivation over many centuries, has prevented the formation of a natural layer of vegetation.

Sometimes, as along the periphery of the entire zone, the soil is hard, tightly packed and clayey, making cultivation with primitive tools difficult. In other places, as in a broad belt along the coast, the subterranean infiltration of sea water gives the soil a high salt content. However, in general the soil is porous, fairly friable and rich is dissolved minerals. It lacks only water to make it immensely fertile.

In the northeast arc of Manchuria, the Liaotung and Shantung peninsulas, the Yin Shan, the mountain ranges of Shansi, Tsinling, Funiu and Tapieh, and the whole of southern China, the soils compounded mainly of lime and calcium elements are replaced by soil rich in aluminum and iron. Soil of this kind contains less humus and dissolved minerals.

North Manchuria has mainly gray soils, similar to those of the forested areas of northern Europe and North America. These soils are covered by a superficial layer of humus formed by decayed vegetation from the forests.

Podsolic soils (light-colored soils found in cold, forested areas) are common in Shantung. They extend as far as the Changpai mountains, the Yin Shan, the hills of the Liaotung

and Shantung peninsulas, part of Shansi and to the mountain chain running from the Tsinling to the sea.

To the south of this area, where there is a higher rainfall, the calcium content of the soil steadily diminishes. The earth takes on a reddish-yellow color and becomes generally hard, compact and clayey.

However, diverse types of soil still occur. These include the purplish-brown soil of Szechwan, which has earned the area the name of the "Red Basin." There are also the old, red soils of Yunnan and Kwangsi; the red, forest soils which predominate in the other provinces south of the Yangtze River; the light and dark chalky soils that form a belt north of the lower Yangtze; and the light, alluvial soils of the ricefields on either side of the middle, lower and lowest reaches of the Yangtze, in the Chengtu plain and in the Canton delta.

The soils of the high pastureland

on the slopes of the valleys of eastern Tibet become gradually poorer toward the mountain desert of northern Tibet and the high mountain chains that surround and traverse the Tibetan plateau.

Flora and Fauna

In relation to the soil formations described above, seven principal zones of vegetation may be distinguished in the territory of China.

The first is a cold-temperate zone made up of the forest belt of northern and eastern Manchuria. This consists of needle-leaved trees in the extreme north and broad-leaved trees and conifers in the northeast and east, interspersed with numerous grassy clearings.

The second zone, of prairies and steppes, includes the fertile black soil area in the central plain of Manchuria, which is surrounded by occasional forests and abundant grassland. It extends into northern and eastern

Peasants gathering the rice harvest in the Yangtze River basin near Wuhan, Hupeh. Rice is a basic dietary item in much of China. Its cultivation is mainly concentrated in the southern tropical areas, the Yangtze valley and the plains of the southwest and southeast. The amount of land under cultivation in China varies from below 20 per cent in some provinces to around 70 per cent in others. The highest percentage of cultivated land is found in Manchuria and Szechwan.

Mongolia as far as northern Dzungaria and, across the Yin Shan, as far as northern Shensi and Ningsia. On the southern extremities of this zone, in Shansi, central Shensi and east Kansu, as far as the borders of the third zone, tall plants become more frequent, interspersed with different types of broad-leaved shrubs.

The third zone, which is temperate, consists of the southern part of Liaoning, Shantung, Hopeh, Honan and southern Shensi. In the hilly peninsulas of Liaotung and Shantung and on the slopes of the Yin Shan and Shansi, where the soil lacks lime and calcium compounds, temperate forests predominate. There are abundant fruit trees of the type most resistant to cold, drought and the alkalinity, or predominance of salt compounds, that often occurs in the soil. The third zone is also the area of the great aluvial plains which have been under cultivation for many centuries, reducing spontaneous vegetation to a minimum.

The fourth zone, a warm-temperate area, takes in almost the whole of the basin of the middle and lower Yangtze. The mountains of Fukien and some parts of the Nan Ling are covered with woods consisting mainly of conifers and broad-leaved trees. In the hilly areas, evergreen plants and shrubs of various kinds predominate, together with bamboo. Wherever the land is level and suitably watered, rice is cultivated.

The fifth zone, which is tropical, extends south of the Nan Ling, taking in Kwangtung, Kwangsi, the southern valleys of Yunnan and the islands of Hainan and Taiwan. Although the conditions favor luxuriant vegetation, the natural primary forests have been greatly reduced, particularly in south Yunnan and in the mountains of Taiwan and Hainan. Instead, an abundance of evergreens is mingled with plantations of tropical trees which yield oils, resin, valuable fibers and timber. Rice is cultivated in the irrigated lowlands and there are thick clusters of mangroves along the coast.

The sixth zone lies around north Yunnan, west Szechwan and Tibetan Chamdo. There are conifer woods on the slopes of the more protected valleys. The more exposed ridges consist of pastureland and scrub, extending up to the desert ranges of the Tibetan basin and mountains. Conifer forests are also found on the slopes of the Himalayans, the Karakorams, the Pamirs, the Tien Shan and the Nan Shan.

At the foot of these mountains, the brief belt of prairies and steppes gives way to sandy deserts (such as the Taklamakan, the Alashan, the Tarim and a part of the Gobi) or stony deserts (such as the Ordos and the greater part of the Gobi). These make up the seventh zone.

The demarcation line between the steppes and the desert is extremely variable, depending on the climatic changes from season to season and year to year. The only permanent vegetation in the area is found on the shores of the meager watercourses and at the oases.

Little more than half of the territory of China is suitable for habitation by wild animals.

Monkeys of various species are found in China as far north as Hopeh, which is the highest latitudinal point at which members of the monkey family are known to live.

China's carnivores, or flesh-eating animals, include tigers, leopards, lynxes, wildcats, various species of bear, pandas, wolves and wild dogs.

Fur-bearing animals include sables, otters, martens, weasels and squirrels.

Among the hoofed animals are a great variety of deer, gazelles, wild goats, oxen, donkeys and wild boars.

Flocks of sheep and goats in the pasture land of southern Sinkiang Uigur, north-eastern China. Stockbreeding is mainly concentrated in the tablelands of Dzungaria, where many of the inhabitants are semi-nomadic herdsmen. Sheep and goats account for roughly 20 per cent of China's domestic animals.

A field of ginseng on a hillside in western Liaoning, Manchuria. Ginseng, an herb of the Panax family, is highly valued for its supposed properties as a cure-all and an aphrodisiac. It is native to Manchuria and also to North America, from where it is exported to Hong Kong for the Asian market. Since the herb is difficult to raise, requiring rich soil and much care, it commands a high price.

The principal rodents include numerous species of rat, hare, wild rabbit, and the pika, a small mammal of the rabbit family which is responsible for the destruction of vast areas of grassland in Mongolia.

China also possesses a number of different species of bat. Since the Chinese word for bat is the same as that for fortune, bats often appear in Chinese art as talismans or signs of good luck.

There are numerous birds, including birds of prey, nocturnal birds, web-footed and aquatic birds and seagulls.

Reptiles also abound, including a large variety of snakes, alligators and water and land turtles. The latter are considered to be symbols of long life and as such often appear on funerary monuments, supporting a pillar bearing the name of the deceased.

China's rivers are rich in aquatic life. There are many varieties of fish, large amphibians and aquatic mammals. The inland waters are marked by an abundance of fish belonging to the carp family and an almost total absence except in Heilungkiang in north Manchuria, of members of the salmon family.

ORGANIZATION OF THE STATE

Land and Sea Boundaries

MOST OF THE TERRITORY OF CHINA IS occupied by the Chinese People's Republic, only a small fraction being occupied by other states. These include the Mongolian People's Republic (Outer Mongolia) which occupies the major part of Mongolia; the Republic of China (Nationalist China), which retains sovereignty over the island of Taiwan (Formosa), the Pescadores Islands, and other small islands in the Formosa Straits and off the Chinese coast; the British crown colony of Hong Kong; and the Portuguese colony of Macao. The last two occupy, respectively, the extremities of the eastern and western promontories on either side of the Pearl River estuary in Kwangtung province.

The northernmost point of the Chinese People's Republic is marked by the location of the Amur river 53°N 124°E. The southernmost point on the mainland is Hoion (21°N 110°E), southwest Kwangtung. The eastern and western extremes are marked by Tungkiang, Heilungkiang (47°N 135°E), and Tash Kurghan, Sinkiang (38°N 75°E), respectively.

The Chinese People's Republic, called in Chinese *Chung-Hua Jen-Min Kung-Ho Kuo*, covers an area of about 3,691,502 square miles, which is about nine-tenths of the whole region of China. Thus it is the third largest state in the world, exceeded only by the U.S.S.R., which occupies an area more than twice as great, and Canada.

The frontiers of China with most of the adjoining countries are difficult to define exactly, since the boundary lines marked on Chinese maps do not always correspond with those shown on the maps of other countries. The question of frontiers is a problem still to be resolved between China and certain of her neighbors.

The Chinese People's Republic has borders with the U.S.S.R. on the northwest and northeast; the Mongolian People's Republic in the north;

A lake in northeast China. This area is rich in lakes which, when used to regulate the flow of the numerous rivers, are often the means of averting floods.

with Korea on the northeast; and with Vietnam, Laos and Burma on the south. It is bordered by the Yellow Sea, the East China Sea on the east and the South China Sea on the southeast; on the southwest its borders extend to the Karakoram and Himalayan ranges, fronting on the Republic of India, Bhutan, Sikkim, Nepal, Pakistan and Afghanistan. These frontiers coincide, for the most part, with those of the historic territory of China.

An important exception is China's frontier with the Mongolian People's Republic. Between the 87th and the 20th Meridian East a wide arc of the Mongolian People's Republic extends southward into China from the level of the 52nd Parallel down to the 41st Parallel. Only the Altai mountains in the west constitute a natural demarcation line, the remainder of the frontier being determined on a non-geographical basis.

COASTAL BOUNDARIES

The entire coast of the territory of China, with the sole exceptions of the colonies of Hong Kong and Macao, is under the sovereignty of the Chinese People's Republic. Some islands, however, remain outside this sovereignty. These include Taiwan, Quemoy, Matsu, the Pescadores, or Penghu Islands, and a number of minor islands such as the Nan Shan group and the coral reefs of the South China Sea.

Administrative Divisions

The Chinese People's Republic is divided into a number of political and administrative units, based on the provinces and areas that make up the territory. In all, if Taiwan is included, there are twenty-nine of these divisions. Twenty-two are provinces, two are the large municipalities of Peking and Shanghai, which are directly dependent on the central government, and five are autonomous regions.

The provinces and central municipalities are largely inhabited by people of the Han (Chinese) nationality. The population of the autonomous regions are mainly peoples of the same racial group as the Han, such as Tibetans or Mongols. With few exceptions, the provinces and municipalities are situated in China Proper and Manchuria, while the autonomous regions are situated in outer China.

The provinces and other areas vary considerably in size, population and density, as the statistical table on page 119 shows. In general, the provinces of China Proper are limited in size and have a very high density of population, while the autonomous regions cover large areas and are sparsely inhabited.

Under the present system, each province and other region is divided into approximately 175 municipalities, or *chou,* and about 2000 counties,

or *hsien.* The *hsien* are further divided into some 100,000 cantons, or *hsiang,* which are in turn grouped into administrative districts, or *chow.*

Apart from the two central municipalities of Peking and Shanghai, the urban population is distributed between some 175 towns and numerous villages.

National Minorities

A section of the Chinese Constitution is devoted to the rights of national minorities within the People's Republic. These are provided with administrative units at the levels of special autonomous regions, districts and counties. Such units are normally of a purely administrative and non-political character. They are found in every locality where national minorities constitute the majority of the population. These localities enjoy a greater degree of local autonomy than corresponding areas occupied by the Han people.

Citizens belonging to national minorities have the right to speak and to be addressed in their own language in all public offices. They also have their own statutes.

Constitution

The Chinese People's Republic was proclaimed on Sept. 21, 1949, and the Central People's Government was innaugurated on Oct. 1, 1949. The detailed structure of the Constitution has been built up gradually by the passing of successive laws regulating the powers and responsibilities of the various organs of the state. The fundamental Constitution was approved by the first National People's Congress on Sept. 20, 1954.

The state system is defined in the Constitution as a democratic dictatorship of the people, directed by the working class and based on an alliance between workers and peasants. This takes the concrete form of an administrative body responsible for expressing and putting into effect the will of the people, acting within the framework of the general principles laid down by the Constitution.

These principles are concerned with the system of state, cooperative and private ownership, in relation to the aim of transforming China into a socialist society; with the planned character of the economic and social life of the country in relationship to its industrialization; with the multinational character of the Chinese state and the right to equality for all nationalities together with the right to autonomy of national minorities; and with the rights and duties of citizens.

According to the Constitution, all power belongs to the people, who exercise it through the people's congresses in accordance with the principles of democratic centralization. The National People's Congress and the three levels of local congress are the organs of expression of the three fundamental politico-administrative units: the provinces, the districts and associated areas.

According to electoral regulations, the members of the National People's Congress are elected for four-year terms by the people's congresses of the provinces, municipalities under central authority, autonomous regions, armed forces and residents abroad. The people's congresses, where the individual right to vote is exercised, are conducted at the *hsiang* or *chou* levels. Elections are conducted either by secret ballot or by a show of hands.

Candidates for election may be put forward by the Communist Party and by other legitimate parties and people's organizations.

All citizens over the age of eighteen who possess political rights may vote in the elections for the congresses of counties and associated areas and are eligible for election as members of these congresses. Particular care is taken to ensure that national minorities are adequately represented at the various levels of congress.

Legislative Branch

The National People's Congress is the highest organ of government and is the only legislative body. It elects the chairman of the Chinese People's Republic and the president of the Supreme People's Court. It approves the appointment of the president of the State Council and the other members of the government and of the vice-president and other members of the National Defense Council. It draws up the economic programs and examines and approves the budget. It is also responsible for all matters relating to provincial and other boundaries, amnesties and other aspects of war and peace.

The National People's Congress consists of 1226 members. They enjoy parliamentary immunity but their mandate may be withdrawn at any time by the bodies which have elected them. A similar principle applies to all public offices. Congress is scheduled to meet once every year for a period of one or two weeks.

When Congress is not in session, its powers devolve upon the Standing Committee, a permanent organization elected by Congress for this purpose. In 1959 the Standing Committee was authorized to amend laws enacted by Congress.

As well as arranging and conducting elections and summoning Congress, the Standing Committee has very wide powers. It may issue decrees, interpret laws, supervise the actions of the State Council, confirm the appointment of ministers, vice-ministers, members of the Supreme Court and the procurator - general's office, ratify or abrogate treaties, and declare war.

The so-called "Queen's Palace" on the outskirts of Peking. Peking was the imperial Capital of China, with few interruptions, from 1122 A.D. until the fall of the Ch'ing dynasty in the early years of the 20th century. Many of the buildings of the imperial court still remain. The pleasant hills to the west and north of the city are particularly rich in historical monuments.

A timber-felling center in a forested area of Heilungkiang, Manchuria. The northeast is the main forest area of China; pines and firs, used for building boats, houses and smaller articles, are common in the region, especially in hilly areas.

The Standing Committe is scheduled to convene twice a month, but this arrangement is subject to change should the need arise.

Executive Branch

The chairman of the republic is elected by Congress from among its members. He represents the state in its foreign relations, promulgates laws and decrees and, as chairman of the National Defense Council, commands the armed forces.

The State Council is the highest executive and administrative organ of the state. It is composed of a president, vice-president, ministers, commission directors, a secretary-general and a large number of vice-ministers and vice-chairmen of committees and commissions. These officials are all elected by and subject to recall by the National People's Congress.

The State Council draws up laws and decrees for submission to Congress or the Standing Committee, makes decisions regarding the proper application of laws and decrees and carries out the directives of the current economic plan and budget.

Local Government

Local government is the responsibility of the various levels of People's congresses. They are responsible for the application of the state's laws in their respective areas, approving local economic plans and budgets, and electing the members of the local people's councils.

The people's councils are presided over by governors at provincial level, by mayors in provincial capitals and by chiefs in other subdivisions. They are responsible either to the local people's congress or to the people's councils above them. They have three distinct functions: to execute the resolutions of the people's congresses in the field of local administration; to exercise the powers of the people's congresses when they are not in session; and to execute the decisions of the people's councils above them on matters of administration.

National Defense

The chairman of the people's Republic of China, as chairman of the National Defense Council, commands the army, navy and airforce. The vice-chairman and members are elected by the National People's Congress and are subject to recall by the Congress. A fourth branch of the armed forces, the Public Security Force, is controlled by the Ministry of Public Security.

Judicial System

The Chinese Constitution provides for judicial powers to be vested in two government organs. These are the Supreme People's Court, which is the highest judicial organ and has supervisory powers over the local and special people's courts, and the Supreme People's Procuratorate, which exercises supreme supervisory power over local people's procuratorates, all departments of the government and the people.

The people's courts are organized on a three-level system—basic, middle and high—and each is controlled by the court next superior to it. According to a law of 1954, these courts are independent and "subject only to the law."

The people's courts are competent to judge penal, civil and administrative cases and to adjudicate according to the law wherever relevant legal dispositions exist. In the absence of these, when no law with a bearing on the case in hand has been promulgated, they adjudicate according to analogy with other cases and with reference to the general principles of the Constitution and the laws.

SUPREME PEOPLE'S PROCURATORATE

The Supreme People's Procuratorate enforces the observance of the laws and supervises their application by the state bodies of various types. It is responsible for supervising the promotion or investigation of penal trials and for representing the state's interests in any legal action in which they are at stake.

The Procuratorate is presided over by the procurator-general elected by the National People's Congress and its Standing Committe. The local procuratorates are independent in the exercise of their authority, and are not subject to the supervision of state organs on the same level.

Communist Party

The dominant role in the political life of the Chinese People's Republic is taken by the Chinese Communist Party. The Communist Party instigated the revolution and civil war from which the new republic arose and was the guiding force behind the formation of the Constitution and the legal system.

The Communist Party holds the largest number of seats in the People's Congresses at the highest levels and also occupies most of the offices in government bodies. Thus, it is able to carry out, it claims, according to its own ideology and principles, the will of the people.

In mid-1961 the Chinese Communist Party was estimated to have around 17,000,000 members.

Religion

The Chinese Constitution does not recognize any state religion and

A gorge on the middle reach of the Yangtze above Ichang in central Hupeh. Because of gorges and rapids, ocean-going craft can ascend the Yangtze only as far as Ichang. Because of the speed and volume of the river at Ichang a large hydroelectric power station was built there.

makes no particular provisions for the establishment of clergy or for the pursuit of any religious activities. The Chinese government, which controls all aspects of life, is dedicated to doctrinaire Marxist-Leninism and, as such, is atheistic and dedicated to the elimination of religion. It is true to say, however, that the Chinese people have never been religious in the way of other peoples. Their predominant social philosophy, Confucianism, is an ethical system with no theology. In the past, the Chinese have tolerated many religions because they have been deeply involved in none.

No great religion has originated in China, although it has been the cradle of a great philosophic tradition. Three of the great religions— Buddhism, Islam and Christianity— were imported from India and from the West.

China's spirit of religious toleration was shown in the way in which many different religious-philosophical movements were able to exist side by side for centuries or to succeed each other without violent upheavals. Among these were the Confucian, Neo-Confucian, Moist, Legalist, Skeptic and Idealist schools.

Followers of widely differing religions—Taoists, Buddhists, Moslems and Christians of various sects— erected their temples and practiced their rites without incurring anything approaching the bloody religious conflicts which took place in the West.

BUDDHISM AND TAOISM

The two most widely spread religions of China, Buddhism and Taoism, have been mainly dominated by small sectarian movements dedicated to convent life and solitude. Neither religion has a centralized authority or an organized hierarchical clergy, and their ties with the mass of the people and with the state authorities have always been much weaker than those of the religions of other countries.

The dominant religious observances of the Chinese people were, and to some extent still are, limited to the cult of ancestor worship which was formulated by Confucius and for the expression of which the various Buddhist and Taoist sects, with their temples, monasteries, shrines, legends and ceremonies, provided an outlet. The Jesuit missionaries of the 17th century recognizing the strength of this religious cult tried to make provision for it.

THE EMPERORS' RELIGION

The emperors of the various Chinese dynasties, except for a few brief periods, never established a state religion. Instead they maintained a cult of the emperor as the guiding divinity and father of his people, which subsequently became the social philosophy of the Confucians. The emperor cult was thought to provide a sufficient ideological basis for the unification and guidance of the professional and literate members of the ruling class.

BUDDHISM AND ISLAM

The situation in China's border territories—in Tibet, Tsinghai, Mongolia, Ningsia and Sinkiang—presents a somewhat different appearance.

In Tibet, Tsinghai and Mongolia, various Buddhist sects were able to acquire a great deal of economic and political power and succeeded in establishing themselves at the head of a feudal system. In Tibet, especially, religion ruled the country, and the Dalai Lama, whose seat was at Lhasa, was recognized by most Lamaists as their spiritual and temporal leader. The richest of all Buddhist temples is the Potala at Lhasa.

In Sinkiang and Ningsia the multiracial population consists mainly of Turkic speaking Uigurs and Chinese speaking Hui, most of whom belong to various Moslem sects. Religious discipline in these areas is much stricter than in China Proper.

Many Moslems also live in the ancient trading centers of North China, which were used as provision centers for the camel caravans which crossed the desert to trade with the West. Other Moslem centers are the south coastal towns such as Canton, which were reached by sea from the ports of the Levant and India.

CHRISTIANITY

Beginning in the 13th century, and to a much greater extent from the 18th century onward, Catholic missionaries were responsible for introducing Christianity into many parts of China. They were later joined by missionaries from the Protestants and Orthodox Christian churches.

Christianity gained its greatest footholds in towns which contained foreign trade concessions, notably in Shanghai, Peking, Tientsin, Canton, Harbin, Dairen, Tsingtao and Wuhan, but it also spread to rural areas. Thus, the Tai P'ing revolution of the 1840s had among its slogans a number of concepts clearly inspired by Christian teaching.

Catholicism was particularly widespread in areas where there were French, Portuguese, Italian and German concessions. Protestantism flourished around British and American concessions. The Orthodox faith centered around the Russian-influenced towns of Manchuria in the northeast.

The Christian missionaries were hampered by the fact that Christianity was the religion of Western powers that had for centuries attempted, with partial success, to subjugate China by reducing her to the status of a semi-colony. The resurgence of Chinese nationalism in the 19th and 20th centuries became a barrier against the further spread of Christianity. There are now about three million Catholics in China and about the same number of Christians of other denominations, including around one million Protestants.

Since 1952, the many excellent Christian educational establishments in China have been absorbed into the national university system. Many foreign missionaries have been repatriated and some have been imprisoned.

OTHER RELIGIONS

There are also a number of pagan tribes which survive in the more remote areas of China, notably among the national minority populations of Yunnan. Until about a century ago, a number of descendants of Jewish immigrants were concentrated in a fairly large community in Tsinan, but these are now mostly dispersed and have been assimilated into the mass of the population.

ATTITUDE TOWARD RELIGION

In modern China, the older generation has remained attached, to a considerable extent, to the beliefs and religious practices of the various ancient cults and to the ideals of traditional moral philosophy. The

Right: A section of the Great Wall in northwest Hopeh. Construction of the Wall, built both as a defense and as a boundary marker, was completed in 246 B.C. under Emperor Shih Huang-ti of the Ch'in dynasty. The height of the Wall, which stretches for some 1500 miles, varies between 15 and 30 feet. Along it, at intervals of 600 feet, are watchtowers ranging from 30 to 40 feet high. The Wall is about 20 feet wide at the base, narrowing to around 12 feet across the top.

situation of the younger generation is different.

Although it must not be assumed that organizations of a militantly atheistic nature exist in the Chinese People's Republic, there are certain factors which combine to cause the youth of the country to become increasingly detached from religious concepts and practices. These include the secular character of state education, the prestige enjoyed by the Communist Party and its ideology and the limitation of ecclesiastical activities to purely religious fields.

Education

In the past, China had made as great a contribution to world civilization as any other country and it has one of the richest cultural traditions. However, over the last few centuries its culture has been much less widely diffused than have those of the European countries and North America. When the Communist regime came to power the level of higher education in most fields was very low and illiteracy was widespread.

One of the principal objectives of the government of the Chinese People's Republic has been to raise the standards of education as quickly as possible, both in order to produce the professional and technical material necessary for the industrialization of the country and to further China's cultural development in all spheres.

Considerable progress has already been made. By the end of 1958 there were 86,400,000 pupils in elementary schools, 8,520,000 in secondary schools, and 660,000 students in universities.

ELEMENTARY AND SECONDARY EDUCATION

Elementary schooling in China lasts for a period of six years, accommodating pupils between the ages of six and twelve. Almost all Chinese children in the appropriate age group attend elementary schools, since attendance is both compulsory and

free of charge. The curriculum of elementary schools is uniform throughout the country.

Secondary, or middle schools, correspond to American high schools, and are divided into junior and senior middle schools. They include vocational middle schools, including polytechnic colleges, and workers' and peasants' short-term middle schools. In general, their curriculum consists of political indoctrination, languages, literature, mathematics, agricultural techniques and other vocational courses.

In 1958 an experimental amalgamation of factories and secondary schools was introduced. Under this scheme, students work in factories for a few hours each day while factory workers attend school. In rural areas, the same principle is applied to students and farmworkers.

HIGHER EDUCATION

University courses constitute the highest grade of education. They are broadly divided into various faculties, including languages, especially Russian, engineering, agriculture, forestry, economics and finance, political science and law, medicine, physical culture, natural sciences and arts. These faculties are further divided into a wide variety of specialized fields, ranging through such diverse subjects as oil engineering, cattle breeding, rail transport, diplomacy, interpreting and classic opera. These specialized courses are designed to prepare persons for immediate employment in the appropriate fields of production, social services or administration.

UNIVERSITY ENTRANCE AND INSTRUCTION

Efforts are being made to increase the number of elementary schools and to make the middle schools, especially the junior middle schools, accessible to a larger section of the population. University entries, however, although continuing to increase, are regulated by a system limiting

The tableland of Shansi, northeast China. The province forms the most easterly part of the loess region. It is traversed by the 430 mile course of the Fen River, which rises in the Luya range. The river is navigable for much of its course across Shansi and provides an important communication route.

annual intakes into the various faculties according to the personnel requirements of the different branches of the administration for which the students will be prepared.

Among the most important qualification for university entrance are political ideology, academic merit and moral conduct. A particular effort is made by the government to provide university places for the greatest possible number of students from the artisans and peasantry.

Studies and practical work are closely linked, both in the senior middle schools, as has already been mentioned, and in the universities. Practical experience in the workshops, farms or factories where the students eventually will be employed is interspersed with academic studies.

The cost of instruction at the universities is borne by the state. Additional expenses, such as board and lodging, books and other scholastic materials are normally the responsibility of the students and their families. However, if they are unable to meet these financial commitments adequate state

grants can usually be obtained.

The most promising graduates from scientific faculties are able to take courses of post-graduate studies at various institutes for scientific research. In 1959 and 1960 a long-range program for scientific development was inaugurated, with the aim of improving facilities for scientific research. The highest research body in China is the Academia Sinica, which has institutes of history and philology, chemistry, botany, zoology, ethnology and modern history.

NEW UNIVERSITIES

The old universities of China were mostly concentrated in the ancient coastal cities and commercial centers, including Peking, Shanghai, Tientsin, Canton, Chungking, Nanking and Shenyang. A particular effort has been made to build new university complexes in the provinces and inland regions, taking into account the local personnel requirements for graduates. A large number of engineering faculties have been set up in places where, due to the existence

of natural resources, new mining and industrial projects are under construction.

In 1962-63 there were fifteen universities in China. These were the People's University of China (Peking); Peking University; Amoy University (Fukien); Futon University (Shanghai); Inner Mongolia University (Huhehot); Lanchow University (Lanchow); Nankai University (Tientsin); Nankin University (Nanking); People's University of Northeast China (Changchun); Northwestern University (Sian); Shantung University (Tsingtao); Sun Yat-sen University (Kwangchow); Szechwan University (Chengtu); Wuhan University (Wuhan); and Yunnan University (Kunming).

Language

In China, with its many ethnic groups, many different languages and dialects are spoken. The principal group of languages are those spoken by the Han, or Chinese, who constitute more than 90 per cent of the population. The other groups are those of China's national minorities.

HAN DIALECTS

Like all languages, Chinese, or Han, has continually evolved and has changed greatly throughout the centuries. The process of evolution and change is particularly notable in the spoken language, which includes a large number of dialects and can be divided into ten principal groups, which often differ considerably from each other.

The ten groups are:

a) Northern Mandarin, spoken in North China, Manchuria and Sinkiang.

b) Southwestern Mandarin, spoken in Szechwan, Kweichow, Yunnan, northern Kwangsi, western Hunan, Hupeh and southern Shensi.

c) Southern Mandarin, spoken in Anhwei and in Kiangsu, north of the lower Yangtze.

d) The *wu* dialect, spoken in Chekiang, Kiangsu and eastern Kiangsi, south of the lower Yangtze.

e) The *kan* dialect, spoken in Kiangsi, around Lake Poyang.

f) The *hsiang* dialect of Hunan.

g) The *min* dialect, spoken in Fukien, Taiwan, Hainan and northeastern Kwangtung, and including northern *min*, centering on Foochow, and southern *min*, centering on Amoy and Swatow.

h) The *hakka* dialect, spoken in northeastern Kwangtung, southern

Kiangsi, western Fukien and parts of Kwangsi, Hunan, Szechwan and Taiwan.

i) The *yueh* (Cantonese) dialect, spoken in Kwangtung and Kwangsi.

j) Minor dialects, spoken in southern Anhwei, southwestern Hunan, northeastern Kwangsi and other areas.

Compared with the spoken language, written Han, which is based on the dialects of northern China, has evolved slowly.

LITERARY HAN

The literary Han language was richer, more complex and more disciplined and refined than was the spoken language. Its geographical distribution covered all China but its use was limited to the educated classes and professional writers.

The literary language has two distinct branches. The first is the *wenyen*, or classical language, which is over 2000 years old. Its use has not yet been abandoned, for the poems of Mao Tse-tung, published in 1957, were written in *wenyen*.

The second branch is the *paihua*, or spoken language. This began to spread in the 13th century, under the Mongol dynasty, and reached its peak in the 16th century, at the end of the Ming dynasty. It continued to be enriched with expressions from the Peking dialect and during the 19th century, under the Manchu dynasty, it became known as the Mandarin language, or *kuan-hua*.

The most important national minority languages are Uigur, spoken mainly in Sinkiang; Tibetan, spoken in Tibet, Tsinghai and west Szechwan; and Mongolian, spoken mainly in Mongolia. Manchu, which was one of the principal languages spoken under the last Ch'ing dynasty, has become a dead language since the fall of the Ch'ing, or Manchu, dynasty in 1912.

A final non-Han linguistic group, which is large and extremely varied, is the collection of the languages and dialects spoken by the national minorities in Yunnan, Kwangsi, Kweichow, Hunan, Sinkiang, Kirin and Heilungkiang. Most of these are similar to the languages spoken in the respective bordering countries—Vietnam, Thailand, Burma, Tadzhikistan, Korea and eastern Siberia.

COMMON LANGUAGE

In 1912, after the fall of the Manchus, the Mandarin language became known as the *p'u-t'ung-hua*, or common speech. It has gradually become the dominant Chinese literary language. In 1956 the government began a program for all Chinese to learn Mandarin.

In the present period of transition between a backward feudal society and a modern industrial state, the Chinese language has been continually enriched by new words and phrases designed to meet new needs. The literary language has also become increasingly influenced by the spoken language.

Chinese words are generally short, averaging about two syllables. The number of phonetic sounds is relatively limited, and the same sound may have a wide variety of meanings. This has led to the use of tones and musical inflections in the pronunciation of vowels. The number of tones varies between three and seven depending on the dialect; Mandarin, for example, has four.

IDEOGRAPHIC SCRIPT

The Chinese literary language has developed side by side with the scripts in which it is written. These have been the means of spreading the language and have also contributed to its evolution. Each word in Chinese script, which is ideographic, is expressed by one or more signs. These do not represent sounds, but ideas or concepts.

There are a very large number of these signs, or word pictures. The great dictionary of the Emperor K'anghsi, dating from the beginning of the 18th century, lists some 40,000. However, a large number have now fallen into disuse while an increasing number of phonetic elements has been introduced into the script.

Nevertheless, it is true to say that

The summit of the Hwa Shan, at 7218 feet the highest peak in the Hwa mountains, lying to the south of the Wei River in south-central Shensi. The Hwa Shan is a sacred mountain of the Buddhist faith and is topped by a shrine. The Hwa mountains are, together with the Tsinling range in the south, the chief mountain masses of Shensi province.

NORTHEASTERN CHINA

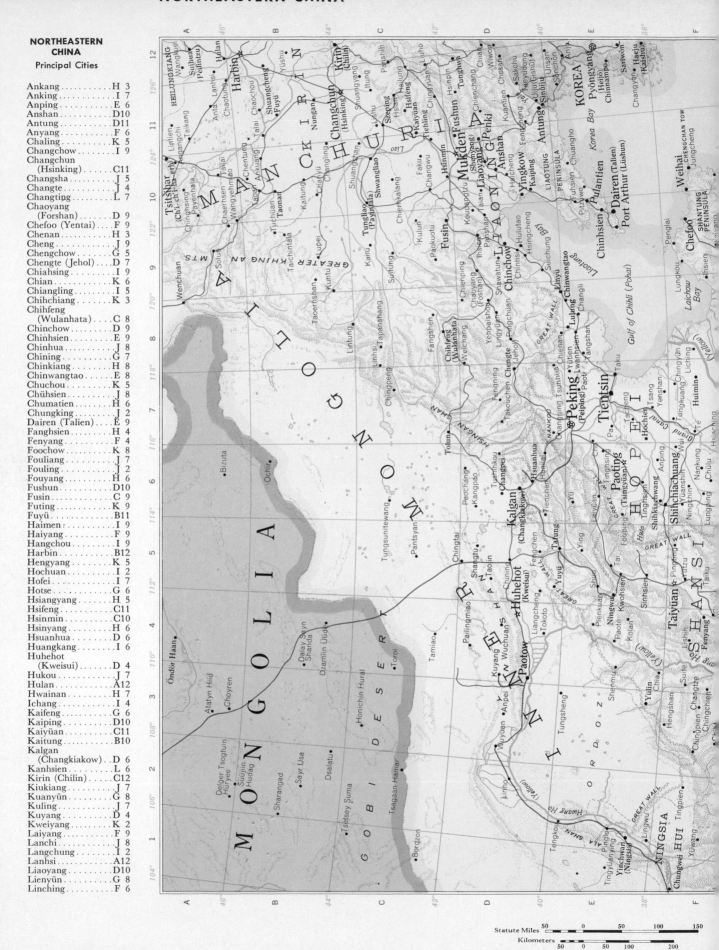

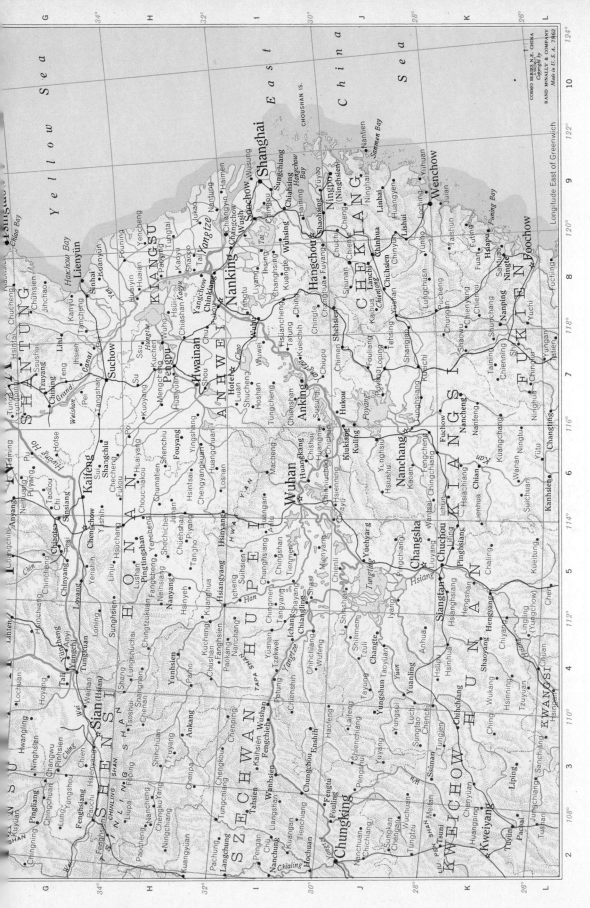

Lambert Conformal Conic Projection
SCALE 1 : 8,000,000   1 Inch = 126 Statute Miles

the correspondence between the writing of words and their pronunciation, an important part of most modern languages which enables words to be read even if the sense is not understood, is almost entirely missing in Chinese.

There is, however, one considerable advantage in this aspect of Chinese. Anyone who knows the meaning of Chinese characters can understand a written text even though he cannot pronounce it. In a country with so many different dialects, this has been a valuable element in cultural and political unification.

MINORITY ALPHABETS AND SCRIPTS

The Uigur, Tibetan, Mongolian and Manchu languages had an established alphabet and script during the whole course of their development In the last few decades the populations of other national minorities have been enabled to have their own script, based on the Latin alphabet.

These scripts were originally introduced by European missionaries and have since been adopted, with improvements, variations and elaborations, by the Chinese authorities. Like the great majority of scripts in use in the modern world, the scripts of the national minorities are based on the phonetic system, in complete contrast to the Chinese script, which is still fundamentally ideographic.

MODERN PHONETIC SCRIPT

In 1912, after the overthrow of the Manchus, a movement was begun which advocated the substitution of a phonetic script based on Latin characters for the traditional script. This movement was opposed by the educated classes, whose hard-won knowledge of the traditional script was an important factor in preserving their privileged position.

After a number of abortive attempts at reform a commission was set up to study the problem. In 1956 a new phonetic alphabet with Latin characters was completed. This was accepted by the government, which put into action a plan designed to ensure its gradual adoption by the masses. At the same time, measures were introduced to reduce the number of ideographic characters in the traditional script by several hundred, so that the traditional common language might become more widely diffused.

Over the past few years, progress in the Latinization of the Chinese language has been very great. However, the new script still serves more as an auxiliary for the diffusion of the common language than as a substitute for the old, traditional system of writing.

Numerals

The Chinese system of counting is less complicated. The Western *O* is used to indicate zero, and Chinese characters indicate the figures from one to ten, the latter being written as a cross (X).

The numerals between ten and twenty are formed by adding the appropriate number to ten. Thus, eleven is "ten-one" and fifteen "ten-five." Twenty and further multiples of ten up to 100 are expressed as "two-ten," and so on.

Special characters are used for large numbers above 1000, and these characters are deliberately made more complex when used on banknotes, as a safeguard against forgery.

Monetary System

Since 1951 the official coinage of the Chinese People's Republic has been the *Jen-Min-Pi* (J.M.P.), or popular currency. Since the revaluation of 1955, the basic monetary unit has been the *yuan*, the unit introduced in 1948 by the Nationalists.

Lake Tai 40 miles long and 35 miles wide, is one of the largest lakes in China. It is linked to the navigable Grand Canal, which crosses Kiangsu from Chingkiang on the Yangtze to Soochow on the Whangpoo river. The inhabitants of the area surrounding Lake Tai are mainly engaged in growing cereals and in fishing.

The *Jen-Min-Piao* (People's Bank dollar) generally called *yuan*, is divided into ten *chiao*, each *chiao* being further divided into ten *fen*, or cents. Notes to the value of one, two, five, ten, twenty and fifty *fen* are issued as paper currency, although since 1957 coins of one, two and five *fen* value have also been issued. The text on banknotes is printed in Chinese, Uigur, Tibetan and Mongolian.

Since 1951, the circulation of *Jen-Min-Piao* has been strictly limited to the Chinese People's Republic. The foreign exchange market is limited to the People's Bank of China, which can change foreign currencies into *yuan* for legitimate possessors of currency, both foreign and Chinese.

Although there is, at present, no official rate of exchange for the *Jen-Min-Piao* and the United States dollar, it may be assumed that since the pound sterling is worth 6.86 *Jen-Min-Piao*, the dollar is worth about 2.45 *Jen-Min-Piao*.

Measurement

Although the work of converting the traditional system of weights and measures to the metric system was completed some time ago, the metric system still · is not in general use. Since the old system is still used in many publications and is still in current use, a few examples may be given.

LENGTH AND AREA

One *shih chih* = 1.094 feet
One *shih li* = 0.311 miles
One square *shih chih* =
  1.195 square feet
One *shih mow* = 0.1647 acres

WEIGHT AND VOLUME

One *shih catty* = 1.102 pounds
One *Taiwan catty* = 1.333 pounds
One *picul* = 110.231 pounds
One *shih sheng* =
  0.264 U.S. gallons
One cubic *shih chih* =
  1.308 cubic feet

Calendar

The Gregorian solar calendar, as used in the West, is in official use in modern China. The only deviation from Western usage is that months and days of the week are not designated by names. Instead they are given numbers according to their position; January = 1, Monday = 1, and so on.

However, in rural areas where the calendar has always been arranged on the basis of agricultural pursuits, conforming to the seasons for sowing or harvesting, the traditional Chinese calendar is still in general use.

The traditional calendar is arranged in sixty-year cycles, divided into equal periods by the signs of the zodiac. The month was indicated by the moon, and usually consisted of thirty days, with twelve months in each year. A Chinese scientist has calculated that the average length of the old Chinese year was 365¼ days.

The Chinese year is normally made up of twelve lunar months of thirty days each, the odd days accumulated being inserted as an extra month every third year. The year is divided into twenty-four *chieh*, or divisions. Four fixed points, the equinoxes and solstices, divide the *chieh* into four equal seasons of six *chieh* each. The *chieh* are further divided into *chieh-ch'i* and *chung-ch'i*.

The Chinese day has twelve *shih*, or divisions. Each *shih* lasts for two hours, the day beginning at midnight.

PHYSICAL GEOGRAPHY

Geographical Divisions

CHINA IS DIVIDED INTO TWO PRINcipal parts. Eastern China, consisting mainly of the area known as China Proper, includes practically the entire area east of the 100th Meridian East. This area possesses the most favorable conditions for human habitation. In Western China, west of the 100th Meridian East, conditions are far less favorable.

Western China is usually summarily divided into only two natural regions—Tibet-Tsinghai and Sinkiang. Eastern China requires a more complicated analysis. It is divided into two parts—northern and southern China—each of which has four natural regions.

NORTHERN CHINA

THE CHIEF CHARACTERISTICS OF northern China are its great stretches of level land interspersed with hills. Cold, rainless winters are followed by hot, wet summers with about 25 to 30 inches of rainfall. The soil is rich in lime and calcium compounds and is dark and friable. The growing season lasts for between four and six months, with one or two harvests. Agriculture is precarious, with yields falling sharply in seasons of flood or drought,

A Buddhist monastery in Szechwan.

since most fields are not artificially irrigated. The principal crops are rice, millet and sorghum. There are few forests.

The Yellow River Plain

The plain of the Yellow River is the largest and most densely populated in China. It stretches along the coast from the Gulf of Chihli at the 40th Parallel North to the coast of Kiangsu around the 33rd Parallel North, a distance of about 500 miles. Its inland boundary is marked by a broad arc of mountains which runs from the Mongolian border to Shanhaikwan, through the ranges of Yen, Funiu, Tungpeh and the hills of Hwaiyan, and into the plains of Kiangsu.

The greater part of the Yellow River plain was probably originally a large gulf, which was gradually filled in by the alluvial deposits carried down by the Yellow River and the other rivers of the basin.

The region can be divided into five principal areas. These are the belt of hills and mountains, the hills of Shantung, the Hopeh basin, the lower reach of the Yellow River, and the basin of the Hwai and its tributaries.

THE HILL AND MOUNTAIN BELT

The hill and mountain systems that define the plain of the Yellow

Isolated farmsteads in southeast Tibet. Although the climatic conditions of central and northern Tibet are such that vegetation is scanty, in some areas of the south, particularly near rivers, luxuriant vegetation is found. It is in these more fertile areas that isolated farms surrounded by small cultivated fields are situated.

River consist of the outer escarpments of the Mongolian and loess plateaus in the north and west and the continuation of the massive Tsinling range beyond the Yellow River in the south.

North of the Chinwangtao-Peking line, the Mongolian plateau descends to plains through broad, rectangular valleys running between gently sloping mountain ridges rising to about 3000-4000 feet.

WEST OF THE YELLOW RIVER

To the west of the Yellow River plain, the loess plateau towers above it in steep parallel chains including the Heng mountains, the Wutai range near the Chahar-Hopeh line, which rises about 10,000 feet, and the Taihang mountains which continue southward to the Yellow River.

To the south of the river, the Tsinling range enters the province of Honan, where it becomes gradually lower, reaching a height of between 4000-6000 feet as it runs through the Funiu, Tungpei and Tapieh mountains. The southeastern branch forms the Tienmu mountains beyond the Yangtze River while the northeastern branch forms the Hwaiyan hills, which separate the Hwai Ho basin from that of the Yangtze River.

The whole of this mountain belt is among the most sparsely vegetated areas in China. It is considerably marked by erosion, particularly in the mountains and hills of Honan, which are covered with a layer of loess. Most of the watercourses in the plains below originate in the mountain belt.

The Hills of Shantung

The hills of Shantung are of the same geological formation as the Changpai mountains on the Korea-Manchuria line and the hills of Liaotung in Manchuria, of which they are a continuation. They form the backbone of the peninsula and hinterland of Shantung.

The zone consists of two regions, peninsular and continental. These are divided by a strip of sedimentary lowland, through which a canal runs, joining the bays of Kiaochow and Laichow, at the southern and northern extremities of the neck of the peninsula.

The highest point in the peninsula is in the Lao Shan near Tsingtao, which reaches a height of 3707 feet; and the highest on the mainland is in the Tai Shan, one of the sacred mountains of China, which is situated to the south of the provincial capital of Tsinan and reaches a height of 5069 feet. Elsewhere, elevations seldom exceed 3000 feet.

As well as extensive erosion, the hills of Shantung have suffered considerable denudation of vegetation. These factors would have been even more damaging but for the moderate slopes and very solid rock surfaces. The coast of Shantung, like that of Liaotung, is very irregular in comparison to the low, sandy shores of the rest of the regions.

The Hopeh Basin

The Hopeh basin, which is fan-shaped, centers on the Gulf of Chihli and is bounded on the west and northwest by the Shansi and Inner Mongolian plateaus. Its minor rivers, the Lwan, Pai, Yungting and Huto, descend from bare mountains in areas where precipitation varies considerably according to season and locality and where heavy erosion has occurred. Consequently, their flows are irregular and torrential.

Some of these rivers make their way to the sea independently. The most important is the Lwan which, together with some of its tributaries, rises in the Mongolian plateau, crosses the Jehol mountains and flows into the Gulf of Chihli through a large delta. Most of the rivers cross the plain by devious routes and form a collective estuary after joining the Pai River, in the Tientsin region.

THE LONGEST RIVER

The longest river that flows into the Gulf of Chihli is the Yungting, which rises in northern Shansi and flows to the west of Peking.

Next in importance is the Wei Ho, which rises in the southernmost part of the Taihang mountains. The Huto Ho, called the Tzeya in its lower course, flows down from the slopes of the Wutai mountains. The Peh Ho rises north of Peking and flows to the east of the city, while the Chaopai, east of the Peh Ho, takes an independent course to the sea but is linked to the Hai Ho system by canals.

NUMEROUS SWAMPS

The great quantity of eroded soil and rock carried down by these rivers, especially during heavy rains, has caused them to change their courses frequently. Poor natural drainage has given rise to numerous swamps.

A number of projects for the control of these rivers have recently been put into operation. The Yungting has been contained by a dam, which has formed a large artificial lake, and the Chaopai by a dyke. Numerous other barricades have been built, involving the removal of billions of cubic yards of earth and stones. Since modern earth-moving machinery often is not available, much of this work has had to be done by manual labor, making the process of averting floods and improving drainage and irrigation a slow, laborious task.

THE LOWER REACH OF THE YELLOW RIVER

In the Sanmen gorge, the bed of the Yellow River leaves the well-defined valley running through the foothills of Shansi and Honan and enters a wide plain. Further along the gorge, near the provincial capital of Chengchow, all natural barriers to the river's course disappear; from this point it becomes erratic.

Almost all the northern Chinese plain has been, at some time or other, the plain of the Yellow River. Because of its high level, the river has no tributaries flowing into its lower reaches. The local watercourses are collected by other rivers running parallel to the Yellow River.

There have been elaborate schemes to eliminate the recurrent flooding caused by fluctuations in the volume of the Yellow River in this area by making its course more regular. The latest of these projects is a plan to regulate the whole basin. This calls for soil conservation works and reforestation along the middle reach and its principal tributaries, for the construction of flood basins, irrigation canals and numerous hydroelectric plants. The first stage of the project is scheduled for completion in 1967, and it is hoped that by that time the risk of flooding will be eliminated, hydroelectric resources developed, the irrigated area considerably increased and the navigable length of the river extended by about ten times.

The third most important basin in the Yellow River plain is that of the Hwai. The Hwai collects the waters of the tributaries which flow from Honan, southern Shantung and southern Anhwei and spread out into a fan shape towards the depression of northern Kiangsu.

The rainfall and terrain of the Hwai basin are similar to those of the Yellow River basin, and the river and its tributaries have the same irregular pattern of flow. The problem of insufficient flow is, in fact, so serious that for centuries the Hwai has had no proper outlet to the sea.

THE BIG LAKES

This has resulted in the formation of big lakes. These include the great lake of Hungtze, the smaller lake of Kaoyu, on the Kiangsu-Anhwei border, and many minor lakes along the middle reach of the Hwai. The size of the lakes vary according to the season or year. At many

Rice fields in western Shantung. The province of Shantung is bounded on the east by the Yellow Sea and is traversed by two great mountain ranges, the Lao Shan and the Tai Shan, around which lies a wide belt of flat, intensely cultivated land. Agricultural production is fairly high, since the region is irrigated by canals fed by the Yellow River. The main crops of the area are cereals, cotton and fruit

points, large areas remain flooded for long periods after heavy rains. When these areas dry out, they are desolate wastelands unfit for agriculture.

Honan is the principal lake district of China. In addition, subterranean infiltration of both running and stagnant water has caused the formation of one of the largest areas of underground watercourses and water eroded channels in the country. This area covers about 130,000 square miles in western Honan, northern Anhwei and Kiangsu.

One of the main problems for northern China is the regulation of the Hwai and its tributaries. A large scale project for the construction of dams and canals is now under way. Among the most important of these constructions is the Grand Canal in Kiangsu, linking the Hungtze and Kaoyu lakes.

CLIMATE AND VEGETATION

The Yellow River plain has a dry, temperate climate, influenced by dry air masses from the Mongolian deserts. The rainfall is limited and the winters often severe. The growing season lasts from four to six months and usually yields only one crop annually.

Temperatures are milder in the province of Shantung, which has a continental climate and benefits from its proximity to the sea.

Taking the region as a whole, there are usually about 2500 hours of sunshine every year and 100 to 150 days on which the temperature falls below freezing point. The rivers and the Po Sea are frozen for three or four months of the year.

During the winter, the dry winds are strong and a high level of sunshine is maintained. However, this increases evaporation and restricts the formation of organic substances in the soil. These factors explain the lack of pastureland and woods, not only in the cultivated plains but also in the mountain belt of northern China, which is among the barest landscapes in the country. The dominant colors of the landscape are those of the red sandstone rocks and yellow soil.

The most common of the trees in the area are pine, oak, cedar, ash, cypress, acacia, willow, poplar, walnut, chestnut, pear, plum and, particulary in Shantung, apple, peach and apricot.

The soil of the plain, continually enriched by wind and water-borne deposits, is still fertile after many centuries of cultivation. The mountain and hill zones are less fertile, although the grayish-white soil, typical of cold, coniferous wooded areas, is suitable for orchards. The least fertile areas are the sandy and saline stretches along the coast.

However, modern methods of improving the condition of the soil are gradually doing a great deal to change the aspect of the region.

The Loess Plateau

The mountainous plateau crossed by the middle reach of the Yellow River and its tributaries extends over Shansi, Shensi, eastern Kansu and the autonomous region of Ningsia Hui. It is covered by a layer of loess, a fine, yellowish loam produced by erosion and windborne sedimentation, varying between 25 and 250 feet in depth.

Loess is extremely porous but also has strong cohesive qualities. Thus, it does not crumble away when it is cut or excavated. Wherever the layer is sufficiently thick there is a profusion of ditches and gulleys worn by water or the passage of man, together with caves excavated for use as dwellings or storehouses.

Unfortunately, the western part of the plateau around Lungsi, where important Quaternary formations are

Laborers repair breaches in the levees of a river in flood in Kwangtung. Much damage is caused in low-lying areas by the flooding of China's great rivers, though considerable advances have recently been made in controlling the flow of the rivers and diverting their waters for agricultural and hydroelectric purposes. In tasks such as that illustrated here, China makes up for a lack of modern earth-moving machinery by the utilization of the country's vast resources of man-power.

A view of the Gobi desert in northwest China. The Gobi occupies an area of some 500,000 square miles; it is about 1000 miles long and 500 miles wide. On the borders of the province of Kansu extensive reforestation work has been initiated in order to prevent the sands of the Gobi from encroaching on cultivated land. A belt of shrubs of a type suitable to dry, sandy soil stretches along the edge of the desert, its thickness increasing near villages and agricultural settlements.

mingled with those of older periods, is one of the regions of China most subject to violent earthquakes. These cause serious landslides in the loess layer. The earthquake which occurred in 1920 was one of the most disastrous ever recorded, claiming thousands of victims and changing the appearance of large areas.

MOUNTAINS

The plateau is bounded on all sides by moutains of varying heights. The most important and complex of these ranges is the Tsinling in the south, which rises to over 12,000 feet in the Tapai Shan. The Taihang and Wutai mountains to the east dominate the plain of the Yellow River. In the north and west the mountain chains are more irregular, but they are linked together by the line formed by the central part of the Great Wall. This runs from the boundary between Hopeh, Shansi and Mongolia to the eastern flanks of the Nan Shan, north of Lanchow.

THE GREAT WALL REBUILT

The Great Wall is not only a colossal piece of military architecture which has at times constituted the boundary of an empire, but also one of the most important geographic barriers between the various regions of China. After the unification brought about under Emperor Shih Huangti of the Ch'in dynasty in 221-206 B.C., it was repeatedly rebuilt and reinforced up

to the time of the Ming dynasty (1368-1644). Its course corresponded to permanent elements dividing the arable loess lands from the deserts and steppes of Mongolia. These elements included geological, climatic and anthropological characteristics.

OTHER MOUNTAINS

There are numerous other mountain groups in the loess region, the most important being the Luliang in western Shansi and the Liupan Shan, with the Lungsi plateau, in eastern Kansu.

The loess plateau may be divided into three main zones; the Shansi plateau, around the axis of the Fen River valley; the valley of the middle Yellow River; and the plateau of Shensi-Kansu, including the valleys of the Wei and the other tributaries of the Yellow River.

The Shansi Plateau

The plateau of Shansi lies between the Taihang and Wutai mountains. It is bounded by Shensi on the west and by the part of Honan lying along the Yellow River. It has an average height of between 2500 and 5000 feet and has a corrugated surface forming numerous mountain groups interspersed with valleys. The Fen River bisects the area, flowing

in a north-south direction through a series of valleys. Between the Fen valley and the Yellow River lies the Luliang range, which extends in a north-south direction to form the western edge of the plateau.

ARC TO PEKING

To the north and east of the Fen valley there are a number of mountain complexes, among them the Taihang and the Wutai at the edge of the plateau. The Luliang chain descends steeply, in short, perpendicular valleys, to the Yellow River valley, but the eastern mountain groups have a more complex structure. They enclose several extensive inland basins in the north, east and south, including the valley of. the Sangkan, which descends in a broad arc to Peking, the valleys of the Huto and the Tsang, which descend into the plain of Hopeh, and the valley of the Tsin Ho, which descends to the south to join the Yellow River.

Because of its relatively uneven formation, Shansi is the area where the distribution of the layer of loess is least uniform. Loess accumulates in the valleys and on the gentler slopes, especially those facing northwest, while the ridges and rock faces, formed through denudation and erosion, project above the main loess bed.

Beneath the layer of loess in Shansi are found thick, horizontal layers of coal, the largest deposits of this commodity in China.

The Valley of the Middle Yellow River

A little above Lanchow, where the outskirts of the Nan Shan range meet those of the Tsinling, the Yellow River enters its middle reach. It flows in the shape of an inverted "U", first north, then east, then south, with its center in the Ordos desert plateau. The northernmost part of its course, from Yinchwan to Hoku, is outside the Great Wall in Mongolia.

At Lanchow, the bed of the Yellow River is about 4927 feet above sea level. At the end of its middle reach, in the Sanmen gorge, it is about 650 feet. A fairly high average gradient is maintained over a course of more than 1250 miles, but this is unevenly distributed between different reaches. From Lanchow to Yinchwan the river flows fairly rapidly. From the Yinchwan plain to the end of its southward progress, near Hoku, it flows through gently sloping valleys broadening out into wide plains like those of Paotow and Huhehot in Mongolia. This is the only navigable stretch of the river's middle reach.

MEAGER SUMMER STREAMS

Very little water flows in from tributaries on the middle reach, the only important sources being the streams descending from the Liupan mountains in Kansu, on the right bank. Further north, also on the right bank, a few meager summer streams flow in from the Ordos desert. On the left bank, no important tributaries descend from the Holan mountains or the Yin Shan and between these mountains the sands of the Alashan desert extend to the banks of the Yellow River.

The evaporation rate in the middle reach is very high and large quantities of water are diverted for irrigation purposes. Thus, the flow of the Yellow River is reduced rather than increased.

OVER THE GREAT WALL

After recrossing the Great Wall at Hoku, the Yellow River passes through a series of precipitous gorges chiseled from the soft loess and the harder rock beneath. These are full of rapids, making navigation impossible. However, the increased rate of flow makes this region ideal for the production of hydro-electric power. Work is in progress to regulate the flow of the waters and to construct the necessary dams.

This reach of the Yellow River marks the boundary between Shansi in the east and Shensi in the west. Shansi provides only one important tributary, the Fen, which joins the Yellow River almost at the end of this reach. However, a number of important tributaries flow from Shensi through long valleys set at right angles to the river.

The Plateau of Shensi and Kansu

The drainage basin of the rivers flowing through Shensi to the Yellow River extends between the Ordos desert, the Liupan range, the Yellow River and the Tsinling, and forms the heart of the region. Surrounded by mountains and desert, it was one of the original areas of human settlement and plays an important part in China's early history. It has often been a most important strategic stronghold for the domination of China, both for its geographical position and the fertility of its valley.

GENTLE LANDSCAPE

The plateau has an average height of around 4900 feet, reaching its highest point around 10,000 feet in the Liupan Shan. Compared with neighboring Shansi, the landscape is less corrugated and more gentle. The valleys are broader and the country is hilly rather than mountainous.

The most important valleys are the Wei, which extends from west to east at the foot of the Tsinling, the King Ho in Hupeh, between the Han and Yangtze rivers, and the valley of the Lo River, which has its source on the edge of the Ordos desert. Both the King Ho and Lo Ho have torrential courses. They converge into the valley of the Wei River, the King Ho flowing into the Wan and the Lo Ho flowing straight down to the Yellow River.

Other minor tributaries from the eastern rim of the Ordos desert join the Yellow River further up in the mountains. The most important of these is the Wuting Ho.

Although the Shensi plateau is mainly an area of water-borne rather than wind-borne deposits, the Wei basin, especially in its lower reach, is a zone of both wind-and water-borne deposits and is thus one of the most level areas and the finest for agriculture of the northwest. It possesses an irrigation system dating back more than 2000 years.

CLIMATE

Although the loess plateau is more exposed than other areas of China Proper to the cold, winter winds from Mongolia, it is more sheltered than most from the wet, southeast monsoons. This is mainly due to the great barrier formed by the Tsinling in the south.

The clear air of the high plateau accentuates seasonal and daily fluctuations in temperature, making the climate colder and drier than that of the adjoining Yellow River plain. The average annual temperature varies between 50° and 60° F. from area to area. The number of days on which the temperature falls below freezing point varies between 125 and 150 annually.

Annual rainfall varies between about 20 inches in the plain of the Wei to about 7 inches in the Ningsia plain. The tempestuous nature of the precipitation increases toward the Yellow River plain, and the rivers of this area are thus subject to periods of disastrous flooding.

SOIL

The natural green covering of the soft loess is sparse, while the forest areas have been mostly destroyed and the cultivated area extended even into the hilly zones where the gradients permit. Recent hydraulic erosion is thus more marked in this area than elsewhere in China. Most of the detritus that the Yellow River carries down through the Sanmen gorge, amounting to about one billion tons annually, comes from the loess region, and it is the yellow color of this soil that gives the river its name.

The fertility of the layer of alluvial loess in the Yellow River plain has already been mentioned. The same fertility exists in the superficial wind-borne deposits of the plateau, but it is strictly dependent on an adequate supply of water. Since rainfall is infrequent and of a torrential nature, and as the slope of the land facilitates rapid drainage, the area is, in fact, very dry.

VEGETATION

Because of the prevailing directions of the winds, the peripheral zones of the north and west, bordering on the deserts, are constantly exposed to the menace of the sand dunes which may advance and bury their meager pastures. Spontaneous vegetation is thus very scarce. The only real forests grow on the slopes of the Tsinling, and the only woods on the slopes of the Liupan mountains and of the mountains of northern Shensi and Shansi.

On the Tsinling mountains, conifers predominate. Elsewhere the most common trees are poplar, oak, linden, birch, walnut, hazel, elm and' cherry. The steppe lands cover a wide area but their vegetation mainly consists of sparse tufts of grass and thornbush.

Large-scale projects aimed at improving the water supply and reclaiming the soil are in progress on the loess plateau. Since the Yellow River receives much of its flood water from the loess basin, dams built on local tributaries will not only improve the area's irrigation but also contribute toward the work of controlling the water of the Yellow River in its lower reaches.

Soil retention and reclamation involves reforestation, protection and extension of grass land, terracing cultivated slopes, cutting terraces in eroded ravines and planting protective belts of trees to slow down the process of erosion and to block the advance of the desert sands.

ANIMAL LIFE

Unlike the intensively cultivated plain of the Yellow River, the loess plateau has uncultivated areas which are the home of numerous wild animals. Among the carnivores are tigers, wolves, leopards, wild dogs and badgers. Hoofed animals include various kinds of deer, wild goats and wild boars. Hares and rabbits are numerous, and birds include the golden eagle and various species of vultures.

Northeast China (Manchuria)

The most northerly region of China is Manchuria. It extends over Heilungkiang, Kirin and Liaoning, and over the most easterly part of the autonomous region of Mongolia.

The western boundary of Manchuria is formed by the Great Khingan ranges and their southern spurs and, further south, by the Jehol mountains extending to Chinwangtao on the Gulf of Chihli. The northern boundary is formed by the Amur

A party of children cross a primitive bridge suspended over a ravine in Tibet.

River. The eastern boundary is formed by the Ussuri and Tumen rivers and their associated lakes, by the Pai-T'ou massif, which is part of the Changpai range, and by the Yalu River. The southern boundary is the coast of the Yellow Sea and of the Gulf of Chihli.

The seacoast, stretching from Shanhaikwan to the mouth of the Yalu River, includes Liaotung, the second great peninsula of China.

It is a characteristic of the river forming the boundaries of this region that only a part of their course flows through Chinese territory. The Argun, Amur and Ussuri flow alternately through the territories of the U.S.S.R. and China, with about 50 per cent in each region. The greater part of Lake Khanka is in Soviet territory. The Tumen River is almost entirely in North Korea and of the Yalu only the lower and part of the middle reaches are in Chinese territory. Treaties made with the Soviet and Korean governments govern navigation and transport of timber on the rivers in question.

GEOGRAPHICAL DIVISIONS

The area of Manchuria falls into two distinct parts: the mountains and hills stretching into the interior from immediately behind the inland boundaries and the central plain which extends to the bay of Liaotung on the Gulf of Chihli.

The hill and mountain chain in turn divides into two parts: the Great and Lesser Khingan, to the north and west of the plain, and the parallel ranges of the Chang-Kwan-Tsai-Ling and the Changpai, to the east and southeast of the plain.

The plain may be divided into its two main river basins: that of the Nonni and the Sungari to the north, and that of the Liao to the south.

THE GREAT AND THE LESSER KHINGAN

The mountains and hills which form the eastern edge of the Mongolian plateau are known as the Great Khingan. They stretch from the most northerly bend of the Amur to the area of Tolun, where they join the Yin Shan range, in a direction roughly north-northeast to south-southwest. The width of the range sometimes exceeds 125 miles, rising to a maximum elevation of 5670 feet in the peak of Shihwei. Its outline is undulating, with a very slight gradient on the Mongolian side and a much steeper slope on the east, on the edge of the geological subsidence which is said to have formed the Manchurian plain.

Beyond the Liao valley, the Great Khingan is prolonged in the mountains of Jehol, the outcrops of which continue down to the sea. The name Jehol, which means "hot water," was at one time given to the province surrounding the city of Chengteh. The name derives from a spring in the city which is said never to freeze over, even in the coldest weather.

At its northern extremity, the Great Khingan range turns abruptly to the southeast, continuing in the hill and mountain system called the Lesser Khingan. Most of the Lesser Khingan system is under 3000 feet in elevation, but it rises to 4665 feet in a peak some eighty miles to the northwest of Kiamusze.

THE CHANG-KWAN-TSAI-LING AND CHANGPAI MOUNTAINS

The Sungari River valley divides the outcrops of the Lesser Khingan from the mountains of eastern Manchuria. These are divided into two main parallel ranges about 300 miles long. The lower of these flanks the Manchurian plain, while the other, higher and more rugged, follows the Korean border.

The highest peak in Manchuria is the Ch'ang-Pai Shan, which rises to 9003 feet and is situated almost in the center of the Korean border. It is the only characteristically cone-shaped volcanic mountain in China and its crater is filled by a small lake. The Ch'ang-Pai is the center of considerable volcanic activity, which occurs in the Changpai mountains and on the western borders of Manchuria.

Lake Khanka, the principal lake of Manchuria, lies in the hollow between the Changpai and Chang-Kwan-Tsai-Ling ranges, as do a number of other minor lakes.

The hills of the Liaotung peninsula are an extension of the Changpai range. They have an average elevation of between 700 and 1600 feet. Their slopes often extend down to the sea, giving the coast an irregular outline fringed by rocks and islets, similar to the coast of Shantung.

The Northern Plain

At Latitude 45° N., the furthest slopes of the Chang-Kwan-Tsai-Ling are joined to the Great Khingan by

A desolate landscape in the Taklamakan desert in the Tarim basin, Sinkiang Uigur. The Taklamakan is uninhabited, although oases linked by caravan routes lie along the foot of the Kunlun mountains in the south and the Tien Shan in the north. The most important settlements to have grown up around these oases are Yarkand and Khotan. Shown here are the remains of an attempt at human settlement.

Agricultural workers cutting sugarcane on a farm in southwest Kwangtung, southern China. The tropical monsoon climate of the region, with rainy springs and summers and cool, dry winters, is favorable to the cultivation of sugarcane, which is a major product of the area around Swatow.

a ridge with a maximum elevation of 1650 feet. This forms a watershed which divides the central Manchurian plain into two separate basins.

The northern basin is the larger, and is divided into two zones. The zone in the southwest, which is between 150 and 650 feet above sea level, is enclosed by the Chang-Kwan-Tsai-Ling and the Great Khingan. The northeast basin, lying outside the mountain ranges, is bounded by the confluence of the Amur and the Ussuri. Its elevation is mainly below 150 feet above sea level.

Two great rivers drain into the northern basin. These are the Nonni, which flows from the junction of the Great and Lesser Khingan ranges in the north, collecting numerous tributaries, mostly from the Great Khingan, and the Sungari, which rises in the Paitow massif in the south and collects much of its water from the mountainous region in the east.

The two rivers meet almost in the center of the northern plain, where the single river formed takes on the name of the Sungari. It then flows north-northeast through the narrow corridor separating the Lesser Khingan from the Chang-Kwan-Tsai-Ling and crosses the eastern plain to join the Amur river. The eastern plain is the result of a silting-up process which is not yet complete, as is shown by the extent of the marshes which still cover more than half its area.

The flow of the Sungari is one of the most regular of all Chinese rivers and that of the Nonni is also generally good. Thus, the part of the Sungari from its confluence with the Nonni to its junction with the Amur, together with the Amur and the Ussuri, forms the second most important navigable waterway in China, second only to the Yangtze.

The Southern Plain

The southern plain, consisting of the valleys of the Liao and its tributaries, is bounded on the west by the southernmost part of the Great Khingan and by the mountains of Jehol and on the east by a continuation of the Changpai range.

The Liao and its western tributaries have more affinity with the rivers of Hopeh than with those of northern Manchuria. They rise either in the same parts of the Jehol mountains as does the Lwan, or in the Khingan ranges, where climatic conditions and rainfall are unfavorable to a regular flow. In addition, widespread deforestation in these areas has led to erosion on a very large scale, disturbing the balance of flow of the rivers and contributing to the drying-up of the grass lands.

The Liao, especially in its upper and middle reaches, is torrential in character. It is liable to flood or to dry up with results just as disastrous as those caused by the rivers of the Yellow River plain, and like them it carries down a large quantity of detritus. To the south of the eroded valley through which the middle reach of the Liao flows, this detritus has been deposited to form a wide alluvial plain. The Liao flows through this plain in its lower reaches where, augmented by several tributaries, it is navigable by quite large craft.

The coastal plain of the Liao was the first part of Manchuria to be colonized or cultivated. In the 17th century fortifications, consisting of

a ditch surmounted by a willow palisade, were built to protect the colony from the attacks of the nomadic tribes which dominated the rest of Manchuria. These fortifications stretched for 750 miles and were pierced by twenty gates.

CLIMATE

Manchuria, which lies approximately between Latitude 40° and 50° N. on the eastern margins of the Asian continent, has short summers and the longest and coldest winters in China. The winter monsoon brings dry, cold air from Siberia. The summer monsoon brings warm, humid air from the South Pacific, raising temperatures in July to around 80° F. Northern Manchuria is a sub-arctic region with an average January temperature of 21° F.; such low winter temperatures do not occur elsewhere in the same latitudes. On the coast of the Liaotung peninsula, however, the climate is temperate, and 60 miles from the coast it becomes continental.

In southern Manchuria the rivers are frozen for about six months of the year, only the harbors of Port Arthur, Dairen and Hu-lu-tao re-

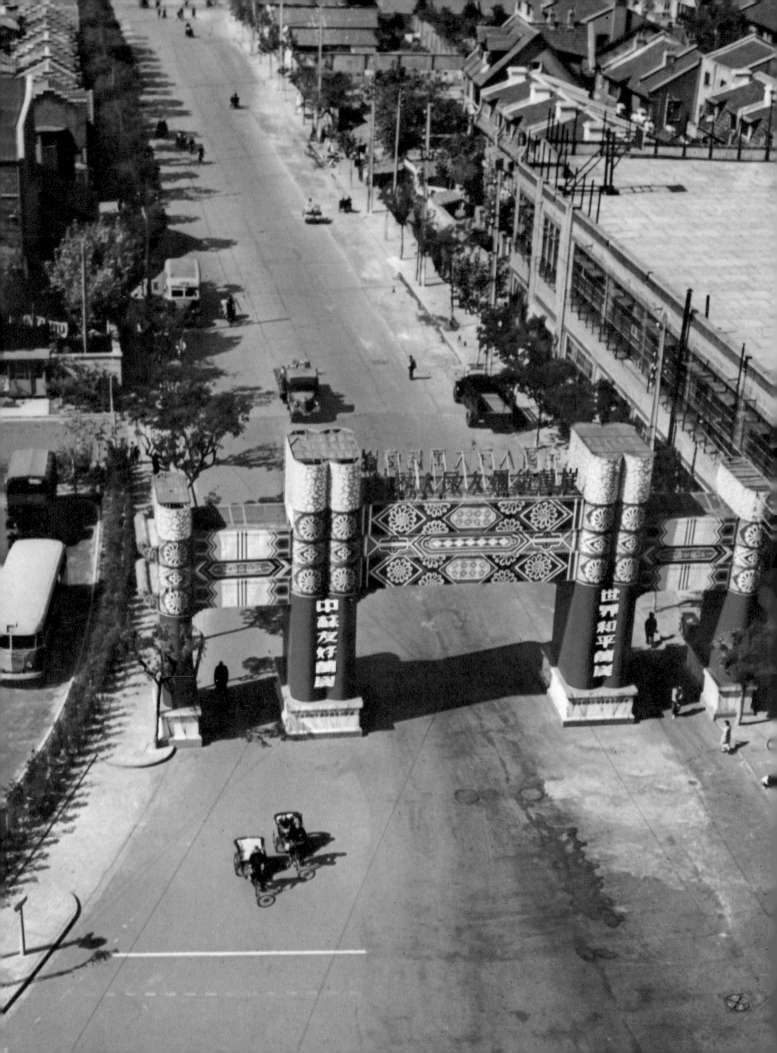

maining ice-free. Summers never last for more than two or three months in the south and they are almost non-existent in the north.

RAINFALL

The volume of rainfall in Manchuria is unevenly distributed. It ranges between 40 inches in the southeast to about 15 inches in the northwest. The wettest area is the Changpai mountains and rainfall is lowest on the plains.

The Changpai mountains have a heavier rainfall because they are exposed to the damp winds blowing from the Sea of Japan. The rainfall in this area is also more evenly distributed than in any other part of Manchuria, and the Changpai range is notable for having larger snow caps, in relation to their size, than any other mountains in China.

Even in the areas with the lowest rainfall, however, the humidity is sufficient to provide good growing conditions. This is because average temperatures are generally low and evaporation is thus much less than in other regions.

LANDSCAPE AND VEGETATION

The favorable balance between rainfall and evaporation has made Manchuria the richest arable land of China, covered with thick forests and rich grass land. The black soil of the grass lands was discovered in the last century to be the best land in China for growing cereals, and the greater part of the Manchurian plain is now under cultivation.

The forests which cover the greater part of the mountain belt consist mainly of conifers on the higher elevations and the northern slopes and conifers mixed with deciduous trees in the valleys and to the south. These forests are the richest in China and constitute about 35 per cent of forest in the entire country.

The only large gap in the forest belt is in the valley of the upper Liao. In this area large-scale reforestation is in progress. The scheme involves the planting of a forest belt 620 miles long from north to south which should halt erosion and the drying-up of the soil and thus improve both the water supply and the vegetation of the basin of the Liao and its tributaries.

The Liaotung peninsula is par-ticularly suited to fruit growing, since both the nature of the soil and the temperate climate are favorable.

The trees most commonly found in Manchuria are fir, Korean pine and larch among the conifers, and poplar, willow, birch, alder, oak, elm, maple, lime, ash and juniper among the broad-leaved trees, at different heights and latitudes. The *ginseng* shrub is notable, since it is widely used for medicinal purposes and is traditionally a cure-all. The aromatic root grows wild in woods and fields and is also cultivated.

FAUNA

The forest areas and grass lands form an excellent environment for wild animals and birds of many different kinds. Manchuria is the habitat of the largest-known species of tiger and the largest wild boars in China are also found in the region, together with black bears, lynxes, wolves and wild dogs.

Hoofed animals include the large stag known as the *wapiti*, the *sika*, or spotted deer, which appears in many Chinese paintings and is famous for the medicinal qualities of the powder made from its horns, the *goral*, a species of wild goat, the antelope and roebuck.

Characteristic birds of the region include Manchurian cranes and the green herons of the Amur River.

Many fur-bearing animals are also found in Manchuria. These include sables, martens, otters, ermine (weasels), badgers and the *kolinsky*, a species of Asiatic mink.

Inner Mongolia

Chinese Mongolia, or the Inner Mongolian Autonomous Region, consists of a broad belt of land on the northern border of China, extending from the northwest border of Heilungkiang to the northeast border of Kansu. It is bounded on the west and north by the Mongolian People's Republic, and on the east, south and southwest by the provinces of Heilungkiang, Kirin, Liaoning, Hopeh, Shansi, Shensi, the autonomous region of Ningsia Hui and Kansu.

The northern frontier of Chinese Mongolia with Outer Mongolia runs through the heart of the Gobi desert to the Great Khingan. The eastern boundary with Manchuria runs south-east almost to the coast of Liaotung Bay. The southern boundary runs parallel to the Great Wall, along the mountains northwest of Peking, traverses the Ordos plateau, and runs northwest into the Gobi desert, forming the northern border of the Kansu corridor.

CHARACTERISTICS OF THE REGION

The Mongolian region comprises a series of enclosed hollows, called *Tala* in the Mongolian language, in the center of which the hill streams form lakes and marshes which are almost always salt. The only exception is the unenclosed valley to the north of the loess plateau, which is formed by the great curve of the Yellow River.

CURVE OF THE YELLOW RIVER

Most of Inner Mongolia lies between 3000 and 5000 feet above sea level. Its surface appears as an immense plain of uniform height on which atmospheric action, especially wind erosion and wind-borne detritus, have, in recent geological eras, razed practically every considerable elevation and filled up the larger hollows.

The highest remaining mountain masses are those situated along the curve of the Yellow River. The peaks of the Yin Shan range rise to about 7000 feet, while the Ala Shan range attains elevation of over 10,000 feet. In general, Inner Mongolia is a region of steppes and deserts, with the former predominating in the eastern basins and the latter in the western. Well-watered areas are found only in the great curve of the Yellow River and in the valleys running down from the Nan Shan mountains.

The division of Inner Mongolia is based on the characteristics of the soil rather than on the position of mountain masses and rivers. The region may thus be divided into three principal areas: steppes, deserts and well-watered areas.

GRASS LANDS AND STEPPES

The steppe areas occur mainly in eastern Mongolia, forming a wide belt on the Manchurian border. The most northerly part of this belt, which is sometimes called the Hulunbuir, is the area known as the Barga. In this area there are more rivers and richer vegetation. In the Barga, the forests of the Great Khingan thin out into wide grass lands, especially in the valleys of the Argun. This constitutes an area of black earth

A street in central Shanghai. The modern factory on the right and the bus on the left contrast strangely with the ornate archway, decorated with slogans in Chinese and abstract designs, which spans the highway.

A view of Hwangshihkang, a modern industrial center in southeast Hupeh. Hwang-shihkang is situated on the navigable middle reach of the Yangtze some 13 miles northeast of the mining center of Tayeh. Much of its recent development is due to its importance as a port for the iron ore mined at Tayeh and to its river communication with the great industrial conurbation of Wuhan.

which, in the basin formed by the Kerulen river and the lakes of Dalai Nor and Buir Nor, becomes steppe land.

In eastern Silingol in the southwest and Jooda, sometimes spelled Chau Uda, in the south, steppes predominate over grass lands. The earth gradually becomes drier as one moves from east to west. The volume of rainfall in Silingol is as low as in the Barga, but the average temperature, and consequently the evaporation, is considerably higher. The narrow streams that descend from the southern outcrops of the Great Khingan are of a torrential nature.

BARE DESERT

Toward the center of Inner Mongolia, in the areas of Erhlien and Chahar, the arid nature of the land increases and the steppe gives way to bare desert. Only on the slopes and at the foot of the Yin Shan range, particularly to the north and east, does a considerable belt of grass land and steppe reappear. There are also a few conifer woods in the higher areas. This area includes the hills of Ulanchap and the northern part of Suiyuan.

Finally, both desert and steppe areas are found in the Ordos plateau.

AGRICULTURE

The main steppe and grass land areas of Mongolia, particularly those on the borders of Manchuria and Shansi, have been under cultivation since the 18th century. However, since the climate is far less favorable than that of Manchuria the results archieved in Mongolia have been much inferior, and agriculture in the region remains an uncertain process.

In certain limited areas the vegetation is much richer. These areas contain a sufficiency of water and are made up of grass land and steppe. From ancient times they have been cultivated by man. One such area lies between the northern curve of the Yellow River and the Yin Shan range. A second is the tract of the Yellow River valley in Ningsia, between the Alashan mountains and the Ordos plateau. A third consists of a group of oases scattered along the Kansu corridor.

The most northerly part of the curve of the Yellow River forms a wide valley which broadens into the plains of Ho-Tou to the west and Huhehot to the east. It is protected from the cold winds from the north by the Yin Shan range. Numerous branches of the Yellow River flow through it in an area extending to about thirty miles north of the present course of the river. Over the centuries a network of irrigation canals has been constructed, making this area into the most fertile land in Mongolia. Similar conditions exist further up the river in the fertile plain around Yinchwan.

The Kansu Corridor

Conditions are different in the Kansu corridor, which consists of a strip of land about 400 miles long, running from the neighborhood of Lanchow as far as Yumen, or the Gate of Jade, at the foot of the northern slopes of the Nan Shan range. The Nan Shan are the highest range on the Mongolian border, with an average elevation of around 13,000 feet reaching to around 20,000 feet at the highest peak.

The Kansu corridor is actually the tract extending from the central block of the Nan Shan to the edges of the Little Gobi and Alashan deserts. It is traversed from end to end by the famous "Silk Road," which has formed the principal communication route between China and the West for over 2000 years.

All along the corridor, rugged valleys run down from the Nan Shan. The mountain streams flowing through them vary in size but very seldom dry up, since they are fed by water from the snow fields and glaciers. A few of the streams are absorbed by the desert sands, but most of them flow into the Etsin Gol. This is a fairly vigorous watercourse which has succeeded in cutting a deep bed for itself through the desert before finally flowing into the Gashiun Nor depression.

Rich, spontaneous vegetation and conditions suitable for agricultural development are found only in valleys provided with level alluvial ground and a good water supply. Small valleys of this kind form a string of oases scattered along the corridor.

The Mongolian Deserts

The Gobi desert, one of the largest in the world, is 300 to 600 miles wide and over 1000 miles long. It straddles the boundary between the Mongolian People's Republic and the autonomous region of Inner Mongolia. It extends southeast from the eastern borders of Chinese Turkestan and the Mongolian Altai range, and then east and northeast to the Khingan ranges of Manchuria. It is bounded in the south by the Yin Shan, the Tibetan plateau and the Alashan mountains.

The greater part of the Gobi, a typical rock desert, lies within the boundaries of the Mongolian People's Republic, but a considerable area forms part of the autonomous region of Inner Mongolia. The rock desert is a region where wind erosion has reduced the surface to bare rock and shingle, while the sand desert is an accumulation of fine detritus carried by the wind in enormous quantities from one place to another. Since the prevailing winds in the Gobi are from the north or northwest, the sand dunes have accumulated mainly in the south.

SAND DESERT

The desert regions of Erhlien and Chahar form a wedge between the steppes, stretching about 120 miles north of the Great Wall above Peking. Rock desert predominates in the Erhlien region, while the south, in Chahar, is mainly sand desert.

The widest tracks of sand desert are situated in southwest Mongolia. This area includes the valley of the Etsin Gol, the most important Mongolian river, to the west. This is surrounded by the sand desert of the Little Gobi, while to the east the valley and desert of the Alashan stretch as far as the Alashan mountains and the bend of the Yellow River.

THE BIGGEST DESERT

The Alashan and Little Gobi deserts constitute the largest tract of sand desert in China after the Taklamakan desert of Sinkiang Uigur. Like the Taklamakan, the region is partly surrounded by high mountains, and this factor, together with certain climatic characteristics, makes this part of Mongolia resemble Sinkiang Uigur more than any other region of China.

Another desert region is the Ordos plateau, which lies between the bend of the Yellow River and the Great Wall. In the Ordos, rock desert prevails over both sand desert and

The façade of the building in Peking that houses the National People's Congress, the highest organ of state authority. This modern building stands on the west side of the broad T'ien-an-men Square, which is reached from the south through the gate of the same name.

steppe. The sand desert is concentrated to the south of the plateau, where it has buried a large section of the Great Wall, and constitutes a constant threat to the fields and pastures of neighboring Shensi.

CLIMATE

Mongolia has the driest climate of the regions of China which have so far been considered. The volume of rainfall diminishes as one moves further into the region. On the eastern and southeastern borders, on the slopes of the Great Khingan, extending from Jehol and Chahar to the plain of Huhehot, there is a narrow strip with an average rainfall of between 10 and 20 inches annually, which is approximately the same as that of Shansi, Shensi, Kansu and most of Hopeh.

However, in the southwest, in the Barga, in northern Silingol, in Ulanchap, in the deserts of Alashan and Ordos and in the Kansu corridor, annual precipitation falls to between 3 and 10 inches.

MONGOLIAN WINTERS

The Mongolian winters are colder than those of adjacent regions. There are great variations between summer and winter tempratures and considerable temperature variations according to latitudinal position and distance from the sea. At Hailar, in the extreme north, the temperature varies between an average of 18° F.

in January and 69° F. in July, the average annual temperature being 27° F. The average annual temperature in the Kansu corridor is 46° F.

UNCEASING WINDS

Mongolia is a land of perpetual wind. The scanty rainfall is concentrated into a few showers during the summer monsoon season, but the winds are unceasing, with the winter cyclones predominant. A clear indication of the domination of the wind is given by the hours of sunshine, which average about 3000 a year in almost all parts of Mongolia, the highest average in all China.

VEGETATION

The fundamental problem to be solved by agricultural experts in Mongolia is how to widen the area of ground at present held in place against erosion by vegetation and how to extend it into areas which are now desert. The most ambitious projects aim at the creation of great belts of forest. The longest of these is to form the northern border of the Kansu corridor, while another is to follow the southern edge of the Ordos desert on the borders of Shensi.

Other methods which are being used to stabilize the soil include the improvement of irrigation both on and below the surface and the planting of large areas with various types

Gathering the rice harvest in the province of Kiangsu, eastern China, one of the most heavily populated of China's agricultural regions. Rice growing is concentrated in the southern part of the province where the silk industry also flourishes.

of plants and shrubs suitable to the hot, dry climate.

It will be apparent that in the present conditions few varieties of tall trees grow spontaneously in Mongolia. They are limited to the fringes of the Great Khingan and to certain valleys in the Yin Shan and Nan Shan ranges. Small thickets are found by the sides of streams, around villages and at oases.

The commonest trees of the extreme north are elm, birch and various conifers, which are also found on the mountain slopes. Elsewhere juniper, poplar, lime and tamarisk occur.

FAUNA

The Mongolian steppes provide ideal conditions for animal life, and no region in China is richer in wild animals. Tigers of a smaller species than those of Manchuria are to be found in the Kansu corridor and Suiyuan, together with wolves and desert foxes.

Hoofed animals include wapiti, gazelles, Siberian and four-horned goats, together with other species of goat and wild asses. The domesticated animals include the hardy breed of horses for which the area is famous and the large, two-humped Bactrian camel.

Fur-bearing animals of the area include marmots, squirrels, polecats, hares and rabbits. The birds include the steppe eagle, pheasant, bustard, partridge and demoiselle crane.

Eastern Mongolia is the greatest natural game reserve of China, and many of its products are exported to zoological institutes all over the world.

SOUTHERN CHINA

SOUTHERN CHINA IS MAINLY MOUNtainous, interspersed with occasional plains. It has a subtropical, monsoonal climate, with an abundant rainfall of about eighty inches a year. The cool winters are succeeded by warm, wet summers, and the vegetation remains green throughout the year. Bamboo predominates in the abundant vegetation and the soil is free from lime and calcium compounds. Intensive agriculture in the well-watered fields produces two or three high-yield harvests every year. The principal crops are rice, tea and mulberry trees.

The Middle and Lower Yangtze Basin

As the Yellow River plain forms the central part of northern China, so does the hill and lake region of the middle and lower reaches of the Yangtze River form the central part of southern China. The northern boundary of the region is marked by the ridge of the Funiu, Tungpeh, Tapieh and Hwan mountains. The western boundary is marked by the Wu Shan and Wu Ling mountains and the edges of the Kweichow table-land. The southern and eastern boundaries consist of the Bohea Hills, or Wuyi Shan, the Tienmu mountains and the sea.

The average height of the mountains bordering the region is about 3300 feet. The great river and its tributaries are the unifying element of the region, which is divided into a number of valleys by the chains of mountains and hills that radiate inward from the surrounding ranges. The most important of these chains is the one which extends from the Nan Ling mountains in the south to the Tapieh Shan in the north. This separates the two main valleys of the region: that of Hupeh and Hunan to the west and that of Kiangsi and lower Anhwei in the center. The third great valley of the region, that of the lower Yangtze and its delta, stretches over the whole of southern Kiangsu.

The lower parts of the first two valleys and the whole of the third are formed of a series of alluvial plains which together form the third greatest lowland area of China. It contains more water resources—in rivers, lakes, marshes and canals—than any other Chinese plain, and it is this characteristic that sets it apart from all others.

The axis of the region is the 1000 mile stretch of the Yangtze River which runs from the Wu Shan mountains to the sea. In this tract the river reaches its full magnitude, running through the gorges which it carved out in the last geological era, through the Szechwan basin to the alluvial plain which it has now almost filled up, and through an immense estuary to the sea.

The gorges of the middle Yangtze extend for about 190 miles between Wanhsien and Ichang. Towering precipices fall sharply to the river, providing some of the world's most impressive landscapes. The river is forced into so narrow a bed that . at Wushan, about halfway along the reach, the difference between the maximum and minimum water levels is more than 180 feet.

Between Wanhsien and Ichang the river descends very steeply. This causes a large number of rapids and at some points the speed of the current approaches ·about 15 miles per hour. Thus, Ichang has ideal conditions for the building of one of the largest hydroelectric plants in the world. This great project, first outlined by an American engineer, involves the building of two or three successive dams above Ichang. The power stations thus established will have a capacity of 14 million kilowatts and an even greater potential.

The importance of the part of the Yangtze River that lies between Ichang and the sea may be gauged from the fact that although this distance is scarcely one-third of the river's course the size of its basin becomes almost doubled and the average volume of its discharge is two and a half times as great as in the upper reaches.

The gradient of the Yangtze gradually decreases between Ichang and the sea. In the 445 miles between Ichang and Wuhan the height of the river above sea level falls from 145 feet to less than 65 feet. In the 430 miles between Wuhan and Nanking it falls from 65 to 20 feet.

The depth of the Yangtze between Wuhan and the sea is so great that sea-going vessels of up to 10,000 tons are able to navigate the river as far as Wuhan, making this town one of China's major ports.

Altough the Yangtze river has a much more regular flow than the Yellow River, it also has great variations in discharge which can, in times of flood, cause the inundation of great tracts of land. However, the Yangtze floods are less feared than those of the Yellow River, the Hwai and the other rivers of the northern Chinese plain, since they occur less frequently and the flood water drains away faster.

Since rainfall and running water are moderately abundant in the low-lying regions along the course of the Yangtze, the problem of drought, which weighs heavily on much of northern China, is confined to the hilly areas. For this reason, and also because a river with a discharge as great as that of the Yangtze needs an extraordinary amount of study and technical resources to control, large-scale hydroelectric projects are much more limited in extent on the Yangtze than on the rivers of northern China.

Hupeh, Hunan and Poyang Basins

The two principal basins into which the middle and lower course of the Yangtze is subdivided are each made up of an area of alluvial lowland, a hilly area and an outer mountainous fringe. The alluvial lowlands are in the process of gradual formation, and since this process is not yet complete it has given rise, in low-lying areas, to the major lake areas of China.

To the west, the plain of Hupeh and Hunan, which in former times was occupied by a huge lake, has gradually been reduced to the present Tungting lake and a large number of other lakes and ponds, which are numerous to the south of Wuhan.

To the east, the plain of lower Kiangsi and lower Anhwei contains the large, fresh-water Lake Poyang. There are numerous small lakes of which Lake Chao in northern Anhwei is the most important.

The alluvial lowlands are also characterized by numerous other watercourses, some of them formed by the secondary branches of the Yang-

Boats on the Si, or West, River, in western Kwangtung. The Si, the chief river of southern China, rises in east Yunnan. It has two branches, the Hungshui and Yu rivers, which meet at Kweiping. The course of the river totals about 1250 miles and the lower reaches, before it flows into the South China Sea, are navigable by ocean-going steamers.

Log rafts on the Pearl, or Canton, River in southern Kwangtung. The Pearl River is the main waterway of the Canton delta. Its 110 mile course begins at Canton with the confluence of rivers rising to the north and forms an estuary between Macao and Hong Kong. The Canton delta itself is a flat, alluvial plain with an area of about 2890 square miles.

tze and its tributaries and some of them canals cut by man.

The lakes mentioned above vary considerably in size. Among the factors affecting these variations are the season of the year, the relative discharge of the rivers flowing through the basins and the amount of rainfall. The Yangtze receives its main tributaries in these basins, the major ones being the Min and the Han, from the northwest, the Yuan, from the southwest, and the Hsiang, Wu and Kan from the south.

THE HAN VALLEY

The Han, which is one of the largest tributaries of the Yangtze, rises south of the Chin mountains. It flows through the valley between the Tsinling and Tapa Shan ranges, crosses northern Hupeh and, after a course of around 750 miles, flows into the Yangtze near Wuhan.

The high valley of the Han in northern Hupeh forms an area of transition between northern and southern China. The rainfall, soil and vegetation of this area resemble those of the Hwai basin, as does the flow of the river. Like the Hwai, the Han is subject to great variations in discharge and to disastrous floods. For this reason the largest hydroelectric operations in the region have been concentrated upon it.

One of the largest dams in China is being built on the Han at Siangyang, where it is hoped to create a massive reservoir which will supply irrigation works in upper Hupeh, and to establish power stations of very high output. In due course, it is planned to cut a canal through the passes of the Funiu mountains and to lead a part of the Han waters into the Yellow River, thus connecting the two largest river systems in China with a view to regulating the flow of each with the other.

THE YUAN, HSIANG AND KAN

The Yuan and Hsiang rivers flow down from the valleys of Hunan and from the main outlets of Lake Tungting. Because of the abundant natural vegetation covering the hills from which they receive much of their water and because of the comparatively regular rainfall of the locality, these rivers are much less subject to flooding than is the Han. For this reason, the main purpose of the minor hydraulic works along their courses is to improve irrigation.

The characteristics of the last great tributary of the Yangtze, the Kan, are similar to those of the Yuan and the Hsiang. The Kan flows through the province of Kiangsi from south to north and is the principal river flowing into Lake Poyang.

A FEW SHORT STREAMS

In lower Anhwei, the Yangtze receives no tributaries of any importance but only a few short streams of variable flow which form basins of minor importance.

The entire vast area traversed by the great rivers, tributaries and streams detailed above is dominated by the surrounding hills. Their average height is between 165 and 1650 feet, with a more rugged outline to the south of the Yangtze river, in Hunan, Kiangsi and the Tienmu mountains, and a gentler outline in Hupeh and the Hwan hills.

Only on the borders of the region, in the great central fold of the mountains of southeast Chekiang, do the serrations become sharper and more prominent, and hill country gives way to mountain regions.

The Yangtze River Estuary

The great fan-shaped area of lower Kiangsu, which opens out beyond the provincial capital of Nanking, is partly delineated by the mouth of the Yangtze River. At Nanking, the minimum level of the Yangtze is six feet above sea level and the bottom of the river is below sea level. Thus, the ebb and flow of the tides has a noticeable effect on the river.

Lower Kiangsu consists of a large, flat alluvial plain. Its outline is broken only by a few scattered hills, in ancient times the peaks of islands, that become less frequent as the coast is approached.

Vast areas of the plain are occupied by lakes. The most important of these are Lake Kaoyu, and Lake Tai Hu to the south. A part of the waters of the Hwai flow through Lake Kaoyu into the Yangtze, thus making the Hwai the last of the important tributaries of the Yangtze.

The Yangtze is connected to the various lakes by a large number of streams which, over the centuries, have been canalized and increased in size and number by man. It is estimated that about half of China's canals are concentrated in this area. By centuries of work, men have reclaimed much of the plain from the river, marshes, lakes and the sea, protecting their hard-won territory with dikes and locks in much the same way as the Dutch have done.

The great island of Tsunming, in the middle of the Yangtze estuary, has been transformed from a bleak sandbank, rising just above the water at low tide, into an area of magnificent agricultural land. Since very early times the same transformation has been brought about in a great part of southern Kiangsu. No area of China is better irrigated and more fertile over such a wide area and no area can support a denser population.

The coast of the Kiangsu region is the flattest in China. Vast sandbanks lie along it, and for more than 60 miles the sea is no more than 65 feet deep. The coastal ships which come from the port of Shanghai or sail down the Yangtze are obliged to stand more than 60 miles out to sea when navigating the Kiangsu coast.

CLIMATE

The region of the middle and lower reaches of the Yangtze River has the most balanced climate of China. The average rainfall of around 50 inches a year is more regularly distributed than elsewhere and it is sufficient to ensure regular crops in almost every part of the region.

The area has a temperate, continental climate with hot, wet summers and cool winters. Temperatures are mild; in January, even in the most northerly areas, they vary between 0° and 36° F., while in the south they average about 46° F. Snow falls only in the north and much of the year is free from frosts.

The winds, including the cold winter winds from the northwest, have spent much of their force by the time they reach the Yangtze plain. This is favorable in winter, and in summer, when the average temperature over much of the region rises to around 82° F., and there is considerable evaporation, the absence of strong winds helps to produce the most humid atmosphere in China.

The temperate climate and moist heat of the Yangtze plain are extrem-

A view of Kweilin, situated on the right bank of the Kwei River in Kwangsi Chuang, some 250 miles west of Canton. The beauty of the city's setting along the river is enhanced by the surrounding mountains which are often picturesquely shaped due to erosion. Kweilin is a cultural and commercial center of the Hunan-Kwangsi region. It possesses a university and a medical college and its main industries are textiles and the processing of sugar, tung oil and rice.

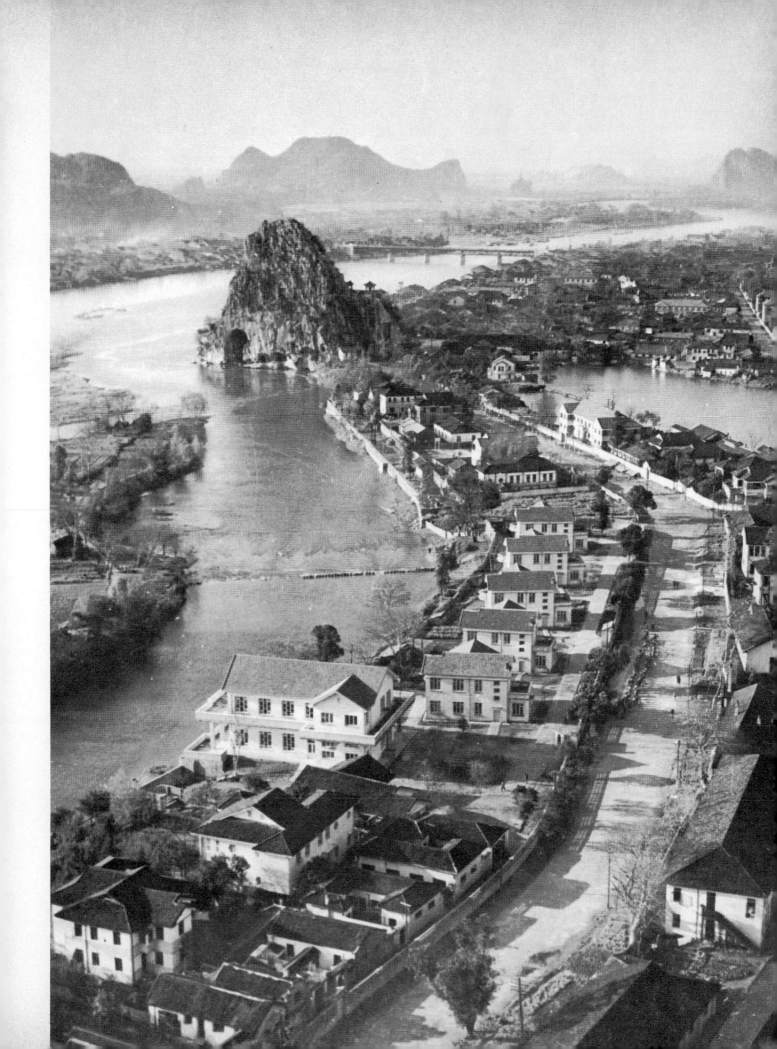

ely favorable to both spontaneous vegetation and to agriculture. Brown and gray-brown soils predominate in northern Hupeh and lower Anhwei, gray alluvial soils in the plains of the Poyang and southern Kiangsu, and soils of various shades of red, from brown to purple, in the high valleys of Hunan and Kiangsu.

A great expanse of saline sand stretches along the coast of Kiangsu. Apart from this strip, the remainder of the region has a good average fertility. Fertility is at its height in the alluvial lowlands due to the detritus carried down by the rivers, the decomposition of water-plants and the labors of men over many centuries.

Fertility in hill and mountain regions is less good, since the natural compounds and mineral deposits of the soil have been washed away by rainfall and evaporation. However, because of the abundant rainfall and temperate climate, trees and shrubs which can sink deep roots into the soil are able to flourish luxuriantly.

Extensive tracts of natural forests cover a great part of the Wu Shan mountains and the mountains encircling Hunan and Kiangsi. The most common trees are pine, elm, cunninghamia (a small evergreen tree of the pine family), liriodendron (a tree belonging to the magnolia family), beech, chestnut and juniper. On the hills, vegetation is richer still, including maple, cypress, box, hornbeam and medlar. Trees and shrubs from which valuable substances may be extracted include bamboo of various types, camphor, sassafras, tea and ginger. On the plains there are many willow and mulberry trees, while the lotus and many varieties of rushes abound in and around the lakes and ponds.

FAUNA

The animal life of the Yangtze River area is numerous and varied. Among the carnivores are the tiger, civet and sun badger, and the ungulates, or hoofed animals, include the Yangtze deer, the *Muntjac* deer, the *goral,* a kind of goat antelope, and the wild boar. The pangolin, a species of scaly anteater, is also common.

Among the domesticated animals, the water buffalo is typical of the

Pinkiang park, a public recreation center in Shanghai. The red stars on the façade of the building on the right suggest that it is a government office.

region and, indeed, of all southern China.

The abundance of water gives rise to a large number of aquatic animals. Among the largest of these are the dolphins of Lake Tung, the Yangtze seal, the pilot whale of the Yangtze estuary and the small Yangtze alligator, which attains a length of about six feet. Reptiles are also common, among them the black cobra, the green bamboo viper, the deadly *krait* snake and various species of land and river turtles.

Among the birds of the area, aquatic species predominate. These include the Japanese ibis, wild swans and geese, the water pheasant, the black stork and various kinds of pelican. Mention should also be made of the cormorants, which are trained to catch fish for their owners.

Red Basin of Szechwan

Around the upper and middle reaches of the Yangtze lies the basin of Szechwan, which is called the Red Basin because its soil, made up of particles of sand and eroded rock, is purplish-red in color.

The Red Basin is surrounded on all sides by mountains. Because of its well-defined natural boundaries it formed an independent kingdom on the occasions in history when China was dismembered into separate states. More recently, during World War II, it was the only important region which the Japanese invaders were unable to penetrate.

The name Szechwan signifies "four rivers" in the local dialect. Besides the upper and middle reaches of the Yangtze, three of the Yangtze's important tributaries flow through the region. These are the Min in the northwest, the Kialing in the northeast and the Wu in the south.

Szechwan is the largest province in China Proper and is the most populous in the whole of the Chinese People's Republic. Owing to the geological formation of the Szechwan basin, which is thought to have been a great lake at the beginning of the Tertiary era and to have become gradually filled up by the end of the Cretaceous period, there are widespread deposits of natural gas, petroleum and saline water. The last-named resource has been used since the earliest times for the production of salt.

The biggest mountains surrounding Szechwan are those on the west,

which are the last outcrops of the huge chain of mountain ranges which begins on the Tibetan plateau. Immediately above the basin, the Min Shan massif rises from north to south with an average height of about 8200 feet. The Chiunglai range and the sacred mountain of Omei, which rises to 9957 feet, complete the barrier.

HILLS OF HUNAN

Behind these first ranges rise the Tahsueh mountains, their tall, snow-covered peaks culminating in Minya Konka at 24,900 feet. From the Min Shan massif, the Tapa Shan ranges stretch eastward almost as far as Tzekwei in western Hupeh; the northern boundary runs along their crests. The eastern boundary is marked by the hills of northern Hunan, while the edge of the high Kweichow-Yunnan plateau forms the southern boundary of the region.

Four principal passes connect the Szechwan basin to the neighboring regions. The first of these is the Kialing valley, which runs between the Min Shan and Tapa Shan ranges to communicate with the Han valley and then goes on across the Tsinling mountains to communicate with the Wei valley. A railroad and a good highway, suitable for heavy traffic, run through the Kialing valley, connecting Chengtu with Sian and Lanchow. Its position has made the Kialing valley the site of some of the greatest battles in Chinese history.

THE CHIEF WATERCOURSE

The natural way of access from the Szechwan basin to the eastern plain is provided by the Yangtze gorges. The southern bend of the higher reach of the Yangtze provides a way to Yunnan. The Kweichow plateau is reached through the Wu Kiang valley.

The Yangtze River is, naturally, the chief watercourse of the Szechwan basin. Although it has already flowed for 1750 miles when it enters Szechwan, it is only in this area that the Yangtze becomes a major river. Further upstream it flows through a narrow, deep valley full of gorges and ravines and receives only one important tributary, the Yalung. However, in the 440 miles between Pingshan and Wanhsien the extent of the Yangtze basin increases from about 180,000 square miles to about 386,000 square miles, and its average discharge is almost trebled.

A number of important tributaries

A view of a modern part of Peking, the capital of China. The present city of Peking dates from the 13th century and its street plan is based on the system laid out by Kublai Khan. Historically it consisted of four separate cities: the Tatar city, the Mandarin city, the Chinese city, where the bulk of the population lived, and the Forbidden city, the seat of the imperial court. The new modern suburbs are concentrated in the west, where there are educational and research institutes, and in the north, a mainly industrial area.

flow into the Yangtze river after it enters the Szechwan basin. The Tatu River rises in the Min Shan mountains and flows through the valley between the Tahsueh Shan and the Chiunglia mountains. The Tatu then joins the Min River which also rises in the Min Shan, crosses the plain of Chengtu and, after joining the Tatu, flows into the Yangtze at Ipin.

The Yangtze is also joined by the To River, which flows across the center of Szechwan, and by the Kialing with its two tributaries, the Fow and the Chu.

The height above sea level of the Szechwan basin varies between 660 feet and 1650 feet in the central and western areas, between 1650 and 3300 feet in a fairly broad strip at the foot of the mountains, particularly wide on the eastern side, and between 3300 and 10,000 feet in the mountainous border country.

THE HIGH MOUNTAINS

The high mountains of the north, west and east borders are harsh and rugged in outline. The region at the foot of the mountains is made up of rounded hills. The floor of the basin, being eroded and not alluvial, has a generally hilly landscape, sometimes taking on the characteristics of a rolling plain.

The Plain of Chengtu

The only exception is the plain of Chengtu, which widens out into a fan-shaped area of alluvial land where the Min River descends from the mountains. The Chengtu plain is one of the richest rice-growing areas in China, for an ancient irrigation system was constructed there as long ago as 300 B.C.

In general, the slope of the valleys of Szechwan is sufficient to provide

good drainage. For this reason, there are no lakes or marshes of any size and no need for large-scale drainage works. At the same time, excellent facilities for irrigation are provided by the construction of extensive terraced rice-fields, which are more numerous than elsewhere in China and form one of the most typical features of the landscape.

Along the course of the Yangtze and its tributaries in Szechwan there are huge reserves of potential hydro-electric power which so far remain untapped.

CLIMATE

The Szechwan basin, which is surrounded by high mountains, is probably better protected from the winds than any other part of China. It is sheltered from the cold northwest winds by the Min Shan massif and by the mountain chains which branch off to the east and south. As a result, snow is rare during the Szechwan winter and the growing season lasts for eleven months of the year. The average January temperature is about 45° F. and snow falls only on the high mountains to the north and west.

However, the geological formation of Szechwan is not so favorable in summer, when the concave shape of the basin causes a great concentration of the sun's rays and the resultant humidity becomes the greatest in China. Rainfall in the basin is fairly heavy, the average for the year being about 40 inches, but is largely concentrated in summer. The average July temperature of about 80° F. may not seem excessive but it becomes overpowering to man because of the excessive humidity and the very slight variation between day and night temperatures.

Except on the high mountains encircling the basin, where there is more wind, mist and fog throughout the year make Szechwan the region of China with the smallest annual total of hours of sunshine.

VEGETATION

The red earth of the Szechwan basin, from which natural substances are washed by the rain, is deficient in humus, as are the brown soils of the mountains to the north and west. An important exception is the Min Shan highlands, where climatic conditions have allowed the growth of large areas of grassland. However, because of the moderate temperatures and the humidity, perennial plants flourish even in the red and brown soils, making Szechwan one of the richest areas in evergreen vegetation.

The mountain trees include pine, fir, yew, oak, juniper and Tibetan cedar. In spring, red rhododendron blossoms cover wide areas on the mountain slopes. Lower down on the foothills there is an abundance of bamboo, tung trees, from which tung oil is extracted, lacquer trees, elm, willow, mulberry, medlar and magnolia. Trees from which valuable natural products are derived include camphor, cinnamon, cardamom, ailanthus, sumach, mustard and tea plants and orange trees.

A view of the harbor of the river port of Tientsin, in the province of Hopeh, situated on the Hai Ho some seventy miles southeast of Peking. Tientsin developed from a garrison town in the 19th century to become the leading transportation and commercial center of north China. It is an important railway junction, but since only small craft are able to navigate the Hai Ho with ease, larger, ocean-going ships now tend to use the new port of Sinkang on the coast.

FAUNA

Various species of hoofed animals inhabit the mountainous regions of Szechwan. These include wapiti, *serow*, a type of long-haired goat, the musk-deer, a ruminant like the small roebuck which is sought after for the musk it secretes in a special gland, and the great *takin*, a goat-like antelope reaching a height of over four feet at the shoulder, which the Chinese call the wild ox.

The carnivores include snow-leopard, lynx and civet. There are numerous monkeys, among which are the brownish-gray langur and the macaque which feature in many Chinese folk tales.

The birds of prey include the great imperial eagle, the largest in China, and among aquatic creatures the otter, which, like the cormorant, is sometimes domesticated and trained to catch fish for its owner.

Southeastern Maritime Provinces

From the Hangchow Bay at Latitude 30° N. to the area bordering the Gulf of Tonkin, a long strip of hill and mountain country about 200 miles wide stretches along the coast of the East China Sea and the South China Sea. It covers the provinces of Chekiang, Fukien, Kwangtung and the southeastern part of the Kwangsi-Chuang autonomous region.

This area is separated from the hinterland by a series of mountain ranges, the chief of which are the Wuyi Shan, running northeast to southwest, and the Nan Ling, running from west to east. These mountains respectively join the Tienmu

Shan in the northeast and the edges of the Kweichow plateau in the southwest. Beyond these ranges lie the great valleys of the middle and lower Yangtze.

CLEFTS IN THE MOUNTAINS

The geological characteristics of the area are extremely complicated, since successive chains of mountains follow upon each other and run parallel to the coast. The mountain ranges are broken in places by deep clefts, through which the valleys of the interior run down to the sea.

The maximum height above sea level of the coastal region is not much above 6600 feet in either the Wuyi or Nan Ling ranges, and the height is between 650 and 1650 feet in Chekiang and Kwangtung and 1650 and 3300 feet in Fukien.

The Wuyi mountains are rugged in outline, while the Nan Ling and the hills and mountains nearer the coast have a gentler, more rounded appearance. In the southwest part of the region it is hills rather than mountains which predominate. The coast is rocky and deeply indented with gulfs and bays, particularly in the north, and is fringed by over 3000 islands of varying sizes.

Among the more important bays along the coast, moving from north to south, are the bays of Sanmen, Taichow, Wenchow, Samsa, Hinghwa, Swatow, Kitchioh, Hunghai, Taya and Kwangchow. The most important islands include Chushan, Matsu, Haitan, Quemoy, Tungshan, Namoa, Shangchuan and Hainan.

There are few alluvial plains in the area and those that exist are fairly limited in area. The single exception is the alluvial plain of the Canton delta.

The coastal region may be divided into three parts. The first part corresponds approximately to the provinces of Chekiang and Fukien. The second part consists of the Pearl River basin. The third part is made up of the Luichow peninsula and the island of Hainan.

Chekiang and Fukien

The provinces of Chekiang and Fukien are crossed by numerous

A street in the commercial district of Peking. In recent years, trade has become increasingly the preserve of state owned companies, but street markets and peddlers still survive in many areas. Trade in foodstuffs is still often a matter of private commerce between peasants and peddlers still take goods from the large cities to sell to the people of the rural areas.

mountain ranges which divide them into a number of rainy basins. Each basin has a direct opening to the sea, which penetrates deeply into these openings to make bays which often resemble the fjords of Norway. Since access from one basin to another is generally difficult, the region is effectively divided into closed areas.

One result of this division is that a very large number of widely differing dialects are spoken in the region. The main communication route between the two provinces has long been the sea, since conditions on the coast are favorable to navigation.

RIVER BASINS

The principal basins into which the two provinces are divided, beginning in the north, are as follows; the basin of the Fuchun which flows into Hangchow Bay, the only basin bordered by a wide, alluvial plain; the basin of the Wu River which flows into the sea at Wenchow; the basin of the Min River which flows into the sea at Foochow, the most important basin of the region; the basin of the Kiulung which flows into the sea at Amoy; and the basin of the Han River, which flows mainly through the province of Kwangtung and reaches the sea at Swatow.

Since the mountains through which these rivers and their tributaries flow are formed of very hard, ancient rock and are generally covered with luxuriant vegetation, erosion is limited and the rivers are clear and swift flowing. They generally have a steep gradient which gives rise to frequent rapids and waterfalls which greatly echance the beauty of the landscape.

With the exception of the Fuchun, the rivers of Chekiang and Fukien are only navigable for short portions of their courses, and then only by the local junks with their shallow draft. However, their torrential nature makes them a great source of hydroelectric power which is now being exploited by the construction of large dams like that at Kutien on a left-bank tributary of the Min.

Since natural drainage facilities in this hilly area are good, there is at most times little danger of floods. However, in seasons of typhoons and heavy rains the combination of rivers in flood with high tides can cause great damage to the narrow plains lying on either side of the mouths of the largest rivers.

In the southwest of the Chekiang-Fukien region the mountains are less rugged and not so high and the

A boatman propels a pleasure craft across one of the lakes in the vicinity of the Summer Palace to the northwest of Peking. The Summer Palace was built in the late 19th century as a pleasure resort for the imperial court. In recent times, the beauty of the surrounding lakes and hills has made the area a popular holiday resort.

valleys are wider. The rivers are thus able to attain greater length and form wider basins.

A range of mountains stretches for about 600 miles along the coast, extending from near Swatow to the Gulf of Tonkin. This range is broken only by the Canton estuary, south of Canton, and streams flowing from all over the region have their only outlet to the sea at this break in the mountains. Thus they flow together to form the Pearl, or Canton, River.

THREE GENTLE RIVERS

Three main rivers join to form the Pearl River. These are the Si River from the west, the Peh River from the north and the Tung River from the east. The Si is by far the largest; it is some 1250 miles long and is swelled by many tributaries flowing from the plateau of Yunnan and Kweichow. All three rivers flow gently through wide valleys, their course is fairly regular, their waters

are generally clear and they are all navigable.

The Pearl River is the main branch of the complex network of channels and estuaries through which the three rivers cross a great delta plain and flow into the Canton estuary. The estuary itself is dotted with many islets.

The plain of the Canton delta is the most fertile in southeast China. Its many man-made drainage and irrigation canals form a system second only to that of lower Kiangsu.

Luichow Peninsula and the Island of Hainan

To the west of the Canton estuary, beyond the plain of the delta, the coast becomes flatter and more regular. Many short rivers and streams flow into the sea along the coast. The most important of these are the Foshan River, which flows into the sea at Ngchun, and the Lien River, which flows to the Gulf of Tonkin

north of Pakhoi. This stretch of coast is a formation of the Quaternary period and differs from the more recent alluvial formation of the Canton delta by being the result of a rising of the earth's surface rather than a subsidence.

About halfway along the coast the peninsula of Luichow projects into the sea. It is about 90 miles long and 30-45 miles wide. Liuchow is the third largest peninsula in China, after the Shantung and Liaotung peninsulas in the Yellow Sea.

The Luichow peninsula is a low plateau with an undulating surface; its maximum height above sea level is less than 1000 feet. Its east coast bends in a great curve to form Kwangchow Bay. The islands in the bay provide, between themselves and the coast, the best harbor of the region.

South of the Luichow peninsula, and across the 14-mile wide Hainan Strait, is the large, tropical island of Hainan, the second largest in Chinese waters. To the west of Hainan and the Luichow peninsula is the Gulf of Tonkin, the second largest in China.

Hainan, like most of the region to

which it belongs, is formed mainly of rock of the most ancient geological eras in an advanced state of erosion. Slightly to the southwest of the center of the island are the Wuchi mountains, a massif with five main peaks which rise to around 6000 feet. To the south, the Wuchi fall steeply to the sea, while to the northeast they fall gently in rolling hills toward the plain. Also on the northeast of the Wuchi is the most important river of Hainan, the Nantu.

The coast of Hainan is generally flat and regular. It is formed mainly from alluvial deposits and is fringed with sandbanks and coral reefs. The other islands of the South China Sea differ from Hainan in being formed mainly of coral reefs. They are the Sisha, or Paracel group; the Chungsha, or Macclesfield Bank group; and Pratas Island. These are all fishing centers and are rich in guano deposits.

CLIMATE

The northwest boundaries of the Chekiang-Fukien region are marked by the Wuyi and Nan Ling ranges, which afford protection from the cold, winter monsoons. On the other hand, no part of China is so exposed

to the damp summer monsoons or to the sea. Although these characteristics give the area a certain climatic unity, the difference in latitude between its various areas tends to complicate the general picture.

Fukien has the heaviest rainfall in China. The annual amount is from 60 to 70 inches but the area has received up to 200 inches of rain in one year. There are also occasional typhoons.

Chekiang has a subtropical climate like that of Fukien, except in the north, where the winters are very cold.

The Luichow peninsula and the island of Hainan have high temperatures and abundant rainfall throughout the year.

Rainfall over the area occurs almost entirely in summer and is often occasioned by the cyclonic disturbances accompanying typhoons. In the wettest areas the humidity is very high, and the resultant mist and fog mean that Fukien has only a limited number of hours of sunshine every year.

TEMPERATURES

Since the region lies across the Tropic of Cancer, the temperature is generally high and varies little either according to the season or the time of day or night. Temperatures on the coast are much influenced by the sea.

In north Chekiang the minimum January temperature is around 40°F. and the maximum July temperature is around 83°F. In Amoy these temperatures are respectively 58° F. and 84° F., and on the island of Hainan they are 68°F. and 86°F. In the extreme north the temperature is more variable but there is still a high percentage of days free from frost.

The high temperatures and heavy rainfall of the Chekiang-Fukien region give rise to the growth of luxuriant vegetation. The greater part of the Wuyi range and the western Nan Ling range are covered with forests and the hill areas are rich in fruit trees, including orange, lychee and mulberry trees. There are also numerous aromatic plants from which essences and medicines are extracted.

The Chekiang hills are an important center of tea production, and the coast to the south of the Tropic of Cancer is covered with expanses of mangrove and bamboo. Luxuriant meadowlands cover the hills of Kwangtung, the peninsula of Luichow and eastern Kwangsi, while the island of Hainan is rich in tropical vegetation, including cocoa palms, betel, spice and coffee plants and *hevea,* from which india-rubber is obtained.

FAUNA

Animals of many kinds are numerous in the area. Among the carnivores are tigers, clouded leopards and mongooses.

Fur-bearing animals include sand and sun badgers, polecats, otters and a number of species of monkey.

Hoofed animals include various kinds of small deer, and among the reptiles are the Chinese python, giant salamander, large marine turtles and various large species of frog and toad. Finally there are the bamboo rats, the largest Chinese rat, and venomous giant centipedes.

The indented coastline of the area offers excellent facilities for fishing. The fishing grounds extend from the extreme north of the region, where the Chushan Islands, offshore from the Bay of Hangchow, provide the largest fishing base in China, to Hoppo, in the Gulf of Tonkin, where pearls are cultivated. Pearls, mother-of-pearl and coral are all sought for among the coral reefs of the islands in the South China Sea.

The Southwest

The limestone plateaus of southwest China are situated south of the province of Szechwan, extending down to the borders of Vietnam, Laos and Burma. They cover most of the provinces of Yunnan and Kweichow and the western part of Kwangsi.

These great tablelands are formed of crystalline rocks dating from the earliest geological eras, mainly Paleozoic. They have been subject to a continual process of erosion by the elements, which has given the landscape its characteristic and unusual appearance.

To the northwest of the region lie a series of great, parallel, mountain ranges, an extension of the Chamdo mountains in Tibet, running from north to south. These have been eroded by surface water, which has deepened the folds and valleys and has formed them into impressive canyons equalled only by those in Arizona and Colorado and in the Zambezi region of Africa.

In the center of Yunnan, the mountain ranges decline into great tablelands with a fairly even surface cut into by deep valleys. Surface erosion is reinforced in this area by subterranean erosion; underground water dissolves the calcareous rocks by chemical action. This process is intensified to the east and south, giving the region an appearance more typical of limestone formations than any other in the world.

Subterranean erosion has created a labyrinth of caves which, over the years, have collapsed to form dolines, or hollows, and trenches of ever-increasing size. As a result, the depth of the valleys below sea level tends to be greater than the height of the mountains above sea level.

The various phases of the process of erosion are well illustrated by comparing the relatively compact plateau of central Yunnan with the regions of Kweichow and Kwangsi. In Kweichow, the work of breaking down the mountain mass by erosion is about half completed; the area of the mountains is about equal to that of the valleys, giving rise to a relief of the most complex kind. In Kwangsi, the work has gone much further; the mountain mass has been reduced to rocky ruins which rise from the rolling plains.

As a result of this process, the landscape takes on a characteristic appearance; high peaks and cones of broken rock rise from the flat valley bottoms, often pierced by caverns and carved by erosion into fantastic shapes.

Apart from its limestone formation, Yunnan is also notable as representing, together with eastern Kansu, one of the most important centers of seismic activity in China. Earthquakes occur most frequently in the area where the mountain ranges extending from the north meet the main plateau in the west.

RELIEF AND HYDROGRAPHY

Unlike the loess plateau and the plateaus of Tibet and Mongolia, the Yunnan-Kweichow plateau does not have its boundaries clearly marked by encircling mountains. In the northwest, the Yunnan-Kweichow plateau merges with the ranges running from the Tibetan plateau. In all other directions it gradually becomes lower until it merges into the mountains of the neighboring regions.

Nor is the height of the plateau above sea level uniform. It varies from 6300 feet around Kunming, rising to 13,000 feet on the northwest borders, and falling to 1650 feet in other areas. With the exception of the western borders, it is difficult to distinguish any mountains of a size worthy of

The city of Loyang in northern Honan, situated on the lower reach of the Lo Shui River, a tributary of the Yellow River. Loyang was the capital of the Chou dynasty (770-255 B.C.) and of the Eastern Han dynasty (25-221 A.D.) but was eclipsed in importance by Kaifeng in the 13th century. The city was temporarily the capital of China in 1932.

note from the complicated mountain formations of the plateau itself.

RIVERS

The same is true of the rivers; the region is broken up into numerous basins none of which are of outstanding size and none of which play any part in the geographical unity of the region or even of any single part of the region.

Northwest Yunnan, which is a continuation of the mountain belt beginning in Tibet, is also a continuation of the drainage basins which follow the long valleys of the mountain range. The principal rivers of the area are the Salween, Mekong and Yangtze. The first two follow the western edge of the Yunnan plateau, flowing from north to south, and continue into Burma and Laos. The

course of the Yangtze lies further east and the height of the Yunnan plateau compels the river to double back, taking a south to north course instead of a north to south and flowing into the Szechwan basin.

A large number of other rivers rise on the plateau itself and descend from it in various directions determined by the prevailing slope of their area of source. In the southeast the Yuan,

flow gently through wide valleys but in other places they flow through gorges and ravines which give rise to boiling rapids and magnificent waterfalls.

LAKES

Natural drainage facilities are generally good and lakes of considerable size are found only on the central plateau. Notable among them are Lake Tien Chih near Kunming, Lake Fusien about 30 miles further south and Lake Ehr Hai near Tali, on the western edge of the plateau. As has already been mentioned, this limestone country possesses a great system of subterranean rivers and streams, which as yet have been little studied or explored.

There are great potential reserves of hydroelectric power, as yet untapped, throughout the region. These, together with the rich mineral deposits which are also known to exist, afford an excellent basis for the industrial development of the area.

CLIMATE

Since the various parts of the limestone plateaus vary considerably in their latitude, height above sea level and exposure to the wind, the climate of the whole region is not uniform. For example, the average January temperature is 39°F. in the valleys of the northwest, 50°F. in Kunming and 61°F. on the borders of Laos. In July, these localities have average temperatures of 64°F., 68°F. and 79°F. respectively.

Similarly, the number of frost-free days varies from region to region. Almost the whole year is free from frost in the south, while in the northwest frosts occur on about 100 days in every year.

THE MONSOONS

Western Yunnan, Kweichow and Kwangsi have the heaviest rainfall, since they are most exposed to the wet, summer monsoons coming from the Bay of Bengal and the Gulf of Tonkin. Their average annual precipitation of between 40 and 60 inches is concentrated in the summer. However, the center of the plateau around Kunming is more exposed to

the cold, winter monsoons and is thus drier all the year round.

In summer there is a particularly noticeable contrast between the climate of the Szechwan basin, which is constantly oppressed by damp heat and mist, and the open mountain valley of Kunming, about 6600 feet above sea level, which has a clear sky, mild temperatures and strong winds. Kunming, in Yunnan, has twice as many hours of sunshine annually as does Chungking, in Szechwan. Yunnan is south of Szechwan, and the name Yunnan means, in fact, "south of the clouds."

Although Kweichow and northern Kwangsi, because of their elevation, have a cooler climate than the more low-lying areas on which they border, they are no less damp, for the winds are usually so light that mists linger over them for long periods. The mists combine with the eroded shapes of the limestone mountains and the changing nature of the rivers to produce landscapes in this area which are the most beautiful in China.

VEGETATION

The soil conditions of the limestone plateau are not very different from those in other parts of southern China which have already been described. There are, however, very few alluvial tracts in the area. The old, red soils of the plateau have not been subjected to intensive cultivation and have preserved their natural covering of vegetation.

There are extensive forests and woods on the edges of the plateau. They are most widespread in the northwest, the great valleys of the west, on the borders of Burma and Laos and on the borders of Szechwan and Hunan. Pine, fir, *tsuga* trees, yew, Tibetan cedar, maple, oak and beech predominate in the higher regions, intermixed with thickets of rhododendron and azalea and with green meadows. In the lower, more southerly areas are rosewood, sandalwood, tung trees, camphor and lacquer trees, bamboo and the rubber-producing *hevea*. On the borders of Burma and Laos, the tropical jungle penetrates fairly deeply into the valleys of southern Yunnan.

FAUNA

Cultivated land on the plateau is extremely limited and this, together with the rich natural vegetation, provides ideal conditions for a great variety of wild life. Deer, roebuck and musk-deer are common in the

or Red, River and its tributaries flow down to cross the frontier of Vietnam and form the Tonkin basin. In the east, the Si River and its tributaries flow down toward the Canton delta. In the north, the Wu River flows to join the Szechwan basin.

The volume of the waters of these rivers is fairly stable, but the complicated mountain system gives them variable gradients. Sometimes they forests and grasslands of the northwest. Elephants, wild oxen and snakes and tropical birds of many kinds are found in the jungle of the southern valleys. Tigers, leopards and civets, together with many different kinds of monkey are found throughout the region.

However, the most interesting animal of the region is the panda, both the common and giant variety. The giant panda is rare, representing the only surviving species of a family which is becoming extinct. It is the size of a bear, its fur is white with large black spots and its staple diet is bamboo shoots. The panda's comical appearance has made it a favorite with children in zoos all over the world, though it is one of the hardest animals to breed in captivity.

TIBET AND SINKIANG UIGUR

TIBET, WITH TSINGHAI, IS THE highest and largest of all the natural regions of China. Its boundaries are marked by the Himalayas in the south; the Karakoram mountains in the west; the Kunlun, Altyn Tagh and Nan Shan mountains in the north; and by the Min Shan, Tahsueh Shan and the western buttresses of the Tsinling range in the east. Also on the south is the short range joining the southern outcrops of the Ting Shan to the Burmese frontier.

This natural zone contains within its borders the autonomous region of Tibet, the province of Tsinghai and the western part of the province of Szechwan.

MOUNTAIN DIVISIONS

High mountains in the interior of the region divide it into five principal basins. Two of these are closed; the northern Tibetan basin and the Tsaidam-Koko Nor basin. Three are open; the southern Tibetan basin, the Chamdo basin and the basin of northeast Tsinghai.

The autonomous region of Tibet is bordered by the Kunlun mountains in the north, the Karakoram mountains in the west, the Trans-Himalayas and the Kailas ranges in the south, and the Tanglha and Nyenchen Tanglha ranges in the east. The Kunlun mountains separate northern Tibet from the autonomous region of Sinkiang Uigur.

OPEN VALLEYS

In southern Tibet a series of open valleys runs lengthways between the

A view of the civic center of Sian, called Ch'ang-an until 1943, in northern Liaotung. The ancient walled city was the capital of the Han dynasty (202 B.C.- 220 A.D.) and of the Tang dynasty (618- 907 A.D.), and a large number of important historical remains, mainly of religious monuments, exist. It is now a cultural center, with a university and a college of engineering, and a modern industrial area, specializing in textiles, flour milling, tanning, printing, glassware and chemicals.

Kailas and Himalayan ranges. The rest of the region east of the Tanglha mountains is divided into two basins by the Bayan Kara range, a branch of the Kunlun mountains. These basins are the Chamdo-Sikang basin, which consists of a strip of long, open valleys extending southeastward as far as the borders of Yunnan and Szechwan, and a smaller basin formed by the high valley of the Yellow River and its tributaries.

Basins of Northern Tibet

Northern Tibet is the highest and largest plateau in the world, and is often popularly called "the roof of the world." Is is also known to the Chinese as Changtang. Its elevation varies between 13,000 and 20,000 feet, with a number of peaks in the peripheral ranges and central massifs which are higher still.

The greatest elevation within Chinese territory occurs on the northern border, where the peak of the Ulugh Muztagh, in the Arka Tagh group of the Kunlun mountains, reaches a height of 25,340 feet.

The complex mountain system of the plateau divides it into a large number of separate closed basins. Depending on their supply of water, these basins culminate in lakes of fresh or brackish water, marshes or salt plains or plains of alkaline earth. The two largest lakes are the Nam Tso, or Tengri Nor, and the Ziling Tso, both of which are brackish, lying between the Kailas and the Tanghla ranges.

The landscape of Tibet is full of vivid contrasts. Rugged hills, some formed by volcanic or glacial action, alternate with rolling downlands and rocky expanses of sparse pasture land.

ICE CAPS AND SNOW

The highest peaks of the Kailas, Kunlun and Tanghla ranges are topped by large caps of ice and snow which provide the main water supply of the rivers of the Tibetan plateau.

To the northeast of the Kunlun

range the height above sea level decreases considerably until, at about 10,000 feet, another great closed basin is formed. This is the Tsaidam basin in Tsinghai. It is bounded on the west by the Kunlun mountains and by their continuation eastward, which is formed by the Tsishih Shan or Amne Machin range whose highest peaks, reaching 25,000 feet, are the greatest elevation in Tsinghai. On the east, a low ridge separates the Tsaidam basin from the open valley of the Yellow river.

CHINA'S BIGGEST LAKE

The Tsaidam basin is made up of one very large basin, the Tsaidam basin proper, and a number of smaller basins to the west and east, the chief of which is that of the Koko Nor. The Koko Nor is 10,515 feet above sea level and has an area of over 2000 square miles. It is a salt lake and is the largest lake in China.

The Tsaidam basin itself provides a contrast to the high plateau of Tibet in that it is a flat, monotonous expanse made up of sand and rock desert to the west and a large alluvial salt marsh to the east. It is watered mainly by the rivers which descend from the Kunlun and Amne Machin ranges.

Further enclosed basins are for-

med by the complex mountain systems of the Nan Shan and Altyn Tagh ranges. The Nan Shan mountains, whose highest peak reaches to over 20,000 feet, have a breadth from north to south which sometimes approaches 200 miles. The small enclosed basins lying between its corrugations generally culminate in lakes, most of them salt.

The Altyn Tagh mountains are simpler in formation. They have an average elevation of under 13,000 feet with the highest peak reaching 17,000 feet. The basins enclosed within their corrugations are, like those of the Nan Shan, generally small and contain salt lakes.

Open Basins of the South and East

Between the Kailas and Himalayan ranges lies a great depression, about 1000 miles long and never wider than 125 miles. The large main valleys and their collaterals which open into it form the valleys of southern Tibet.

The Himalayan range is the larger of the two that border the region. It includes the highest peaks in the world; Everest at 29,028 feet, Kanchenjunga at 28,168 feet, Dhaulagiri at 26,810 feet, and a number of others ranging between 20,000 and 26,000 feet. The southern slopes

of the Himalayas are very steep; over a distance of less than 60 miles the elevation falls from 25,000 feet to 650 feet on the edge of the plain of the Ganges River. The northern slopes, fronting on Tibet, are more gentle; only at the eastern extremity do the Tibetan valley bottoms fall below 10,000 feet.

RIVERS

Three rivers flow through the great depression between the Himalayas and the Kailas. They rise at a height of almost 16,500 feet, north of Nepal. The chief of these rivers is the Brahmaputra, known in Chinese as the Matsing Tsangpo, which flows eastward through about three-quarters of the depression. The other two, the Indus and the Sutlej, flow westward in the two more or less parallel valleys into which the western quarter of the depression is divided.

The Brahmaputra descends from a height of about 16,500 feet at its source to about 5000 feet at the foot of Mt. Namcha Barwa. At this point it bends sharply to flow through the ravines which cut through the Himalayas and lead it into the plain of Assam. About halfway along the Brahmaputra's course, at a height of about 10,000 feet almost exactly north of Bhutan, the

valley broadens out and the gradient of the river becomes less steep. At this point it becomes navigable for local craft.

It is also at this point that a number of important secondary valleys enter the main valley. The most important of these descends from the north and contains, at a height of 12,087 feet, the city of Lhasa, the capital of Tibet. The freshwater lake of Yamdrok, the most important lake of the southern Tibetan valleys, lies in the same region.

CHAMDO AND SIKANG

The relief of Chamdo and Sikang is somewhat different from that of the areas already detailed. In this region, a series of great parallel ranges branch out from the Tanglha and Bayan Kara ranges and make a wide sweep to the south before joining the Yunnan plateau. In the valleys between the corrugations of these mountains the canyons of higher Yunnan are continued, forming the upper reaches of some of the greatest rivers of China and southeast Asia.

Among these rivers are the Yangtze and its longest tributary the Yalung, the Mekong and the Salween. The Yangtze is the one whose sources penetrate most deeply into the Chamdo-Sikang region, lying to the north of the Tanglha range. The Yangtze skirts the Bayan Kara mountains and bends gradually southward, flowing through the canyons of the Yun Ling range to the borders of Yunnan.

RIVERS AND MOUNTAINS

The Yalung rises to the south of the Bayan Kara mountains, and the Mekong and Salween rise on the eastern slopes of the Tanglha mountains. After taking a short southward course, they all bend to flow more or less parallel to the Yangtze.

The mountain system of the Chamdo-Sikang region is such that there are very wide differences in elevation between the various mountain crests, plateaus and valleys. The greater part of the Bayan Kara range has an elevation exceeding 15,000 feet and the eastern spurs of the Tanglha mountains rise to above 20,000 feet. The valley bottoms of the southeast, however, do not exceed 10,000 feet in elevation.

The Yellow River rises to the north of the Bayan Kara range. It encircles the Amne Machin and its adjacent

massifs and then flows northeast to the pass on the border of the loess plateau where its upper reaches end. Not far from its source, the Yellow River forms two of the largest lakes of the region, the Tsaring Nor and the Ngoring Nor, both of which are fresh-water lakes.

The steep gradient of the rivers of the Chamdo-Sikang area, together with the narrowness of the valleys and the hard rocks which form the river beds, gives the area one of the greatest potential reserves of hydro-electric power in China. These resources have not yet been properly exploited for several reasons: they have not yet been sufficiently studied; they are situated in areas to which access is very difficult; and they are often a very great distance from

A view of the Yangtze River at Chungking, the great river port and commercial center which stands at the confluence of the Yangtze and the Kialing. Chungking, an ancient city, became commercially important after it was opened to foreign trade concessions in 1891. It is a leading communications center and its industries, developed since World War II, include textiles, iron and steel, chemicals and paper. Chungking was the capital of China during World War II, when most other parts of the country were occupied by the Japanese.

A view of one of the docks in the harbor of Shanghai. For some time after the Communist revolution, Shanghai was rendered inactive by Nationalist bombardment and in 1949-50 it was replaced as a center of foreign trade by Tientsin. The U.S. embargo on trade with Communist China has also affected Shanghai's international importance. The city now handles around 60 per cent of China's exports, a total very much lower than the pre-World War II figure.

centers where electrical power is needed.

CLIMATE

Tibet lies in the temperate zone but its climate can only be described as harsh. Annual rainfall amounts to less than 10 inches and the region has very severe winters and almost rainless summers. The highest peaks are permanently capped by ice and snow and the secondary mountains are free from snow for only about three or four months in every year.

At elevations of less than around 10,000 feet on the periphery of the region, average temperatures are higher. At the same time, however, the latitudinal position and the exposed nature of these areas causes considerable differences between maximum summer and minimum winter temperatures.

For example, Lhasa, at an elevation of about 12,000 feet and with an average annual rainfall of about 18 inches, has fairly mild temperatures. They range from an average of 32°F. in January to 63°F. in June, and the rainfall is distributed between the months of May and September in the southeast monsoon period. However, variations in temperature during the day are very great; the temperature may rise to around 100°F. at midday in summer and drop very sharply in the morning and evening.

TIBETAN WINTERS

The Himalayas constitute a formidable barrier on which the summer monsoons from the Indian Ocean drop most of their moisture. Thus, very little reaches northern Tibet. While the Himalayan valleys receive more than 40 inches of rainfall annually, northern Tsaidam receives no more than about 5 inches.

The Tibetan winters are dry; most of the rain falls in the spring, summer and fall. The main snow falls occur at the beginning and end of summer in the higher ground and in spring and fall at lower levels. However, since falls are light and the sun and wind are strong, the snow leaves little trace after it has fallen except on the higher mountains. Tibet has a high percentage of hours of sunshine annually, due to its height and to lack of moisture in the air.

A panoramic view of the city of Chungking, the most important commercial center of Szechwan. Chungking experienced an economic boom after World War II and is rapidly developing as a center of heavy industry. The area of the city has consequently been much extended in recent years.

COLD DESERT

Its extreme elevation and dryness combine to make the greater part of Tibet the largest cold desert in the world lying in a temperate zone. At elevations of over 16,000 feet, conditions are such that no vegetation can exist, and bare rock and rubble are the dominant elements of the landscape.

In the Tsaidam basin, to the north, sand and rock deserts and vast salt marshes give the region a definite resemblance to the Gobi desert area.

VEGETATION

Only on the plateaus and valleys of the east and south, at elevations below 16,000 feet, does vegetation begin to flourish. Large areas of pasture land and luxuriant growths of rhododendrons and other mountain shrubs are found on the gentler slopes, and under 11,000 feet great forests begin to clothe the sides of the valleys. Fir and larch prevail on the higher slopes, while poplar, birch, maple, juniper and magnolia are found lower down.

FAUNA

Wherever vegetation is abundant many wild animals are found. The best-known Tibetan animal is the yak, or shaggy ox, a domestic beast which provides the main means of transport on the rough mountain tracks and whose milk and meat is the staple diet of the Tibetan people.

Tibetan wild animals include various species of deer, among which the musk-deer or hornless deer is most common, gazelles, brown and black bears and wild horses, donkeys and goats. Among the smaller mammals are the common panda, the desert fox, wild dog and wild sheep.

Among the birds, the best-known are the vultures of the southern valleys which, like those of India, perform the office of scavengers by eating carrion. Other common birds include hawks, gulls, swans, cranes and, in eastern Tibet, pheasants.

Sinkiang Uigur

To the north of the Karakoram, Kunlun and Altyn Tagh mountains lies Sinkiang Uigur, the most westerly region of China. It comprises the autonomous region of Sinkiang and the western end of Kansu. It is bounded on the west by the Pamir mountains and a number of smaller ranges, on the north by the eastern section of the Tien Shan and the Altai ranges, and on the east by the hills of northwest Kansu in the vicinity of Yumen, or the Gate of Jade.

The great eastward curve of the Tien Shan range divides the region into two major basins, that of the Tarim to the south and that of Dzungaria to the north. Their average elevation is much lower than that of the adjacent Tibetan regions, varying between about 2000 and 4000 feet, although the mountains which enclose them are not a great deal lower than those surrounding Tibet.

WORLD'S SECOND-HIGHEST PEAK

In the Karakoram range, Mt. Godwin Austen, or K2, is the second-highest peak in the world at 28,250 feet. Mt. Kungur, in the Muztagh Ata range, reaches 25,146 feet. Khan Tengri, in the Tien Shan mountains, reaches 22,949 feet. The highest elevation reached in the Altyn Tagh range is 17,000 feet and the highest peak of the Altai range is 15,260 feet.

THE DEEPEST DEPRESSION

Both the Tarim and Dzungaria basins date back to the Quaternary period. The Tarim is mainly the result of alluvial deposits, while the Dzungaria basin has been formed by wind and water erosion, giving it an undulating surface.

The Sinkiang Uigur region is extremely dry and contains the

largest sand desert in China. This is the Taklamakan desert, which occupies much of the 300,000 square miles of the Tarim basin.

As well as dividing the region into the two major basins, the Tien Shan range spreads out into the shape of a flattened X to form two smaller basins. These are the Ili valley basin in the west, extending toward Turkestan, and the Turfan basin in the east. The Turfan has an average depression of 940 feet below sea level, making it the lowest point in Asia.

The Tarim Basin

The snow and ice caps of the mountains surrounding the Tarim basin provide the main source of water for the region. Many streams descend the mountain valleys but their courses are unusual. In many cases, on reaching the foot of the mountain they encounter an area of closely packed fragmented rock into which they disappear, to reappear on the surface only in adjacent alluvial regions where the ground is less permeable. Even after this their course is limited, for after a few miles they reach the desert, where their waters are swallowed up by the sands or dispersed over wide areas and subjected to speedy evaporation.

Only in the rainy months of early summer, when rain and melting snow swell the watercourses, can the larger streams penetrate any distance into the desert, carving out a bed which remains dry for the rest of the year.

At the foot of the mountains to the north of the basin, however, the prevailing winds have kept the surface relatively free from great accumulations of sand. In this area the principal watercourses have been able to come together to produce a large river—the Tarim River which gives its name to the basin.

SEASONS OF FLOOD

The Tarim rises in the Karakoram range, receiving much of its water from the ice and snow of the higher peaks. Cutting through the extreme western corner of the plain, it bends eastward at the foot of the Tien Shan range. In seasons of flood it is then joined by the Hotien, which at these times has sufficient volume to enable it to cross the desert sands from the Kunlun mountains, and by other streams flowing from the Pamir range. More regular are the tributaries which reach the Tarim River from the Tien Shan mountains. The most important of these forms the freshwater lake of Bagrash Kol.

The Tarim River has a very variable flow. Its bed often changes course and divides into a number of branches, and in dry seasons it sometimes takes a subterranean course. It is also difficult to define the mouth of the Tarim. A large part of its waters evaporates during its course and the remainder is generally thought to flow into Lop Nor, a lake whose exact area and location vary considerably. The name Lop Nor is also applied to a number of other small basins and depressions in the region. The Tarim sometimes discharges its waters into these depressions, as does the Charchan, which flows from the Kunlun range.

The site of the Lop Nor and its allied depressions is the lowest point in the Tarim basin. The exact location of the discharge of the river's waters is determined by the movement of the sand, which constantly alters the depth of the depressions. About a century ago the Tarim ceased to discharge the greater part of its waters into the Lop Nor and the lake practically dried up. It was thought at the time that the lake had moved from the place where Marco Polo had discovered it over 500 years previously.

A further river, the Shuleh, flows through the eastern extremity of the Tarim basin. It descends from the Nan Shan range, flows past the Gate of Jade and then flows across an area of rock desert. It discharges its waters into a small lake and into an expanse of salt marsh. The salt marsh sometimes spreads until it joins the marshes around Lop Nor.

The Dzungaria Basin

The Tien Shan range forms the base of a great triangle which includes in its area the region of Dzungaria, in the northern part of Sinkiang. Dzungaria is bounded on the northeast by the Altai mountains and on the northwest by a line of isolated secondary massifs whose maximum elevation seldom reaches 10,000 feet and which are separated by broad valleys.

Although the Dzungaria basin is only about half as large as the Tarim basin, it is more complex. This is because there is no single main watercourse to give unity to the area and also, unlike the Tarim, the greater part of the area does not consist of desert.

The driest part of the Dzungaria basin is in the east, in the angle between the Altai and Tien Shan mountains. The discharge of water from the mountains in this region is limited to a number of short-lived mountain streams which evaporate quickly in the surrounding desert. Rock desert predominates in the area.

The western part of the Dzungaria basin has much more water.

RIVERS

A large number of streams descend from the snow capped peaks of the Tien Shan and some of them join together to form rivers. The most important of these is the Manass, which flows into the freshwater lake of Ayran Kol. The more westerly rivers flow into the salt lake of Ebi.

A further basin is formed in northern Dzungaria by the Urungu River, which descends from the Altai range and flows into the freshwater lake of Ulyungur Nor. Not far from this area are the upper reaches of the great Irtysh River of Siberia, which rises in the Altai and flows into Kazakhstan beyond the Sino-Soviet border. The Irtysh flows through the only open valley in Sinkiang.

CLIMATE

Sinkiang Uigur is the driest part of China. No other region is so sheltered from moisture from the ocean. The average annual rainfall is ten inches, falling to five inches in low-lying

areas and rising to nine inches around Kuldja and eleven inches around Ining. In general, rainfall is not evenly distributed throughout the year but occurs mainly in spring and fall.

The average annual temperature is around 55°F., but temperatures vary widely according to season and locality. In the Tarim basin variations in temperature in a single day of over 50°F. have been recorded. Temperatures are higher in the Irtysh valley and in the Turfan depression, which has a summer average of 93°F., the highest in China. In mountainous areas, temperatures naturally vary according to height.

There are over 200 frost-free days every year in the south of the area but less than 150 in the north. The greater part of the territory has a high number of hours of sunshine every year, with a maximum on the Mongolian borders and a minimum on the mountains of the southern boundary.

VEGETATION

Although Sinkiang Uigur has a higher proportion of desert within its boundaries than any other area of China—deserts occupy more than half its total area—there are parts of the region which have luxuriant vegetation.

On the Altai mountains to the north of the Irtysh valley and in the Ili valley there are wide grasslands. The valleys of the Tien Shan and of the larger ranges on the borders are covered with forests of conifers, with deciduous trees on the lower slopes. These are intermixed with pasture lands and expanses of mountain shrubs.

Much of the area is covered by arid steppe land, but wherever there is water, either on the surface or underground, there are salt marshes fringed with tamarisks or, more often, oases. Oases, distributed either singly or in groups or chains, are found all over the strips of land at the foot of the mountains, both around the Taklamakan desert and to the north of the Tien Shan range.

Oases are also found along the courses of the Tarim, the Manass and the other main rivers. For many centuries these fertile patches of ground have been assiduously cultivated by the inhabitants, who employ a method of irrigation by means of water drawn from subterranean channels, thus avoiding loss of water by evaporation.

A number of schemes are in operation to improve the agriculture of Sinkiang Uigur. These involve utilizing all available sources of water to the full, increasing the area of cultivated land, grassland and woodland, cleansing the salt from certain well-watered areas, and protecting cultivated areas against encroaching sand.

FAUNA

Since vegetation in most areas is sparse, Sinkiang Uigur is not rich in wild animals. There are, however, a number of large hoofed animals, including wild oxen, horses and camels, deer, gazelles, antelopes, goats and wild boars. There are also a number of carnivores, among them lynxes, wildcats and otters.

HUMAN GEOGRAPHY

CHINA HAS BEEN POPULATED SINCE remote prehistoric times. The fossilized remains of one of the earliest species of man, called *Sinanthropus pekingensis,* or Peking Man, have been found at the village of Choukoutien, near Peking. Peking Man is thought to have lived during the Middle Pleistocene period and at the present stage of archaeological knowledge, until more detailed examination of recent discoveries in Africa, it appears that the only predecessor of Peking Man is the *Pithecanthropus erectus* of Java, dating from around 400,000 B.C.

The remains of anthropoidal humans thought to date from the Middle Paleolithic period have been found in the area where the Yellow River bends around the Ordos desert.

Remains of *homo sapiens* of the Upper Palaeolithic Age have also been found in Choukoutien, in more recent geological strata, and in Manchuria and the Szechwan basin.

In contrast with the considerable amount of Palaeolithic remains, there have been few discoveries of remains dating from the Mesolithic Age, and these have been limited to Mongolia, northern Manchuria and Kwangsi. Practically no remains from the Lower Neolithic Age have been found, but archaeological discoveries relating to the Upper Neolithic Age abound. These are spread over more than 200 archaeological sites scattered all over China. They may be divided into three main groups representing three types of culture, each of which has certain marked characteristics and a fairly definite geographical location.

The three Upper Neolithic cultures are known as the Yangshao culture, the Lungshan culture and the Southern System.

YANGSHAO CULTURE

The Yangshao culture centered on the middle and lower valleys of the Yellow River. The inhabitants of the area lived in pit dwellings and are known to have domesticated oxen, sheep, pigs and dogs. Their staple diet was millet and they produced light-colored, unglazed earthenware vessels with painted patterns. A characteristic artifact of the culture was a rectangular stone knife with a crescent-shaped edge.

LUNGSHAN CULTURE

The center of the Lungshan culture lay further east, in the coastal plain of the Yellow River and in the Shantung and Liaotung peninsulas. It appears to have occurred a little later than the Yangshao period, since horses were added to the domesticated animals, black pottery was produced and rice was introduced as a food.

A characteristic artifact of the Lungshan culture, which was also used by the people of the Yangshao culture, was a three-legged cauldron which was used to steam cereals. The cereals were placed in a pot with a perforated bottom which was set on top of the cauldron.

THE SOUTHERN SYSTEM

The cultures of the Southern System covered the area between the Yangtze valley and the sea. The people of the Southern System were members of an ethnic group which extended over all southeast Asia. Their culture was characterized by the domestication of the buffalo, the use of bamboo for building and other artifacts, the practice of ancestor worship and the emergence of dragon myths. The latter were to reappear in folk beliefs throughout the course of Chinese civilization.

The first Bronze Age civilization

The lovely Pagoda of Flowers is but one of countless architectural and artistic treasures in the city of Canton. This great metropolis in southern China was for centuries a key point of contact between the Chinese and the Western world.

in China flourished under the Shang dynasty, the first Chinese dynasty which is historically authenticated, between 1766 and 1123 B.C. The Shang were the first of the great dynasties of eastern Asia.

The period was characterized by the introduction of wheat, handwriting, money and the use of chariots as a military weapon. Its predominant features differed little from those of the Neolithic culture, but the influences of Thai and Turkic cultures gradually became more marked, especially after the invasion of the west of China by the Chou rulers in about 1000 B.C.

THE IRON AGE

The transition from the Bronze to the Iron Age between the 7th and 6th centuries B.C. was marked by increased contacts between the civilizations which had grown up in the Yellow River area and in the Yangtze valley. These contacts culminated in the first unification of China under the Ch'in dynasty (221-206 B.C.) and the Han dynasty (202 B.C.-220A.D.).

Migrations

The internal process of fusion in China, which was almost complete by 1000 A.D., was accompanied over the centuries by migratory movements of varying intensity. These were mainly involved with the movement of people from the Yellow River plain to the valley of the Yangtze or, to a lesser degree, to regions further afield.

At the same time there were, throughout the period, movements of populations which were descended from the original Chinese cultures but which had remained more backward. These migrations generally came from the areas of the west, north and northeast. From 700 B.C. onward, the strongest group of barbarians to penetrate Chinese territory and establish themselves were the Huns.

TRADERS AND BARBARIANS

The establishment of the great centralized empires of the Ch'in and Han dynasties halted the invasions of the barbarians, but every time the central power weakened China fell into periods of civil war. At such times new hordes of barbarians penetrated the frontiers, among them the Turks, Tunguses, Tibetans, Tatars, Mongols and Manchus. The Manchus and Mongols finally succeeded in setting up dynasties which ruled over China for long periods in the second millenium of the Christian era.

From the period of the T'ang dynasty (7th to 10th centuries A.D.) there was a considerable influx of Persians and other Moslems from the Middle East. They came mainly as traders, entering China either by the "Silk Road," the main trade route of northern China, or by the sea routes to the provinces of the south.

RECENT MIGRATION

In modern times, the importance of migratory elements in China has been almost negligible. The most compact group of Europeans to have settled recently in China is that of the Russians, who established colonies in Sinkiang and Manchuria in the late 1920s and early 1930s. There is also a noticeable Japanese admixture in the Manchurian population, the result of the long period of Japanese occupation.

Manchuria is also important as having been the scene of one of the most remarkable examples of internal migration in modern history. Toward the end of the 19th century the population of Manchuria was estimated at around 14 million. In the early years of the 20th century, a great movement of people into Manchuria, mainly from Hopeh and Shantung, began to take place, growing until it amounted to about 400,000 people annually. By the early 1960s, the population of Manchuria was estimated at around 50 million.

POPULATION MOVEMENT SINCE 1949

In the People's Republic of China internal migrations have gone on in the traditional manner, the greatest movements being those of rural populations to the towns. The emigration of Chinese has practically ceased. There are, however, large and long-established Chinese communities in a number of countries. Among the more important of these are the Chinese communities in Thailand (3,500,000), Malaya (2,500,000), Indonesia (1,500,000), Singapore (1,300,000), Vietnam (400,000), Burma (300,000), Cambodia (250,000), the United States of America (237,000), Sarawak (225,000), the Philippines (122,000).

Development of the Population

The most densely populated part of China in early times was the lower Yellow River basin. The first census of the area was taken about 2 A.D. under the Han dynasty, at about the same period when Caesar Augustus was making a census of the Roman Empire. The Han dynasty census revealed a population of 59,600,000.

Haichu Square in Canton, the capital of the province of Kwangtung. Canton was one of the main centers of Western influence in China and was a pioneer center of Chinese journalism. Modernization of the city was begun in 1919; the ancient walls were razed, the streets widened, the harbor modernized and a new bridge was constructed across the Pearl River. Canton was formerly noted as a craft center but emphasis in recent years has been on industrial development.

The ancient "Bridge of Ten Thousand Ages," spanning the Min River at Foochow, the capital of the province of Fukien. The bridge, which is 440 yards long and is supported on low granite pillars, links the modern commercial suburb with Nantai, the former center of foreign business interests. The old, walled city of Foochow lies about two miles from the river.

By about 1000 A.D. the Yangtze River valley had become the key economic region of China, and thus the main population center. Over the last centuries, the two areas have merged into one another to form what is now the richest and most densely populated part of China.

Following the Han dynasty census, further censuses were taken under the T'ang dynasty (755), Sung (1102), Yuan (1290) and Ming (1578). Each of these censuses was remarkable in revealing a total population either less than or approximately equal to that recorded under the Han dynasty.

POPULATION EXPLOSION

However, after what appears statistically to have been sixteen centuries of stagnation in population figures, a population explosion appears to have occurred under the Ch'ing (Manchu) dynasty. By 1741 the population had increased to 143,000,000, and at the fall of the Manchus in 1910 it was estimated at around 331,000,000.

In 1929, before the Japanese invasion of Manchuria, the statistical department of the Kuomintang government recorded a population of 420,000,000. In 1947, after the end of the Japanese occupation, the figure was estimated at 463,000,000. This figure appears to have been very low, for the census carried out by the Chinese People's Republic in 1953 recorded a population of 583,000,000. In 1963 the population of the People's Republic of China was estimated at 716,000,000, or roughly 20 per cent of the total world population.

Density and Distribution of Population

In 1957 it was estimated that China had a population of 646,530,000, distributed over an area of 3,691,502 square miles. This amounted to an average density of around 175 persons to a square mile, a figure somewhat below that of most European countries and of India and Japan.

However, it is a fact that China has a higher population pressure than many other countries, and reference must therefore be made to other standards rather than that of simple arithmetic density. A more accurate idea of China's population distribution may be obtained by considering the specific density of population in individual provinces rather than by dealing with the country as a whole.

POPULATION DENSITY

The various Chinese provinces show considerable variation in the average density of their populations. The highest densities are found around the mouth of the Yangtze and in the plain of the Yellow River, while the lowest occur in the western and northern territories.

The population density in the province of Kiangsu is 1105 per square mile. In Shantung it is 913 per square mile, in Honan 755, in Chekiang 643, in Anhwei 621, and in Hopeh 549. Density of population gradually decreases toward the borders of China. In Inner Mongolia it amounts to 20 per square mile, in Sinkiang Uigur 8.9, in Tsinghai 7.4, and in Tibet 2.7.

The greatest factor affecting the relative densities of different provinces is, in China as in the rest of the world, geographic position and its attendant climatic and biological results. Certain differences may be attributed to historical causes, but these are relatively minor.

Until recently, urban development in China was at a low level, and the most important occupation was that of agriculture. Thus the availability of land for cultivation was, and to some extent still remains, the determining factor in the density of population from province to province.

LAND FOR CULTIVATION

It is not too much of a generalization to say that the greater part of land available for cultivation in China is now under cultivation. The reserve of virgin land in Manchuria is now practically exhausted, and Mongolia, Sinkiang, Tsinghai and

Tibet have no reserves which can compare in fertility and generally favorable conditions with those in Manchuria at the beginning of the 20th century.

Since the land at present being developed for agricultural purposes is not as favorable to cultivation as the areas developed in the past, the technical means needed to obtain satisfactory results are correspondingly more expensive. Furthermore, urban developments and the constructions of roads, railways and irrigation lakes and canals, have all cut into the amount of land available for agriculture.

The total area of cultivated land in China in 1953 was roughly estimated at around 430,000 square miles, though this figure has probably been much increased in the last few years. The distribution of agricultural land between one province and another varies according to relief, soil characteristics and the availability of water for irrigation.

The provinces with the largest percentage of land under cultivation are Kirin, Heilungkiang, Liaoning and Szechwan. The second largest percentages are found in Hopeh, Honan, Shantung and Kiangsu. The third largest cultivated areas occur in Anhwei, Hupeh, Shansi, Hunan and Shensi. Fourth in order come Chahar, Fukien, Kansu, Kwangsi, Kweichow, Suiyuan and Yunnan. The areas with the lowest percentage of cultivated land are Inner Mongolia, Sinkiang Uigur, Tsinghai, Sikang and Ningsia.

Ethnic Composition

The very great majority of the population of modern China, some 94 per cent, belongs to the *Han* people, an ethnic group formed by the fusion of a number of basically mongoloid types. This fusion has, however, been on a cultural rather than an ethnographical basis and has been more pronounced in the urban than the rural areas. Thus, the populations of different areas still display considerable variations in physical and psychological characteristics, language and folklore.

The *Han* population has complete predominance in the more fertile and most heavily populated parts of China, for example in the middle and lower valleys of the Yellow River, the middle and lower valleys of the Yangtze and in Manchuria.

MINORITY POPULATIONS

In the poorer, more sparsely inhabited regions of the west, however, minority populations are prevalent. In the autonomous regions of Tibet and Sinkiang Uigur minority populations form about 90 per cent of the inhabitants. In 1953, Chinese belonging to minority nationalities were estimated at 35,320,360, and it is thought that this number had increased to over 40,000,000 by 1961.

Minority nationalities thus account for around 6 per cent of China's population. They vary in size from several million to a few thousand, and may be divided into four basic racial groups: Sino-Tibetan, Turkic, Mongol and Tungus. These may be further divided into a number of major groups with populations of over a million. These are the Koreans, Manchus, Hui, Mongols, Uigurs, Tibetans, Miao-yao, Chuang, Yi and Puyi.

TIBETAN, YI AND MIAO-YAO

The Tibetan group includes both the indigenous inhabitants of Tibet

A view of one of the new workers' residential suburbs which have recently been erected to the west and northwest of Peking. Great expansion since 1949 has caused the city to extend as far as the Great Wall, some thirty-five miles away. The barrack-like apartment blocks shown here, unattractive as they may be to Western eyes, represent an immeasurable improvement over the teeming slums which were formerly a feature of so many Chinese cities.

A village in southwest Kwangtung, the southernmost province of China. Since the Communist revolution the social structure of villages like this has changed very greatly; privately owned land has been abolished and the family system has been broken down by increased collectivization. Agriculture in this area is mainly carried out on the alluvial soil of the river valleys, since the soil on the hillsides is poor. Rice is in short supply in the area, although two crops a year are produced.

and other people of Tibetan stock living in Szechwan, Tsinghai and Kansu.

The Yi form the strongest minority in Szechwan and Yunnan and are associated with a number of other small minority groups, living mainly in Yunnan.

The Miao-yao form important minorities in Kweichow and Hunan.

MANCHUS, HUI, KOREANS AND CHUANG

The Manchu minorities have now become almost completely assimilated into the Han people. They are found mainly in Liaoning, Kirin, Heilungkiang, Inner Mongola and Peking.

The Hui group contains many Moslems of basically Indo-European stock, and is found mainly in the autonomous region of Ningsia. They are also scattered through Kansu and Tsinghai. Further Indo-European minorities are formed by the Tagiks of Sinkiang and the Russians of Sinkiang and Manchuria.

The Koreans, who live mainly in Kirin, form a group basically related to the Japanese people.

The Chuang, who form the largest minority group in China, are concentrated mainly in Kwangsi.

Urban Settlement

In spite of the marked movement of the population from rural to urban areas over the last few years, the population of the cities of China is still a relatively small percentage of the total populaton, estimated in 1953 at about 13 per cent.

In 1956 it was estimated that the total urban population of China amounted to around 89,000,000. More than a third of this total was accounted for by the populations of the fourteen cities with more than 1,000,000 inhabitants. The two largest of these, Shanghai and Peking, have a combined population of more than 10,000,000.

There are twenty cities with a population of between 500,000 and 1,000,000, and about ninety cities

with a population of between 100,000 and 500,000. In addition there are about 1500 smaller areas classed as urban.

The degree of urbanization varies considerably from province to province. Liaoning, the industrial heart of the northeast, has the largest urban population, followed by other northeastern regions of Kiangsu and Hopeh. In the remaining provinces the percentage of urban population is much lower, reaching a minimum in Honan, Anhwei, Hunan, Kiangsi, Kweichow and Kwangsi.

TRADE CENTERS AND SHRINES

Until the 19th century, most Chinese cities were trading centers, situated at the junctions of land and water communication routes. Peking and the provincial capitals were administrative centers, the site of the court in the case of Peking and of the provincial administration in other

A view of the city of Tsunyi in northern Kweichow. Tsunyi is situated on the southeastern slopes of the Talashan range at an elevation of 2723 feet and stands on the main highway to Szechwan. Its main importance was formerly as a wine-growing area and agricultural center, producing rice, cereals and beans. But recent years have seen great developments in the textile, paper and pottery industries.

character was bound up with the work of local craftsmen or the agricultural produce of the area. Other cities were famous because of the proximity of religious sites and places of pilgrimage. Finally, cities on the borders of China often had a predominantly military significance, as garrison towns, fortresses or supply bases.

THE TRADITIONAL CITY PLAN

The traditional Chinese city was a walled complex of buildings arranged to a plan in conformity with the contours of its site. The plan of the city was usually rectangular, divided by two large, central roads at the junction of which stood a tower from which a bell or drum regulated the phases of civic life. The great mandarins with their officials and dependants occupied a separate quarter which was also walled in to create a city within a city.

Trading activities developed in varous districts of the city and sometimes extended to areas outside the city walls. Activities of the latter kind, however, were restricted by the custom of closing the city gates from sunset to dawn.

Streets, with the exception of the two main thoroughfares, were usually narrow. In the case of a city built on a river, as most were, streets would be wider at the landward end

of the town, where goods were brought in by carts, and narrower on the waterside, where goods from boats were unloaded and carried by porters.

RESIDENCES

Houses were generally grouped in rectangular blocks and these blocks were often surrounded by walls, especially in the better residential districts. The traditional Chinese house was rectangular in shape and built on one floor around a courtyard. The entrance to the courtyard thus gave access to the interior of each single block.

In commercial areas, houses were generally narrower and were built on two floors, the window area facing into the street to serve as a shop. The roofs of houses usually sloped.

MODERN DEVELOPMENT

From the 19th century onward, new commercial cities based on the Western type were often grafted on to the traditional urban form. This occurred mainly in the principal ports and communication centers of Manchuria during the period of the concessions, which were, in effect, commercial cities leased to foreign powers.

In the areas subject to the concessions, building was generally car-

ried out in accordance to the usual commercial practice of the countries carrying on trade and industry there. Large urban settlements in which Western styles mingled with traditional Chinese commercial styles often grew up around the concessions. The earliest examples of this kind of development are found in Shanghai, Tientsin, Canton, Hankow, Talien, Shenyang and Harbin.

As in other countries, military, political and economic factors contributed to a continual process of change in the importance of individual towns and to the rise and fall of new urban centers. This process has been particulary marked during the last ten years, when the urban area of China has more than doubled.

However, urban development has been very uneven. While some new towns have been built and others have been enlarged, some have undergone little development and others have fallen into rapid decline. Factors affecting such changes include the position of new railways and other communication networks, the sites of new mines and other sources of energy, and strategic and political criteria.

Rural Settlements

The non-urban population of China consists mainly of peasants. In addition it is estimated that there are still several million nomads, who are occupied in cattle breeding and wander with their herds of sheep, cows, horses, yaks or camels, in the regions of Mongolia, Tsinghai, Tibet and Sinkiang.

BOAT-DWELLERS

Boat-dwellers form a semi-nomadic group of the Chinese rural population. They are chiefly engaged in fishing and in the transport of goods or passengers along the internal waterways. Boatmen and their families, particularly in central and southern China, spend most of their lives aboard their sampans or junks. In recent years, a number of these semi-nomadic families have taken up occupations on land, but a great number still follow their traditional way of life.

A third rural group is formed by woodcutters, foresters and hunters, though this group is probably less numerous than the two previously mentioned. They are found chiefly in the forested areas of Manchuria and the southeastern borders of the Tibetan uplands and, to a lesser extent, in Fukien, Kiangsi, Hunan and Kweichow. In the colder northeastern regions they live in log huts while in the more temperate southern regions their dwellings are usually constructed of boards and wickerwork.

COASTAL FISHERMEN

The last important rural group who cannot be described as peasants are the fishermen of the coasts and islands. Although they spend long periods on their boats, they usually live ashore in the same type of dwellings as those used by the peasants of the same areas.

The rural population of China is mainly distributed in small towns and villages. An important exception to this rule occurs in Szechwan, where some peasants still live in scattered colonies of a few houses.

TOWNS AND VILLAGES

The small towns and villages have populations which may vary between a few hundred and around 20,000. Among the smaller villages some remnants of the ancient feudal system may still be discerned, for the communities retain vestiges of their

A view of the outskirts of Kweiyang in the province of Kweichow, some 200 miles south of Chungking. Kweiyang is an important communications center and its industrial development, notably the production of pharmaceutical goods, has been facilitated by the presence of coalmines nearby. Other products include hides, grain and vegetable oils.

original family system and retainers of the local "great man."

The larger villages serve as market-places for their areas and as centers of local administration. In accordance with the tradition of self-sufficiency in rural life, based on the former paucity of trade relations with the cities, they are often centers of local crafts.

Since the agricultural population is naturally most dense in the more fertile areas, the small towns and villages are distributed evenly over such areas.

The larger villages are usually built in a style resembling the traditional city plan. The scale of planning is suitably reduced, and city walls are replaced by mounds of beaten earth.

Residences take the same form as those in the cities, but the courtyard is generally larger so that it may serve as a sheltered area for such processes as threshing and winnowing grain. The chief building materials used are wood for the framework of the house, and beaten earth, wooden planks, bricks or stones for the walls.

The size and shape of houses and the materials used in their construction varies according to locality and also to the relative wealth of the occupiers. The most elaborate buildings in villages were formerly the chapels dedicated to ancestor worship or to other religious purposes. Great respect was also paid to the shrines and burial places situated in the fields or hills near the village.

THE COMMUNES

Until very recently, the great building developments that were taking place in Chinese cities had little effect on the traditional form of the rural settlements. Only in recent years, with the setting up of the People's Communes and the introduction of farming on a much larger, more industrialized scale, has a change begun to be noticeable in some districts.

The new buildings on the Communes include large grain stores, workshops, modern stalls for cattle-rearing, administrative buildings, dormitories and dwelling houses. They are usually built of red brick in a plain, functional style, providing a contrast to the gray and yellow of the older buildings.

REGIONS, PROVINCES AND CITIES

The Middle and Lower Yellow River Valley

The cradle of Chinese civilization was the middle and lower valley of the Yellow River. This area extends over five provinces: Hopeh, Shantung, Honan, Shansi and Shensi. The economic importance of the region may be judged from the fact that it comprises a third of all cultivated land in China, has large deposits of coal, ferrous minerals and other metals, and a population of 180,000,000.

Four of the provinces are continental in character, only Shantung has a marked maritime character. The alluvial uplands of the eastern plain form a loess region. With the exception of a large part of Shansi and Shensi, western Honan and the hills of Shantung, the region has a mainly level surface which has facilitated agricultural development and cultural and economic intercourse throughout the region. It was in this area that the first roads were built and the first great irrigation works constructed.

To the north, west and east the boundaries of the region are clearly defined by mountains and the sea. Only in the south, toward Anhwei and Kiangsu, is the division with the southern part of the Yangtze valley less clearly marked. The natural boundaries are nowhere impassable, so that in the past northern China, lying beyond the boundaries, was able to enjoy cultural and economic exchanges with the great civilizations of the west.

HOPEH, SHANTUNG AND HONAN

The heart of the region is the province of Hopeh, which is fertile and well provided with natural resources. It is the strategic center for the control of Mongolia and Manchuria and provides an outlet to the sea for the hinterlands of the region.

The province of Shantung, on the southeast, differs in character from east to west. The eastern peninsula forms a maritime frontier, whose economic character is affected by China's international relations. In the past, profitable foreign contacts have alternated with periods of depression. The western part of the province, however, has a deeply rural character and differs little from the similar areas of neighboring provinces.

Honan, more than any other province of the region, has preserved a definite agricultural character. In the past there was little industrial development and even in recent years the province has retained much of its traditional aspect.

FRONTIER PROVINCES

Shansi and Shensi, which are drier and more mountainous, have a smaller cultivated area. In recent centuries they have taken on the char-

acter of frontier provinces and as such have become the site of many fortresses and trading centers. Political and social insecurity, together with the problem of banditry, have served to concentrate the population in large towns and villages to a greater degree than in any other province in northern China.

The Cities of Hopeh

CHANGKIAKOW (Kalgan)
(pop. 229,300)

Changkiakow, or Kalgan, which is situated north of the Great Wall, was formerly a frontier post. Under the Ch'ing dynasty it was an important center for trade between Peking and the Mongols. The present population includes a strong Mongolian minority.

The main business of Changkiakow was formerly the collection and processing of animal products from the Mongolian interior. In recent years it has become a center of heavy industry, particularly textiles.

CHINWANGTAO *(pop. 186,000)*

Chinwangtao stands on the Gulf of Chihli near the boundary of Hopeh and Liaoning. It owes its importance to its position as an export center for coal from the Kailan mines. It is on the northern China-Manchuria railroad and has an excellent harbor with a deep, rocky bed. The harbor is ice-free all the year and the town is an important fishing center.

Chinwangtao has one of the largest plate glass factories in China. The seaside resort of Pehtaiho, on the west, is one of the most popular in China. To the northeast of the town stands the village of Shanhaikwan, the starting point of the Great Wall.

PAOTING *(pop. 130,000)*

Paoting, the capital of Hopeh until 1957, is situated on the Peking-Wuhan railroad. It has a university and a military academy and is a center for a considerable amount of river traffic. In recent years, the cotton weaving industry has been developed but the population of the town has not displayed any great increase.

PEKING *(pop. 4,010,000)*

During the period of the earliest Chinese dynasties Peking was a fron-

tier post. It became the capital of a feudal kingdom during the period of the Warring States (475-221 B.C.), and was created the imperial capital in 1122 A.D. Except for a few short periods, Peking has remained the

A street vendor selling parasols decorated with brightly colored traditional scenes. In ancient times the parasol was a symbol of its possessor's class status and was sometimes made of fine silk with ornaments of gold and precious stones.

cases. In other cities, commercial capital of China ever since.

Few traces of ancient Peking still remain, because of extensive destruction and reconstruction. Most of the older buildings remaining date from the latter years of the Ming dynasty (1368-1644) and from the Ch'ing dynasty (1644-1912). These buildings, however, are more impressive and splendid than any others in China.

In the center of Peking stands the Imperial City, within which was the Forbidden City containing the apartments of the imperial court. Its great palaces are surrounded by parks. The modern government buildings and the Historical Museum stand on an enormous square opposite the imposing T'ien-an-men gate.

Peking has a double square of walls. The first square, on the north, is 15 miles long and forms the boundary of the inner political, administrative and residential area. It is now an impressive ruin whose construction dates back to the Ming dynasty. The second square of walls is 14 miles long and joins the south side of the first square. It encloses the commercial district.

The Summer Palace, which dates from the end of the 19th century, is situated at the foot of the hills to the northwest of the city.

Temples, monasteries, pagodas and tombs dating from various periods of the last millenium are to be found both inside the city and on its outskirts, particularly on the wide sweep of hills to the west and north. These include the Temple of Heaven, to the south of the city, and the Temple of Agriculture. About 35 miles from Peking, to the north beyond the Nankow Pass, lies a section of the Great Wall.

In the old city of Peking, particularly the inner city, the street layout and architecture provide the best examples of traditional Chinese city planning to be found in the country. Since the establishment of the Chinese People's Republic, however, the area of the old city has been greatly extended; many new buildings have been erected and old buildings restored and changed.

In 1957 the population of Peking and its suburbs amounted to 4,010,000, with a further 1,410,000 in the remainder of the municipality. The total area of the municipality of Peking was then 3386 square miles.

The presence of the imperial court in Peking led, in the past, to the growth of a great tradition of craftsmanship in the city. Peking became famous for the production of jade and ivory carvings, furniture, pottery and porcelain, carpets and books. The opera house is the most famous in China and is the home of the Chinese classical opera company which has won wide acclaim in the West.

In recent years, the city and its surroundings have been an area of great industrial development. The production of iron, steel and coal has been greatly increased, and large factories have been established for the manufacture of railroad rolling stock, buses, agricultural machinery, ball bearings, machine tools and wool and rayon goods. Other commercial enterprises include gas works, printing plants and movie studios. About 1,000,000 workers are employed in industry.

The importance of Peking as a center of rail communications has been much increased by the doubling of the lines through Manchuria, Wuhan and Tientsin and the opening of a new line to the northeast, running through Chengteh to Mongolia and Siberia. Peking is also the principal center for both internal and international air traffic.

SHIHKIACHWANG (*pop. 598,000*)

Shihkiachwang is situated in western Hopeh about 150 miles southwest of Peking. It is on the main railroad

The square in front of the railway station at Dairen, on the southern tip of the Liaotung peninsula. The city was originally a fishing village but modernization was begun by the Russians in 1898 and continued by the Japanese after 1905. It is now an important administrative, industrial and commercial center with a modern harbor and thriving shipyards. The city's industrial nature is emphasized by the factory chimneys along the horizon in the illustration.

line between Peking and Te-chou. The presence of rich coal deposits in the area has favored the development of heavy industries and the population has greatly increased in recent years. The town is the major center for cotton spinning and weaving in Hopeh and is also noted for the production of agricultural machinery and fertilizers.

T'ANG-SHAN (pop. 800,000)

T'ang-shan is situated about 60 miles northeast of Tientsin on the railroad line to Manchuria. It is at the center of one of the principal coal fields of China, the working of which was begun at the end of the 19th century and financed by both British and Chinese capital. The development of the city has been closely allied to coal production.

The municipal area of T'ang-shan includes not only coal mines but also coke works, iron foundries, cement works, works for fireproofing materials, railroad workshops, factories producing mining and foundry equipment, wheelwright's workshops and cotton mills.

Architecturally, T'ang-shan is of little interest, since it is an industrial city which has sprung up in the last few decades and thus has little architectural character.

TIENTSIN (pop. 3,220,000)

Unlike Peking, Tientsin, the capital of the province of Hopeh, is a city without ancient traditions or historical remains. It developed from a garrison town into a prosperous port during the 19th century after the establishment of foreign trading concessions.

Tientsin is situated where the Grand Canal and its numerous tributaries unite to form the Hai Ho, at a point about 70 miles from Peking and 32 miles from the coast. It is the most important opening to the sea in the whole region.

Tientsin is also an important railroad junction, with connections to Peking, Mukden and Putai. It can be reached by barges and small craft along the Hai Ho and small ocean-going steamers can berth at Taku and Tangku a little further down the estuary. However, sea traffic now tends to use the new port of Sinkang, on the coast, which can accomodate ships of up to 10,000 tons and is kept open by ice-breakers during the three months of winter frosts.

In 1949, Tientsin was second only

A street in a workers' residential area in Foshan, in the northeast of the province of Heilungkiang. The rehousing of industrial workers is a major project in modern China and it was estimated that in 1952 about $116,000,000 was spent on workers' accomodations.

to Shanghai as an industrial center. Among its many enterprises are salt and chemical works, thermo-electric projects, cotton mills, tobacco factories, plants for processing agricultural products for export and the most famous carpet factory in China.

The population of Tientsin has increased very greatly over the last few years. The greater part of the city consists of relatively modern buildings in the Western style inherited from the period of the trade concessions. New buildings have been erected mainly on the periphery and include large plants for iron and steel production and for the manufacture of tractors, diesel engines and electric cables. Other factories include bicycles, sewing machines, pharmaceutical products and canned food.

Tientsin is also a cultural center with a number of institutes of higher education.

The Cities of Shantung

TAIAN (pop. 80,000)

Taian is situated at the foot of the sacred Tai Shan mountain, some 30 miles south of Tsinan. Formerly it was a small agricultural town but there has been some industrial development in recent years.

TSINAN (pop. 862,000)

Tsinan, the capital of the province of Shantung, is a very ancient city dating back to the 6th century A.D. During this period iron was dis-

covered in Shantung and the province enjoyed great prosperity. A park in Tsinan is famous for its many ancient temples and ornamental fountains and the neighboring hills are the site of early Buddhist rock carvings.

During the last few decades, a new town has developed to the west of the old city. Modern Tsinan, which is still expanding, is important as an administrative center. It stands in one of the richest agricultural zones of the province and has a large market for agricultural produce.

A number of industries have recently been developed in Tsinan, among them meat canning, cotton weaving, the manufacture of paper and agricultural machinery and an iron foundry. The city is also a communications center where the railroad from Tsingtao branches off from the Tientsin-Shanghai line.

TSINGTAO (pop. 1,121,000)

Tsingtao, which is situated to the north of the entrance to the Bay of Kiaochow, is the largest city in Shantung. Its industrial development was begun under German occupation between 1897 and 1914 and was continued under Japanese occupation until 1922. The depth of water in the naturally sheltered harbor makes is one of the best ports in China. The town is on the main rail lines to Tsinan and Yentai.

Tsingtao stretches along a range of low hills and the style of its architecture is predominantly German. To

A view of a village in southern Tibet. This area, which includes the upper valleys of the Indus, Sutlej and Tsangpo (Brahmaputra) rivers, is the most densely populated part of Tibet, since its climate and terrain are more favorable to agriculture than elsewhere. The lower valleys, below about 12,000 feet, are suitable for both cultivation and stockbreeding, but the best pasture lands are found between 12,000 and 15,000 feet, or at even higher elevations during the summer months.

the east, on the coast, is a residential district overlooking a sandy beach which is one of the most popular holiday resorts in China.

In the last ten years many important factories have been erected in Tsingtao and older factories have been extended or rebuilt. The chief industries are railroad rolling stock, tires, cement, iron, aluminum, copper and glass. The city is one of the most important commercial ports in northern China.

Further contributions to local economy are made by the processing of salt, coastal and deep-sea fishing, and the processing of seaweed and other marine products. Tsingtao has a university and an institute of technology which specializes in oceanography.

TSINING (pop. 86,000)

Tsining, which lies to the south of Taian, is a very ancient city. Among its historical remains are the ruins of the Temple of Confucius and His Disciple at Kufow, the ruins of the Temple of Mencius on the nearby hills and the remains of city walls.

TZUPO (pop. 806,000)

During the last decade Tzupo has risen to third place among the cities of Shantung. It is situated in the center of the province on a branch of the Tsinan-Tsingtao railroad. It takes its name from the two large villages of Szechwan and Poshan, which were combined in 1954 to form the municipality of Tzupo.

Tzupo is typical of the centers of heavy industry which have sprung up in recent years. There are large coal and iron deposits around the city and a great number of industries have been set up for the production of coke, pig-iron and similar products.

The Cities of Honan

CHENGCHOW (pop. 766,000)

Chengchow, the capital of the province of Honan, is situated a few miles to the south of the Yellow River, and is one of the oldest Chinese cities. The remains of the ancient city, which is believed to date back originally to the Shang dynasty (1766-1123 B.C.) include fragments of the city wall and ceramic and bronze artifacts.

Until the present century, Chengchow retained little of its early importance. A revival began with the construction of the Lunghai and Pinghan railroads with their junction at Chengchow. Extensive development began in the early 1950s and the area of the city has increased considerably over the last few years.

Modern Chengchow is a well-planned city with wide, tree-lined streets and fine administrative and industrial buildings and dwelling houses. Its major industries are textiles, heavy machinery, thermoelectric power and the processing of agricultural products.

KAIFENG (pop. 299,100)

Kaifeng, to the east of Chengchow, another ancient city, founded in the 4th century B.C., reached its height as the capital of the Sung dynasty from 960 to 1126, when it had more than 1,000,000 inhabitants. During this period it even attracted a number of Jews, who founded a colony there in 1183 and erected the first synagogue in the Far East.

The decline of Kaifeng dated from around the 13th century, when an alteration in the course of the Yellow River led to the eventual silting-up of the waterways on which the city depended for trade. Rebuilding over the last few hundred years has left little of archaeological or architectural interest in the city apart from the Terrace of the Dragons and the Pagoda of Iron.

Kaifeng is the site of Honan Medical College and has a good library and a museum. The chief industries of the area are textiles and flour milling, but agricultural and mineral resources are limited and the size of the city has increased very little over the past few decades.

LOYANG *(pop. 171,200)*

The Loyang area, in a fertile valley watered by the Lo, a tributary of the Yellow River, has a long and distinguished history. The eastern Chou and the Han, Tu'pa and Sui dynasties all built capitals in the area of the present city. All that remains of these past glories are the impressive stone sculptures in the Lungmen gorge, about 10 miles from Loyang, which are among the finest examples of Chinese classical art. Also near the city, a number of monuments dating from the 1st century A.D. are evidence of early Buddhist penetration into China.

From about 1000 A.D., Loyang underwent a steady decline. In the last ten years, however, some of the biggest industrial developments in the area have taken place at Loyang. A new city has been built to the east of the old and the population is steadily increasing.

The Cities of Shansi

ANYANG *(pop. 135,000)*

The city of Anyang, which lies north of the Yellow River on the Peking-Canton railroad, was the capital of the first historically authenticated dynasty of China, the Shang (1766-1123 B.C.). It has been the site of a number of important archaeological discoveries, among them inscriptions carved on tortoise shell and on the shoulder blades of cattle and horses.

Modern Anyang is being developed as a center of the iron and steel industries, due to the richness of natural resources in the area, and the population has considerably increased.

TAIYUAN *(pop. 1,021,000)*

Taiyuan, the capital of the province of Shansi, is situated in the center of the province in the fertile valley of the Fen, one of the largest left-bank tributaries of the Yellow River. The city, which was founded under the Ming dynasty, was occupied by the Japanese during World War II.

Taiyuan's situation as the major town of a frontier province made it an important trade center and the inhabitants gained a reputation as enterprising merchants and skillful bankers. The area is rich in mineral resources and Taiyuan is one of the oldest Chinese centers of the iron industry. It is now an important industrial town, the main industries being steel, textiles, cement and fertilizers.

TATUNG *(pop. 228,500)*

Tatung is situated in the extreme north of Shansi, at the junction of rail and road communications between Shansi, Mongolia and Hopeh. It is an ancient city and was the capital of the Northern Wei dynasty in the 4th century A.D.

A number of ancient temples still exist in the old, walled city of Tatung, and the caves of Yunkang, about 10 miles away, contain a number of very early Buddhist monuments. Southeast of Tatung is the sacred mountain of Heng Shan, another site rich in historical remains.

Tatung is situated in an area which has large coal deposits and in recent years industrial activity in the city has much increased. The main industries, apart from mining, are the

manufacture of cement, locomotives, machine tools and mining equipment.

The Cities of Shensi

PAOKI *(pop. 130,100)*

Paoki is situated on the western border of Shensi in the upper valley of the Wei River. Its importance dates from the construction of the railroad connecting Paoki, Sian and Loyang shortly before World War II. Since the opening of the Paoki-Chengtu railroad in 1956, the city has become an important center of communications and trade. Industrial developments have included textiles, paper and engineering.

SIAN *(pop. 1,310,000)*

Sian, the capital of the province of Shensi, is situated in the center of the Wei River valley. It was the capital of the Western Chou dynasty (1122-771 B.C.), but it was not until the 2nd century B.C. that the Western Han dynasty erected their capital of Ch'ang-an on the site of modern Sian. From that time onward, Ch'ang-an, later Sian, was the capital of a number of ruling dynasties.

Throughout the centuries, Sian retained its importance as an administrative center and as an agricultural and trading center on the route joining northern and western China.

The old city of Sian closely resembles Peking. Its strong walls with their towers and fortifications extend for about 12 miles and the city is rich in archaeological remains and historic buildings. The Shensi Museum in the city contains many important remains, including an ancient

The characteristic square courtyard of a traditional Chinese house. These structures are generally rectangular in shape, facing inward onto the courtyard, the center of domestic activity. In modern China, however, picturesque structures such as these gradually are being replaced by large apartment developments where traditional Chinese family life is abandoned in favor of communal living.

Nestorian tablet, the inscriptions on which record the first Christian penetration of China.

In recent years a great deal of development has been initiated in Sian and a new city has grown up around the old.

YENAN *(pop. 60,000)*

Yenan, a small town with a distinguished past, is situated on the northern border of Shensi. It was formerly an important trading post but owes its more recent fame to having been, since 1934, the headquarters of the Chinese Communist Party. The town contains an ancient pagoda and a museum of the Chinese Revolution.

The Valley of the Yangtze River

The region of the middle and lower valleys of the Yangtze River includes the six provinces of Anhwei, Kiangsu, Kiangsi, Hunan, Hupeh and Szechwan. Kiangsu is the only maritime province, but its coastline is so unfavorable to shipping that there are only two harbors, situated respectively at the extreme north and south of the province.

The area has a higher density of population than the Chinese average; around 238,000,000 people live in an area equal to little more than one-quarter of the country's total area. It is less rich in coal deposits than is

northern China, and although potential resources of hydraulic power are very great they have not yet been properly exploited. Recent industrial development has thus been on a more modest scale than in the north.

The heart of the region is the 1875 miles of the course of the Yangtze River from Szechwan to the sea. However, because of the many complex valleys into which the area is divided, the river is unable to impose a unity on the region in the way that the lower reach of the Yellow River does in the Hopeh area.

From the northern boundaries, the dry plain becomes gradually more suitable for cultivation; it is increasingly broken into lakes, rivers, canals, mountains and hills. Roads and railroads are limited, since their construction is rendered difficult by the nature of the terrain, and rivers provide the basic means of communication. Thus, the sites of the towns often depend on the course of the rivers. Water buffalo replace oxen, horses and donkeys for agricultural work.

In view of its characteristics, the region may be divided into three parts. The eastern part includes Anhwei and Kiangsu, the central part consists of Hupeh, Kiangsi and Hunan, and the third part is formed by the Szechwan basin.

The area of Anhwei and Kiangsu is characterized by having the largest

area of level ground, the largest irrigable area and the highest density of population. It has the best river and rail communications and thus the best trade contacts with other regions, and possesses the only stretch of coast in the area. These factors make it the richest and most progressive area.

HUPEH, KIANGSI AND HUNAN

Although the area of Hupeh, Kiangsi and Hunan is larger and has more mineral resources than the area of Anhwei and Kiangsu, its development has been slow. This is mainly because of communication difficulties caused by the nature of the terrain. The region has, as a result, retained a basically agricultural character.

This situation may soon change. The construction of the Peking-Canton railroad shortly before World War II and the present government's policy of increased industrialization, together with the development of many hydroelectric projects, are likely to lead to the modernization of the region.

SZECHWAN

The third area, that of the Szechwan basin, is isolated from the neighboring provinces by its mountainous boundaries. However, it has abundant natural resources and a good internal communications system. Development before World War II was mainly agricultural, but at present the large reserves of power and raw materials are being directed toward increased industrialization.

A view of the city of Urumchi, called Tihwa in Chinese, the capital of the region of Dzungaria. Urumchi has grown up around an oasis watered by streams flowing down from the Tien Shan range. It stands on the main communication routes between Dzungaria and Sinkiang Uigur and its recent industrial development has been facilitated by the presence of nearby deposits of coal.

A railroad to connect Szechwan with Yunnan and Kansu is at present under construction and Szechwan is destined to become, in due time, the base of the economy of western China.

The Cities of Kiangsu

NANKING *(pop. 1,419,000)*

Nanking, the capital of Kiangsu, is situated on the south bank of the Yangtze River. From the time of the Han dynasty onward it was the capital of China under a number of rulers. It was not known by its present name, which means "capital of the south," until the accession of the Ming dynasty in the 14th century.

The Ming rulers erected a perimeter of walls 20 miles in length and established within them one of the greatest cities of China. From 1853 to 1864, Nanking was the capital of the T'ai Ping regime and in 1928 it became the capital of the Kuomintang regime, which carried out extensive modernization in the city.

The most important monuments of the ancient and recent past are situated outside the city walls. They are the tombs of the emperors of the Ming dynasty and the mausoleum of Doctor Sun Yat-sen, the founder of the Chinese Republic.

The importance of Nanking has been increased in the present century by the construction of railroads to Shanghai and Tientsin. The Tientsin railroad has its terminus at Pukow, on the opposite bank of the Yangtze, and the trains are conveyed to and from Nanking by ferry.

The traditional manufacturing activities of Nanking are silk brocades, cotton goods and pottery. In recent years new industries have been developed, including fertilizers, chemical products, engineering and cement works and food industries.

Since 1949 great advances have been made in the production of agricultural machinery, tractors, trucks, radios and optical instruments.

As well as a political and industrial capital, Nanking is a cultural center and a center of air traffic. It is the seat of the University of Nanking and has a modern airfield.

SHANGHAI *(pop. 7,100,000)*

In ancient times, the great city of Shanghai was simply a small harbor and fishing town. It remained of

An aerial view of part of the city of Nanking which is in the province of Kiangsu. Nanking, which is situated on the Yangtze River, has been a site of human habitation since the 2nd century B.C., though the present city dates from 1368 A.D. One of the traditional cultural centers of China, it is the site of the tombs of the early Ming emperors and of the mausoleum of the great 20th-century Chinese patriot, Doctor Sun Yat-sen.

little importance until 1842, when the granting of foreign trade concessions opened the port to international trade. The foreign concessions were erected about four miles to the north of the old walled city and the great modern city of Shanghai grew up around this nucleus.

Shanghai lies on the left bank of the Whangpoo River, some twelve miles above Woosung, where the Whangpoo joins the Yangtze. The city has excellent rail and river communications with the whole of the Yangtze valley. The Whangpoo is navigable for large steamers and Shanghai's magnificent harbor has made it the main center of maritime trade in China and one of the largest cities in the world.

INDUSTRIAL DEVELOPMENT

The development of Shanghai, which now covers an area of around 270 square miles, was based on foreign investments and trading profits. Before World War II it was estimated that the greater part of personal capital in China, together with about half the country's trade and a

quarter of its industrial production, was concentrated in Shanghai. The city's great office blocks, residential developments and public works create an impressive effect.

The district around Shanghai is relatively poor in deposits of coal and other minerals, but it is rich in agricultural products and provides ideal conditions for the erection of large factories. Shanghai has become China's main center of cotton spinning and weaving, cereal processing, silk spinning, and the manufacture of tobacco, matches, soap, rubber goods clothing and furniture. Industries of secondary importance include iron, engineering and electrical goods.

From 1949 onward, Shanghai was closed to Western economic and cultural influences and was thus obliged to depend for its main business on its contacts with the rest of China. In recent years, therefore, the city has undergone a process of reconversion rather than development.

In the past, Shanghai has had an unhappy history of civic corruption and social unrest. Under the present regime, however, the worst social

Agricultural workers in a sugar cane plantation in the central valley of the Yangtze River. The damp, humid regions of the southeast are well suited to agriculture, in particular to the cultivation of rice and other cereal crops.

evils have been substantially redressed. The greater part of the population has changed from commercial and agricultural activities to industrial pursuits and the number of industrial workers has more than doubled over the past ten years. Along with the great factories, a number of specialized industries have been established, among them iron foundries, shipyards, turbine generator and cable works, and factories for the manufacture of machine tools, textile machinery, bicycles, sewing machines, clocks, dyes, pharmaceutical products, plastics and synthetic fibers.

As foreign trade with the new China has increased, harbor activity has increased also. However, it is not now, as it once was, the most important factor in the life of the city.

Shanghai is also a cultural center and the second most important educational center of China. It has Fu Tan University, several medical and technical colleges, libraries, museums and the Shanghai Conservatory of Music.

SINHAILIEN *(pop. 207,600)*

Sinhailien is situated in the extreme northeast of Kiangsu near the coast of the Yellow Sea. It is an important terminal of railroads from the west. The former village of Lienyun-Kang is the harbor area of the complex and has been in use as a port since the 2nd century A.D. Industrial development further inland is likely to increase Sinhailien's importance as a trade center in the near future.

SOOCHOW *(pop. 633,000)*

The ancient city of Soochow, which is situated 50 miles west of Shanghai and 36 miles south of the Yellow River, was the capital of the Wu dynasty in the 5th century B.C. Soochow is near Lake Tai and is traversed by many canals crossed by arched bridges.

Part of the old city still exists, surrounded by the remains of walls built by the Mongols and containing the 250-foot-high Great Pagoda and a number of charming gardens and villas. In the past the city was called "the earthly paradise" and was famous for its cultural activities and for the elegance of its women.

In recent years, the silk looms which formerly supplied the imperial court have been modernized and the textile industry as a whole has been considerably developed.

SUCHOW *(pop. 676,000)*

The ancient city of Suchow, in northern Kiangsu, was formerly of great strategic importance for the control of the Yangtze basin and has thus been the site of a number of great battles. It now stands at the junction of two main railroads and is the center of a prosperous agricultural zone.

The main industries of Suchow are iron, textiles and the processing of agricultural products. Heavy industry in the area is now developing rapidly. In recent years, factories for

an important commercial center for the rice and salt trades from the 13th century onward. It is still an important trade center and the population has incrased slightly over the past few years.

The Cities of Anhwei

HOFEI (*pop. 183,600*)

Hofei, some 90 miles west of Nanking, has been the capital of the province of Anhwei since 1949. It is situated in the center of the province, north of Lake Chao, and is on the railroad between Pengpu and Wuhu. The modern city was formed by the amalgamation of the old town of Luchow and the neighboring village of Hofei.

Hofei is an example of the determination of the relatively underdeveloped province of Anhwei to become industrialized. It is a center of the food, textile and agricultural markets, and new factories have been built for the production of agricultural and mining machinery, tractors, ball bearings and aluminium.

HWAIYUAN (*pop. 30,128*)

Hwaiyuan lies on the banks of the Hwai River about 10 miles west of Pengpu, to which it is connected by both rail and water. It lies in the biggest coal producing area of Anhwei and its industries are being greatly expanded. In addition to mining activities there are coke works and fertilizer factories.

PENGPU (*pop. 253,743*)

Pengpu, some 110 miles northwest of Nanking, is the most important city in the Hwai River valley. It is situated on the banks of the Hwai at a point where the railway to Hofei branches off the Tientsin-Nanking line. The city is the headquarters of projects for regulating the flow of the Hwai.

Pengpu is a flourishing industrial center with food, tanning, tobacco and textile industries. Iron foundries have recently been built and coalmining developed at nearby Hwaiyuan.

WUHU (*pop. 242,100*)

Wuhu, a river harbor on the Yangtze, is the principal city of southern Anhwei. It is the center of a large river-borne trade in tea, rice, silk and vegetables. It is connected to Hofei by a railroad running to Penghu and a railroad to Kiangsu is under construction.

the production of mining equipment and machine tools have been set up and the textile works have been extensively modernized.

WUSIH (*pop. 613.000*)

Wusih is situated some 75 miles west of Shanghai, in the neighborhood of Lake Tai. For many years it was the most important center of rice distribution in the area. In recent years considerable industrial development has taken place and plants for the production of cotton and silk goods and for the processing of foodstuffs have been established.

YANGCHOW (*pop. 127,000*)

Yangchow is situated on the banks of the Grand Canal about fifteen miles north of the Yangtze river. It was the capital of the Sui dynasty between 589 and 618 A.D. and was

Wuhu has been an important port since the 19th century and lies in a rich coal producing area. Its principal industries are food processing, textiles and boat building and it is the site of a number of large power stations.

The Cities of Hupeh

HWANGSHIHKANG *(pop. 52,000)*

Hwangshihkang is a new industrial town in southeast Hupeh on the right bank of the Yangtze River. It is connected to Wuhan by both rail and water.

The steel plant which has recently been built alongside the large cement factory is one of the most important in China. There is also a new copper refinery and a lime works. The great Tayeh iron mines are some 13 miles to the south of Hwangshih and are the principal sources of supply for the blast furnaces.

ICHANG *(pop. 73,300)*

Ichang is an old, walled city situated on the western borders of the plain of Hupeh, in the area where the Yangtze's gorges make navigation impossible for craft of any size. The city is mainly important as a trade center on the route between Hupeh and Szechwan.

The city lies in a predominantly agricultural area, where the main crops are rice, cotton, tea and beans. To the south of Ichang there are large deposits of coal and ferrous minerals; these are expected to be properly exploited after the construction of a large iron works in the area.

WUHAN *(pop. 2,146,000)*

Wuhan, the capital of the province of Hupeh, is the largest city in the middle and lower basin of the Yangtze river. It is situated at the confluence of the Yangtze and the Han rivers

and has excellent communications by water with neighboring provinces.

The conurbation of Wuhan is made up of the three cities of Wuchang, Hankow and Hanyang. Wuchang was the capital of the Wu and Chou dynasties and has preserved its ancient walls and a number of temples and other monuments. During the last century it has been the political, administrative and cultural center of the province and is the seat of Wuhan University.

The development of Hankow dates from the Sung period, around the 13th century A.D., when it was one of the most important trading centers of the empire. Hankow was modernized in the 19th century when it was opened to foreign trade and became an important river port.

MAJOR PORT

Hanyang developed toward the end of the 19th century, when the largest iron foundry in China was constructed there. It gained in importance with the construction of the Peking-Hankow railroad and later

Breaking up ground with a tractor-drawn harrow on a large collective farm in northwest Szechwan. Large farms such as this are owned either by the state or by farmers' cooperatives, the state being the final authority in both cases. The establishment of large collective agricultural organizations is aimed at achieving the full employment of China's still insufficient supply of modern agricultural machinery.

with the completion of the Wuchang-Canton line.

Since ocean-going steamers are able to navigate the Yangtze as far as Hankow, Wuhan has become one of China's major ports. It is also a cultural center with a large university and a number of technical institutes.

Industrial activity in Wuhan has increased considerably in recent years. It has cement works, cotton and silk mills, oil refineries, tobacco factories, machine tool works, factories for the manufacture of steam boilers, electric turbines and generators and textile machinery, dye works and steel plants. The Hanyang steel plant, one of the largest in China, was transferred to Chungking in 1938, but another plant has been erected recently at Hwangshih. A project is at present in hand for the erection of an automobile factory which will be the second largest in China, after that at Changchun in Kirin.

Wuhan lies on both banks of the Yangtze river and the two halves of the city are connected by a large road and rail bridge. The city is the main center for the control of river traffic on the Yangtze. Its population has greatly increased in the last decade and its area has increased correspondingly.

The Cities of Hunan

CHANGSHA (pop. 703,000)

Changsha, the capital of the province of Hunan, lies on the east bank of the Hsiang and is on the Canton railroad. It was founded in the 3rd century B.C. and was long one of the major political, commercial and cultural centers of central China. It became the capital of Hunan under The Emperor Kang-hsi (1654-1722) of the Ch'ing dynasty.

Changsha has preserved many ancient temples and monuments. These include a temple dedicated to Chu Yuan, a great poet of the 4th century A.D. The city walls were rebuilt in the 17th century and are notable for having withstood the onslaughts of the T'ai Ping rebels in 1852.

The main industries of Changsha are embroidery, bamboo and straw artifacts and cotton weaving. These traditional crafts have been joined by workshops specializing in the production of antimony, lead, zinc and silver. There are also factories for the production of manures, insecticides and machine tools. In spite of increased industrialization, the area

Peasant women working in the hemp fields of the province of Honan. Hemp, which is cultivated mainly in northern and northeastern China, is a tough fiber used mainly for the manufacture of rope and strong cloth. Parts of the plant are used for the production of the narcotic drug hashish.

and population of the city have not increased by any great amount.

CHUCHOU (pop. 127,000)

Chuchou, a junction on the Hankow-Canton railroad, lies about 9 miles east of Siangtan. It is a center for the distribution of coal from the large mines at Pingsiang in Kiangsi. The city has a large plant for the manufacture and repair of railroad rolling stock.

HENGYANG (pop. 235,000)

Hengyang is situated 90 miles south of Changsha at the terminal point of navigation on the Hsiang River. It is on the Hankow-Canton railroad at the junction of the lines to Kwangsi and Kweichow. The sacred mountain of Heng Shan lies to the north of the city.

Hengyang was formerly an important garrison town and trading center but then underwent a long period of decline. In recent years factories have been erected for the production of sheet metal and mining machinery. There are important lead and zinc deposits near the city.

SIANGTAN (pop. 184,000)

The river port of Siangtan lies about 20 miles south of Changsha on the Hsiang River. It is very near the site where Mao Tse-tung, the Chinese Communist leader, was born in 1893. The city was formerly a trading center for hemp, rice, tea, cotton and medicinal herbs but it is now a modern industrial town with coal mines and many factories. Its population has increased considerably during the last ten years.

A street in the old part of Chengtu, the capital of the province of Szechwan. Chengtu, a port and educational center on the Min River, is situated in the middle of a fertile plain. Most of the houses are constructed of wood, since Szechwan is rich in many different kinds of timber.

The Cities of Kiangsi

FOULIANG (*pop. 86,744*)

Fouliang is situated 90 miles northeast of Nanchang, on the Chang River. Until 1931 it was known as Kingtehchen. The city has for centuries been famous for its delicate pottery and porcelain, and is in the center of an area rich in China clay. Pottery is still the basic industry, although in recent years emphasis has been placed on the manufacture of wares for industrial uses. There are coal mines in the area and tea is grown on the hills to the northeast.

NANCHANG (*pop. 508,000*)

Nanchang, the capital of the province of Kiangsi, is situated in the center of the Kiangsi plain on Lake Poyang. The city was founded in the 12th century under the Sung dynasty and was given its present name under the Ming dynasty. It is on the Hangchow-Chuchou railroad and is the terminus of the line from Chiu-chiang.

Nanchang is the center of a rice-growing area. In recent years a number of industries have developed, notably iron works, metal processing, cotton weaving, electroplating, paper and porcelain. The city has a university and a medical college.

To the northeast of Nanchang is the mountain of Lu Shan in the Kuling district. The beauties of this area have been praised by China's classical poets and it is now one of the principal holiday resorts.

The Cities of Szechwan

CHENGTU (*pop. 1,107,000*)

Chengtu, the capital of the province of Szechwan, is situated in a fertile alluvial plain and is in the most densely populated zone of the province. The area is irrigated by a system of canals constructed as early as the 3rd century B.C. The ancient city walls still remain and there are a number of memorials to Tu Fu, the greatest poet of the T'ang dynasty, who was born in Chengtu.

Chengtu is the administrative and political center of the largest province in China. It is the seat of Szechwan University and has a number of technological institutes. The city is also an important communications center; it is on the railroad between Chungking and Pao-chi and on the highway to Tibet and Tsinghai.

Chengtu has long been a center of the food and textile industries and in recent years great industrial developments have taken place. These include the setting up of iron works, railroad workshops, tanneries, and factories for the manufacture of bricks, tiles and radios.

CHUNGKING (*pop. 2,121,000*)

Chungking is situated at the confluence of the Yangtze and Kialing rivers. It was already a flourishing city in the 4th century B.C. and is now the most important and the largest city in Szechwan. It is within easy reach of the principal towns of the Szechwan basin and is connected by rail to Chengtu and the provinces of Hupeh and Kwei-chow.

The development of modern Chungking dates from the opening of the river port to foreign trade in 1891. during 1937-46 the Japanese occupation much of China and the capital of the republic was transferred to Chungking from Peking. The original city was situated on the extremity of the tongue of land separating the two rivers before their confluence, but it has recently extended beyond the rivers where there is space for industrial development.

The ample hydroelectric resources, coal and iron mines and deposits of oil and methane around Chungking afford an excellent basis for industrial development. Among the many activities the most important are iron founding, copper refining and the manufacture of locomotives, tractors, trucks, agricultural machinery, compressors, optical instruments and fertilizers. Expansion has also taken place in the processing of oil, cereals, bristles, silk and ramié, or China grass.

IPIN (*pop. 177,000*)

Ipin is situated at the confluence of the Min and the Yangtze rivers. It is an important communications center since it is the terminal point of steam navigation on the Yangtze and is the terminus of the railroad from Yunnan.

The city is undergoing a process of extensive industrialization. Iron foundries, engineering works and insulating plants have been constructed to join the traditional paper and textile works and an important electric power station is being built on the north of the city.

LOSHAN *(pop. 100,000)*

Loshan is situated about 20 miles to the west of the sacred mountain of Omei. There are rich deposits of coal, iron and oil in the area, favoring the development of industry. Loshan's main industries are paper milling and cotton spinning.

NANCHUNG *(pop. 165,000)*

Nanchung is situated in the center of eastern Szechwan, on the right bank of the Kialing river. Abundant natural resources favor industrialization and the city possesses silk and cotton mills, food processing plants and a factory producing mining machinery.

TZEKUNG *(pop. 291,000)*

Tzekung, 110 miles west of Chungking, was formed in 1942 by the union of Tzeliutsing and Kungching. The area has for centuries been the main center of the salt industry. Saline solution is extracted from the soil, which is rich in chemicals, and processed by continual heating and concentration. Formerly, the primitive methods employed in extraction, handling and transportation employed many thousands of laborers. In recent years the industry has been modernized and expanded. Tzekung is now on its way to becoming one of the main centers of the chemical industry.

The Maritime and Tropical Provinces

The provinces of southeast China are—Chekiang, Fukien, Kwangtung, Kwangsi and Yunnan — extend in a great curve from Hangchow Bay to the borders of Burma. The region has little uniformity, being divided into a number of separate basins between the Yangtze to the north and the coast to the south. Although the basin of the head of the Canton delta is the most important, it occupies only about one-third of the region and cannot be considered a great unifying element.

The population of the area, numbering around 135,000,000, is only about half that of the Yangtze region. It includes, however, a large number of national and linguistic minorities. The population is mainly concentrated on the narrow bands of cultivated land between the mountain ranges, amounting to little more than 13 per cent of China's total cultivated area.

The general characteristics of the population vary widely from province to province. Chekiang, Fukien and eastern Kwangtung are essentially maritime provinces with a predominantly urban population. They have excellent natural harbors which have favored the development of foreign trade and influence.

However, the remainder of Kwangtung and the whole of Kwangsi have predominantly continental characteristics. They center around the great basin at the head of the Canton delta, and their coastline is rocky and unfavorable to navigation.

In Kweichow and Yunnan, the proximity of the frontiers and the irregular terrain, together with the diversity of nationalities among the population, formerly made the area a center of activity for smugglers, brigands and political rebels.

The sea is the most important means of inter-provincial communication; the rivers and roads generally connect the coast or land frontiers with the internal basins, as do the railways constructed during the last few decades.

POLITICAL AND MILITARY TENSIONS

The political and military tensions along the southeast coast in the last ten years, together with the tendency

Tourists inspect the ancient fortifications a section of the Great Wall of China. The Great Wall stretches for about 1500 miles and varies between 15 and 30 feet in height, though in places it has collapsed.

Terraced strips of land in the Hulu Ho valley, Shensi, are plowed in preparation for sowing. In this mountainous region fertile land is scarce and must be exploited wherever possible. The narrow terraces on the mountain side, broken up by ox-drawn primitive plows, are irrigated by the water running down the mountain slopes.

of the government of the Chinese People's Republic to favor development of the internal regions, has somewhat inhibited industrial development in the maritime provinces. In the southwest, however, where there are good water resources and favorable soil conditions, great changes are in process which are likely to transform the region into one of the main centers of heavy industry.

The Cities of Chekiang

HANGCHOW (pop. 784,000)

Hangchow, the capital of the province of Chekiang, is one of China's most famous cities. It was founded in 606 A.D. and became the southern capital of the Sung dynasty, with over 1,000,000 inhabitants. Marco Polo described it as one of the greatest cities in the world.

Hangchow is situated on the shores of Lake Tai on the estuary of the Tsientang River at the head of Hangchow Bay. Its pleasant climate, natural beauties and extensive historical remains have made it the principal holiday resort of China.

The city has good inland waterway connections and is joined by the railroad to Shangai, Ningpo and Nan-ch'ang. However, it has never become a maritime center because of the extensive sandbanks and treacherous currents in Hangchow Bay which, particularly in the spring, are extremely dangerous to shipping.

Hangchow is famous for silk spinning and weaving. Other industries include the manufacture of paper fans, matches, satin goods and, since 1949, jute sacks.

NINGPO *(pop. 237,500)*

Ningpo, situated 90 miles east of Hangchow, is an old, walled city which was formerly an important trading post. It lies on the banks of the Yung River about 12 miles from the sea, where the small town of Chenhai serves as its port. Ningpo was occupied by the Portuguese between 1520 and 1545. It was opened to foreign trade in the 19th century but lost importance with the great expansion of Shanghai.

Ningpo is connected by railroad to Hangchow. Its major industries are silver and straw work and lace manufacturing. It is a center of fish processing, handling the catches made off the Choushan islands to the northeast. These islands, the most important of which is Puto, are the major fishing center of China.

The city of Ningpo was formerly a sacred city of the Buddhist faith and was the object of great pilgrimages. A number of ancient temples and monasteries still remain.

WENCHOW *(pop. 200,000)*

Wenchow, on the south coast of Chekiang, is situated on the right bank of the Wu River estuary. Its development has been limited by the shallowness of the sea around it and by poor communications with the hinterland. However, a railroad to connect the city with the Hangchow-Kiangsi line is now under construction.

Wenchow is a center for the processing and distribution of the agricultural products of the area, mainly vegetables and tobacco. Its present industries include the manufacture of leather goods, straw mats and paper umbrellas, but since there are extensive deposits of minerals, notably aluminum, in the area, further industrial development is likely. A large electric power station is to be erected nearby in the Wu valley.

The Cities of Fukien

AMOY *(pop. 224,330)*

Two large island are situated in the bay in southern Fukien into which the Kiuling and a number of other rivers discharge their waters. The island nearer to the coast is that of Amoy and the other, fifteen miles east of Amoy, is Quemoy.

The city of Amoy is situated at the extreme southwestern part of the island of the same name. It is the second largest city of Fukien. Amoy was opened to foreign trade in 1842 and was occupied by the Japanese during the Sino-Japanese War. It has been a trading center since the 16th century, when it was used by the Portuguese and Spanish. After the establishment of foreign trading stations, the island of Kulangsu, just across the harbor from Amoy, was transformed into a commercial and residential center.

In 1958, after the construction of a causeway linking Amoy with the mainland, the commercial importance of Amoy was increased by the completion of a railroad stretching for 433 miles to northern Kiangsu.

The rich plain around the mouth of the Kiuling River provides the basis of an industry based on agricultural products, including fruit and green vegetable preserving, sugar, noodles, tobacco and bamboo products. Further industrial developments include the construction of a shipyard, a large glass works, and factories producing cod liver oil, fish meal and rubber boots.

FOOCHOW *(pop. 616,000)*

Foochow, the capital of the province of Fukien, is situated near the Min River about 35 miles from the coast. Its foundation dates from the T'ang dynasty (618-907), and it was visited by Marco Polo on his journeys through China. The city was opened to foreign trade in 1842 and became China's main center of tea export.

The old walls of the city, erected under the Ming dynasty, still remain, as do a number of ancient temples, pagodas and shrines. The commercial suburb of Nantai lies on the south of the walled city. The city is situated on both banks of the river, which are connected by a 440-yard bridge set on low granite pillars, known as the "Bridge of Ten Thousand Ages."

The river at Foochow is too shallow for large vessels and this has led to the development about 15 miles downstream, near the village of Mamoi, of a port known as the

Distribution of agricultural activities and utilization of the soil.

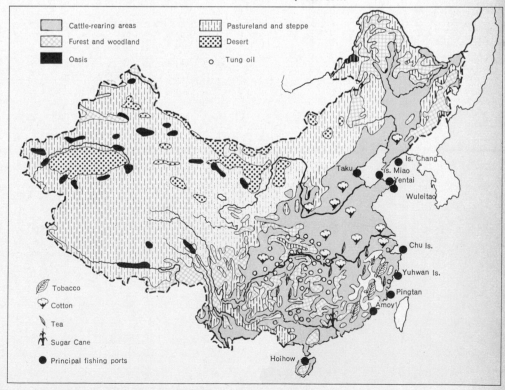

Laying the foundations of a road in the province of Honan. Transport in China has improved during recent years. The construction of modern roads was begun in 1915, although some provinces had no proper roads until the 1930s. Formerly, most merchandise was carried by pack animals or men, depending on the terrain, but by the early 1960s the amount of roads suitable for wheeled vehicles had increased to 275,000 miles.

Pagoda, with shipyards and an arsenal.

The city is famous for the production of lacquer work, preserved fruit, bamboo shoots and goods made of leather, silk and cotton. In recent years, however, industrial development has increased as a consequence of the construction of a railroad link with the Amoy-Yingt'an line. Today the city's industries include sugar refining, iron foundries, and factories producing locomotives, tractors, trucks and plastic goods.

The Cities of Kwangtung

CANTON (pop. 1,840,000)

The history of the ancient city of Canton dates back to the Han dynasty (202 B.C.- 220 A.D.), when it was known as Kwangchow. In the early centuries of the Christian era, Indian, Persian and Arab traders made the city their chief trading center. The Portuguese and Dutch successsively established themselves there in the 16th century, and in 1699 the British East India Company established Canton as the center of the opium trade.

Foreign trade concessions were established in Canton in 1842 and by the end of the 19th century the city was the largest and most modern in China. It was a cultural and political center as well as a center of commerce and in 1912 was the scene of Sun Yat-sen's revolt against the Manchu rulers. In 1927 it was the scene of the first Chinese Communist uprising and the constitution of the Commune of Canton.

LEFT BANK OF THE PEARL

The city is situated on the left bank of the Chu (or Pearl)River, one of the numerous branches of the great rivers which flow into the delta. The old city was surrounded by a wall until 1921, when it was rebuilt on modern lines. The commercial quarter is situated on the river bank to the south and the site of the former foreign concessions was to the southwest, near the Shamen sand bank. New industrial and residential areas have sprung up on both sides of the river, across which are bridges both old and new.

A large population lives in boats on the river itself. The Pearl is not deep enough for large vessels and the main harbor activities are concentrated at Whampoa, about 9 miles downstream. Canton stands in the center of a network of rivers and canals and is the terminus of the railroad from Wuhan.

For centuries Canton his been a center of craftsmanship and manufacturing. The traditional crafts of the city include products of spun silk and silk fabrics, carved ivory, lacquered articles and furniture and gold and silver work. In recent years many new factories have been erected. Among their many products are cement, jute, paper, sugar refining, food preserving, sulphuric acid, fertilizers, machine tools and agricultural machinery. There are also iron works and a shipyard.

CHANKIANG (pop. 166,000)

Chankiang, 230 miles west of Canton, is a new city which is being developed within the sheltered Bay of Kwangchow, on the east coast of the Luichow peninsula. The surrounding territory was formerly under French sovereignty but passed to Chinese possession at the end of World War II.

Chankiang is now the most modern port in China and new railroad constructions may lead to its becoming one of the largest. The 200-mile railroad from Litang has made the city the maritime outlet for Kwangsi, and a continuation of the line is planned in the near future.

The city's shipbuilding industry is being developed as are the chemical and fertilizer industries based on the nearby deposits of salt and phosphates. Chankiang is also a center for the agricultural produce of the region.

KUKONG (pop. 72,693)

Kukong, which is situated in the upper valley of the Peh River on the railroad to Hankow, stands in the center of a district rich in mineral deposits. In recent years it has become a center of heavy industry. It stands at the point where the Wu and Cheng rivers join and marks the upper limit of navigation on the Peh River.

There are mines for the extraction of coal, antimony, tungsten and bismuth on the outskirts of the city.

MOWMING (*pop. 13,566*)

Mowming is situated fifty miles northeast of Chankiang. Its main industries are cotton milling and the manufacture of furniture. There are large deposits of asbestos in the area and gold is also mined.

NAMHOI (*pop. 95,529*)

Namhoi, called Fatshan until 1912, is situated about 10 miles southwest of Canton on the Pearl River delta. It has the biggest silk spinning and weaving industry in the delta. Other industries include iron and steel works, textile and lumber mills and workshops for the production of chinaware, firecrackers, matting and embroidery.

SWATOW (*pop. 200,000*)

Swatow, some 220 miles east of Canton, is the most important city in eastern Kwangtung. It is situated at the extremity of the Han delta on the Swatow Bay of the South China Sea. It has a sheltered harbor where ships lie to anchor and the quays and other harbor services are situated on the south of the city and in the frontier suburb of Kakchioh. Swatow was opened to foreign trade in 1869 and gradually developed into a modern commercial center at the expense of the older town of Chaoan (formerly Chaochow), which lies about 22 miles to the north on the banks of the Han River. The economic development of Swatow has, however, been limited by political tension in the area and by a lack of good rail connections.

Swatow lies in a large sugar-cane producing area and is a manufacturing center producing cigarettes, paper and pharmaceutical goods. It imports cereals, peas, beans and kerosene, and its main exports are sugar, indigo, tobacco and rice.

The Cities of Kwangsi-Chuang

KWEILIN (*pop. 130,790*)

The ancient city of Kweilin is situated on the right bank of the Kwei River some 250 miles north-west of Canton. Like Liuchow, it was an American air base in World War II, and it was occupied by the Japanese in 1944-45. It stands in a natural amphitheater surrounded by mountains and its environs are among the most picturesque in China.

Kweilin is now an industrial center whose chief industries are cotton and textiles, paper and the processing of sugar and tung-oil. It exports rice, wheat and timber. The city is the seat of a university and a medical college.

LIUCHOW (*pop. 158,800*)

Liuchow is situated 300 miles northwest of Canton at the junction of the Hunan-Kweichow railroad. It is in the center of a zone rich in both minerals and timber and is the most highly industrialized city of Kwangsi-Chuang. It was an American air base during World War II and is now a center of air transport with a school of aviation.

Since 1949 new factories have been erected in Liuchow for the manufacture of machine tools, internal combustion engines, cement and

Harvesting rice in the fields of the province of Anhwei, southeast China. Most rice is grown in south Anhwei, along with cotton and ramie (a grass); the north is mainly devoted to cereals and beans. In addition, the province produces around 60 per cent of China's tea. Along with their modern shirts and shorts, the peasants wear the conical straw hats that for centuries have been the traditional headdress of the Chinese laborer.

railway sleeper cars. A medium iron works has gone into production, coal mines in the area have been expanded, and large electric power stations are under construction in the nearby valleys.

NANNING (pop. 194,600)

Nanning, the capital of the Kwangsi-Chuang autonomous region, is situated in the south of the region some 330 miles west of Canton. It was opened to foreign trade in 1907. Nanning is an important communications center, since it is on the main rail and air routes between China and Vietnam. The Hunan-Kwangsi railroad extends to North Vietnam and since 1955 a railroad to the port of Tsamkong has provided direct access to the coast.

In recent years Nanning has become an industrial center and the area of the town has increased very greatly. Its chief industries include cotton and silk goods, sugar refineries, printing, flour milling and meat packing. It is also a center for the agricultural products of the region, which include aniseed, sugar cane and fruit. The development of nearby coal mines had made possible the establishment of new plants for the manufacture of cars, electric generators and chemical and pharmaceutical products.

The Cities of Kweichow

KWEIYANG (pop. 504,000)

Kweiyang, the capital of the province of Kweichow, is situated in the center of the province about 200 miles south of Chungking. It is in the center of an area rich in mineral deposits which will be fully exploited when the railroads to Szechwan, Hunan and Yunnan have been completed. The city has a university, colleges for the training of teachers and doctors and a large number of ancient temples and monasteries.

The Cities of Yunnan

KUNMING (pop. 880,000)

Kunming, the capital of Yunnan, is situated on the shores of Lake Tien Chih about 390 miles southwest of Chungking. It consists of an old, walled city containing many ancient temples and pagodas, a residential quarter and a modern commercial suburb.

The development of modern Kunming began in the first decade of the 20th century. The city was opened to foreign trade and the French constructed a railroad to Haiphong on the coast of Vietnam.

During World War II, Anglo-American forces constructed the Szechwan-Burma truck route, causing the transfer of much administrative business to Kunming. Further development is likely to take place with the completion of the railroad to Szechwan and the construction of a railroad to Kweichow.

Kunming lies in the center of an area which is both fertile and rich in mineral deposits. Its chief industries are silk and cotton textiles, chemical products, iron and copper smelting and food processing. The city is an important transport center and is the seat of Yunnan University, a medical college and an institute of technology.

The Industrial Northeast

The northeastern region of China may be regarded as the prime example of China's transition from a backward agrarian nation to a modern industrial state. The northeast is the smallest of the regions into which China may be divided and consists of the three provinces of Liaoning, Kirin and Heilungkiang.

It is the most unified region of China, unity being imposed by the great central plain of Sungari and Liao. This plain is the richest in both mineral and agricultural resources of any part of the area. There is, however, a considerable climatic difference between the north and south of the region, and this affects agriculture in the area.

Communications are very good by both land and water routes. The excellent harbors of Dairen, Port Arthur and Hulutao are free of ice all the year round and the seas around them are rich in fish.

Fertile arable land amounts to about 15 per cent of the region's total area, while its population accounts for only a small percentage of the Chinese total. The pressure of population is thus lower in the northeast than in any other part of the country.

Until the end of the Ming period, the northeast was a frontier zone which was only sporadically coloni-

Gathering and sorting cotton in southeast Tsinghai, the northeastern part of the Tibetan highlands to the northwest of Szechwan. The most heavily populated part of the area, which is mainly a high, barren plateau, is the valley of the Sining River. As well as cotton, the region produces cereals, potatoes and rhubarb.

zed. The transformation of the region from pasture to arable land began under the Ch'ing dynasty. Industrialization did not begin until the end of the 19th century, when Russia obtained permission from the Manchu government to construct the Chinese Eastern Railway between Irkutsk and Vladivostok.

In 1897 the Manchus gave permission for the construction of a railroad between Harbin and Shenyang (Mukden). At about the same time the British constructed a line between Peking and Shenyang. By 1945, the railroads of the northeast accounted for about one-third of China's railroads.

With the development of the railroads, a great deal of Russian and Japanese capital was invested in agricultural, mining, industrial and building development in Manchuria. As a result of foreign investments and Chinese labor Manchuria became, by the end of World War II, the most advanced industrial region and the first great center of heavy industry in China.

CIVIL WAR DESTRUCTION

However, the removal of many industrial plants by the Russians during the closing phases of World War II, followed by civil war between Chinese Nationalists and Communists, brought great destruction upon the northeast. Most of the railroads were put out of action. Nevertheless, it was Manchuria that made the greatest contribution to the success of the revolution and to subsequent reconstruction and industrial progress.

In 1954 the withdrawal of Soviet troops from Port Arthur put an end to the last foreign concession in the region. During the last decade a great process of integration, both economic and cultural, between Manchuria and the rest of China has been under way.

The Cities of Liaoning

ANSHAN (pop. 805,000)

Anshan, situated on the South Manchuria railroad some 60 miles south of Mukden, is the leading metallurgical center of China. It is near two large iron mines and its development began with the construction of the first blast furnaces in 1919. It was held by the Japanese during World War II and was an important center for war materials. Steel, coke and sheet metal plants were esta-

Preparing manure for spreading before the spring sowing in Hunan. The manure, decayed animal and vegetable matter, is gathered in circular basins of beaten earth and carefully mixed; chemical fertilizers are still in short supply in China. The main crop in northeast Hunan is rice, which is grown particularly in the so-called "rice bowl" area around Tungting.

blished during this period.

After World War II, the plants, already damaged by military action, were dismantled by the Russians. In 1952, however, they were rebuilt and enlarged and by 1956 Anshan was again China's major steel producing center. Complementary industries have also been developed, among them the manufacture of cement, refractory materials, pipes, steel beams and coke.

ANTUNG (pop. 360,000)

Antung is a port on the right bank of the Yalu River, on the Korean border. It is connected to Mukden by rail and joins the Korean railroad system through the small town of Sinuiju on the opposite bank of the Yalu.

Antung was a small fishing center until 1907, when it was opened to foreign trade and became an important commercial link between China and Korea. The railroad connecting Mukden with Korea was constructed in the same year. Antung is now a staging point on the Dairen-Mukden air route.

The chief industries of Antung are timber, fish canning, silk spin-

ning and weaving, aluminum and copper. A chemical fiber plant was completed in 1958. The city is of only minor importance as a port; it is inaccessible to large vessels, which anchor in the outer harbor of Tatungkow.

CHINCHOW (pop. 352,200)

The ancient city of Chinchow was formerly a Chinese military outpost in Manchurian territory. It is situated on the Jehol-Fusin railroad and has long been an important trading center. The city was occupied by the Japanese for much of the first part of the 20th century and it was during this period that its natural resources were first exploited and its industries developed.

By the early 1930s Chinchow was an important industrial center, manufacturing chemicals, synthetic fibers and textiles. In recent years, rapid development has taken place in the coal and iron bearing center of Fusin, 77 miles to the north, and in the area of Chinsi, 27 miles to the southwest, which is a distribution center for the port of Hulutao and has important deposits of lead and molybdenum.

In contrast to the illustration opposite, Chinese engineers operate a motor grader, a modern earthmoving machine. Machines such as these mean that more ground can be reclaimed for agricultural purposes, leading to bigger farms and an increase in production.

DAIREN (*pop. 131,000*)

Dairen, some 23 miles east of Port Arthur, has a sheltered coastal position which protects it from climatic extremes and has made it a popular holiday resort. It is a modern town, with impressive buildings and wide streets, set in attractive scenery.

Owing to the depth of water in its harbor and to the enlargement of the modern port installations erected by the Japanese, Dairen is now the best equipped port in northeastern China. It has also been the site of considerable industrial activity, having the biggest shipbuilding yards and railway workshops in the country as well as factories for the manufacture of electrical and mining equipment, soda, fertilizers and other chemical products, silk weaving workshops and an oil refinery.

FUSHUN (*pop. 985,000*)

Fushun is situated on the banks of the Hsun River about 28 miles east of Mukden. It is in the center of the most important coal bearing area in China and both open cast and underground mine works are in operation near the city. Work on the mines was begun by the Russians in 1902 and continued by the Japanese after 1907. The working of the large oil shale deposits overlying the coal strata was begun by the Japanese in 1929.

The character of Fushun is mainly determined by mining activities but complementary industries are gradually increasing. These include the processing of oil products, the production of synthetic fuels from coal and the manufacture of cement, aluminum, refractory materials and mining equipment.

LUTA (*pop. 1,508,000*)

The municipality of Luta, situated at the tip of the Liaotung peninsula, is formed by the two cities of Dairen (Talien) and Port Arthur (Lushun), discussed here under separate headings, and the villages surrounding them. About 75 per cent of the population is concentrated in Dairen. The two cities were developed by the Russians from the last decade of the 19th century onward —Dairen as a commercial center and Port Arthur as a naval and military base. After the Russian defeat in 1905, the two cities remained under Japanese control until 1945.

MUKDEN (*pop. 2,411,000*)

Mukden, formerly called Shenyang, is the capital of the province of Liaoning. It is the largest city in northeast China and is situated on the banks of the Hun Ho River, a tributary of the Liao.

Mukden was an early capital of the Ch'ing dynasty. The imperial palaces and the tombs of some of the emperors have been preserved and reproduce, on a smaller scale, the grandeur of similar remains at Peking. The development of the modern city began in 1905, when the Japanese were granted a concession to construct a railroad there. Owing to its position at the junction of the Harbin-Talien railroad with the line to Peking, Mukden became the principal commercial center of the province.

The city was the center of distribution for the agricultural produce of the area, notably vegeables, tobacco, furs, beans and cereals, and factories were built for the processing of these products. The heavy industries which have been established at Mukden during recent years have made it the greatest industrial center in China. Among these industries are the manufacure of heavy machine tools for iron works and engineering plants, generators, turbines, boilers, the highest powered transformer plant in China, locomotives and railroad rolling stock, pumps, ventilators, electric cables, auto tires and abrasives. New textile works and factories for the processing of meat, skins and bristles have also been built.

PENKI (PENCHI) (*pop. 449,000*)

Penki, or Penchi, is situated 40 miles southeast of Mukden on the railroad to North Korea. It is an important mining center with coal deposits extending to Tienshihfu, 30 miles to the east. The first blast furnace was erected in 1915 and a large number of industries have subsequently been developed. These include coke, cement, refractory materials, pig iron, special steels, alunite and fertilizers.

PORT ARTHUR (*pop. 377,000*)

Port Arthur, which with Dairen makes up the municipality of Luta, has not been the site of any notable industrial development. It has preserved its character as a military and naval base.

The Cities of Kirin

CHANGCHUN *(pop. 975,000)*

Changchun, the capital of the province of Kirin, is the most important transport and industrial center of central Manchuria. After the Russo-Japanese War in 1905, Changchun marked the boundary between the Russian zone of influence in the north and the Japanese in the south. In 1932 it was made the capital of the state of Manchukuo and during this period the city was greatly extended and modernized.

The major industries of Changchun were formerly limited to timber and agricultural products. Since World War II, however, it has become both a center of light industry and of higher education. Factories have been erected for the manufacture of tractors, railroad rolling stock and agricultural machinery.

KIRIN *(pop. 568,000)*

Kirin was founded in 1673 as a Chinese fortress and an administrative center for central Manchuria. It is situated 60 miles east of Changchun and its position on the left bank of the Sungari River led to its development as a center for the building of junks and other river craft. A number of monuments of the Ming and Ch'ing dynasties still exist in and around the city.

Kirin stands in a zone rich in timber and agricultural products and is provided with power by the Sungari hydroelectric plant at Fengman, some 15 miles to the southeast. It has developed industries for the production of electro-chemical products such as calcium carbide, synthetic rubber and other plastic materials, paper and other timber products, sugar and tobacco.

The Cities of Heilungkiang

HARBIN *(pop. 1,552,000)*

Harbin, the capital of the province of Heilungkiang, is situated on the banks of the Sungari River. It was formerly a small market town, but its development began with the construction of the Chinese Eastern rail-road by the Russians in 1897. Subsequently, a branch of the trans-Manchurian line joined Harbin to Dairen. Harbin remained under Russian influence until 1931, and this influence is still noticeable in the architecture and layout of the modern city. It was a center of Tsarist intrigue after the Russian revolution of 1917.

The Russians' development both of the railroads and of river navigation and port installations made Harbin accessible to large vessels and the most important river port north of the Yangtze River. In recent years, widespread industrial development has led to the establishment of food processing and meat packing plants, vodka distilleries, tanneries, linen and wool mills, sugar refineries, and factories for the production of paper, measuring instruments, generators, turbines, insulators, electric cables, aircraft parts and tractors.

KIAMUSZE *(pop. 168,000)*

Kiamusze, situated about 195 miles northeast of Harbin on the Sungari River, is one of the newest cities of Manchuria. Its development began only a few decades ago and it became an independent municipality in 1934. Recently its great resources of timber and minerals have been much more exploited, a power station has been constructed and flour mills and tanneries have been built.

MUTANKIANG *(pop. 200,319)*

Mutankiang stands on the Chinese Eastern railroad about 170 miles east of Harbin. The process of its development was similar to that of Tsitsihar and with the growth of the railroad network it became an important center for communications with Vladivostok and North Korea.

Mutankiang stands in an area rich in timber, mineral deposits and hydroelectric power. Among the most important of its rapidly developing industries are paper, saw milling, flour milling and the processing of agricultural products.

TSITSIHAR *(pop. 668,000)*

Tsitsihar, a fortified city dating back to the 17th century, is situated on the banks of the middle reach of the Nonni River, on the Inner Mongolian border. Its development dates from the construction of a railroad to Harbin at the end of the 19th century and it now stands on the Chinese Eastern railroad.

Tsitsihar is an important trade center with chemical and automobile assembly plants, an arsenal and a military barracks. Its industries include tobacco processing, flour milling and distilling.

A peasant engaged in cultivating a rice field by means of a primitive harrow drawn by a water-buffalo. The buffalo is the most common of China's draft animals and, in the absence of mechanized farm equipment, still performs a variety of tasks that cannot be accomplished by manpower alone.

Regions of the Future

The fifth great region of China lies roughly to the northwest of a line extending southwest and northeast through the region of Lanchow to the borders of the Chinese People's Republic. Its area is more than half that of the total area of China but its population is lower than that of any other region.

The region consists of the provinces of Kansu and Tsinghai and the autonomous regions of Inner Mongolia, Ningsia Hui, Sinkiang Uigur and Tibet. Except in Kansu and Inner Mongolia, the Uigur, Hui, Tibetan, Mongolian and other national minorities outnumber the people of Han nationality. In addition, these minorities have retained much of their linguistic and cultural traditions. Strong Indian, Russian and Persian influences are intermingled with Chinese influence in the area.

The greater part of the area is covered by steppe and desert. The region is predominantly agricultural and many of the inhabitants lead a nomadic existence. A further barrier to unity is caused by the way in which the terrain is broken up into a number of unconnected basins, and fertile watered plains are limited to the areas around isolated oases. There is no great river to facilitate communications and until recent years the tracks over which the camel, yak and mule caravans slowly proceeded were the only means of communication.

The centers of political and military power in the region were the fortresses and monasteries, while the trading centers grew up around the larger oases. These centers were isolated from one another by the lack of communications. Only recently have a network of roads been created, new railroads constructed and regular air services initiated.

UNEXPLOITED WEALTH

The striking contradiction between the enormous concentration of population in eastern China and the sparsely populated areas of the west and northwest has long occupied the attention of the Chinese government. From the time of Sun Yat-sen plans have been made for colonization, but until recently little has been done to remove the major obstacles to the improvement of the region.

The northwest, by reason both of its climate and terrain, could never become another Manchuria. However, its cultivated lands are capable of considerable extension and its pastures could be more profitably used. Large-scale exploitation of its timber and mineral resources would do much to improve local economy. In all these projects, the improvement of communications is the first essential.

The Cities of Kansu

LANCHOW (LANCHOU) (*pop. 699,000*)

Lanchow, or Lanchou, the capital of the province of Kansu, is situated on the right bank of the Yellow River at a height of 5200 feet above sea level. It is an important point on the main communication route between China and the West, since it marks the beginning of the ancient "Silk Road" to Sinkiang. The Han, Hui, Uigur, Mongolian and Tibetan people have lived together in the city, more or less in peace, for about 2000 years.

Lanchow formerly virtually controlled China's trade to the West and was for this reason of great strategic and economic importance. It was the meeting place for caravans traveling to Ningsia Hui and Mongolia or to Tsinghai and Tibet. During World War II it was a station on the Sinkiang route for Russian war materials and was also a military air base.

The traditional products of Lanchow include goods made from wool, silk, cotton and leather. In 1952, however, a period of major industrial development began. The development of the oil fields of Kansu, Sinkiang and Tsaidam, and the construction of a great hydroelectric works on the Yellow River upstream from Lanchow, are making the city the greatest industrial center of the northwest.

Among the modern industries developing in Lanchow are a large oil refinery and plants for the production of synthetic rubber, fertilizers and plastics. In addition there are iron and steel works, cement works, and a factory for the production of machinery used in the processing of oil and chemicals.

YUMEN (*pop. 28,396*)

The ancient oasis town of Yumen in northwest Kansu has now become the center of the oil-producing region about 40 miles to the east, on the banks of the Shuleh River. An oil refinery and factories to provide oil drilling and processing equipment have been established near the city, which is also becoming a communications center.

Yumen is a center for scholars and tourists who wish to visit the caves of Tunhwang, about 70 miles west of Ansi. The caves contain some of the finest rock paintings and carvings in China, dating from the T'ang dynasty.

The Cities of Ningsia Hui

YINCHWAN (*pop. 85,000*)

Yinchwan has been the capital of the autonomous region of Ningsia Hui since 1958. It is situated halfway between Lanchow and Paotow in a fertile plain irrigated by the Yellow River. The walled city was visited by Marco Polo in the 13th century and was an important Chinese border post, protected by the Great Wall. A number of ancient buildings still survive.

Yinchwan was at one time a center for caravans and for river traffic in wool and skins. It is now a major commercial center whose exports include cattle, wool, furs, grain and sheepskin. The construction of a

large hydroelectric power station and the presence of deposits of coal and other minerals provide good prospects for future industrial development.

The Cities of Inner Mongolia

HAILAR (*pop. 16,140*)

Hailar is situated on the banks of the Argun river, about 400 miles northwest of Harbin. It was founded as a Chinese frontier fortress in 1734 and has developed considerably since the construction of the railway to Harbin at the end of the 19th century. It is an important center for the processing and distribution of the timber and agricultural products of the region and its industries include food processing and canning, tanning, flour milling and wool processing.

HUHEHOT (*pop. 314,000*)

Huhehot, formerly called Kweisui, has been the capital of the autonomous region of Inner Mongolia since 1954. It is situated 250 miles west of Peking at the foot of the Tatsing mountains. The city is made up of the two conurbations of Kweihwa and Suiyuan, situated just over one mile apart. Kweihwa, dating from the 9th century, is a predominantly Mongolian area and was, until 1644, the seat of the Mongolian Lama. Suiyuan has a predominantly Han population and is a commercial center. It contains an ancient monastery and a number of Buddhist temples.

Huhehot has long been important as a trading center for skins, furs, wool, carpets and felt. Its value as a commercial center is increased by its position on the Peking-Paotow railroad. In recent years industrial developments have taken place in the city and factories have been established for wool weaving, fur and hide processing, and the manufacture of soap, bricks, sugar and agricultural machinery.

PAOTOW (*pop. 149,000*)

Paotow is situated on the Yellow River some 230 miles west of Peking. It was formerly a caravan center and a market for cattle, hides, wool and grain. Since the construction of the Peking-Paotow railroad in the 1920s, making the city a distribution center for goods from both Suiyuan and Mongolia, Paotow has become a modern commercial and industrial center.

Large iron and steel works have been erected and a railroad has been built across the mountains to connect Paotow with the iron mines of Paiyunopo, 90 miles to the north. A rail link with Lanchow was constructed in 1958. The major industries of the city, apart from iron and steel and allied activities, include flour milling, rug weaving, oilseed pressing and brewing.

The Cities of Tsinghai

SINING (*pop. 93,700*)

Sining, the capital of the province of Tsinghai, is situated about 110 miles from Lanchow. As one of the principal points of access to the highlands of Tibet, it has long been a center of economic and cultural exchanges between Tibet and China. A number of ancient Lamaist monasteries and temples are situated near

Terraced strips of land in the hills of east Kansu, the southeastern part of the loess area. The strips are divided by banks of beaten earth and are irrigated by channels which distribute rainwater equally between each strip. The agricultural area of Kansu, drained by the upper course of the Yellow River, produces cereals, vegetables and fruit. Important industrial crops include tobacco, cotton and opium.

the city, which is in the center of an agricultural district producing spring wheat and barley.

The construction of the railroad to Lanchow in 1959 considerably increased the commercial importance of Sining. To the traditional exports of wool and skins, the exploitation of natural resources has added the export of oil, salt, timber and precious metals. Industry is also fast developing.

The Cities of Sinkiang Uigur

KASHGAR *(pop. 50,000)*

The ancient city of Kashgar is situated in the extreme southwest of the autonomous region of Sinkiang Uigur, west of the Tarim basin. It is between the Tien Shan and Pamir ranges and is 4000 feet above sea level. Kashgar has long been an important trading center with the neighboring Russian territories of Tadzhikistan and Uzbekistan.

Kashgar is in the center of one of the richest oases of the Tarim basin and is irrigated by means of underground channels. It is made up of the old Uigur city, with its ancient mosques and minarets, and the new Chinese urban development of Laining.

The city is traditionally known for its trade in cotton, skins, wool and silver jewelry. The agricultural produce of the area includes wheat, corn, barley, peaches, apricots, melons and mulberries. Kashgar's external trade is mostly with the Soviet Union, since the city is only 70 miles from the borders of the U.S.S.R. In recent years there has been some industrial development.

URUMCHI *(pop. 140,700)*

Urumchi was one of the greatest cities of the Mongols and was for many years the capital of Dzungaria. It is situated to the northeast of the Tien Shan mountains, at the point where the mountains divide to form wide valleys and easy access to the south. It is in a region rich in water, forest, grassland and mineral deposits, within moderately easy reach of the main economic centers of Sinkiang Uigur by reason of its central position. Communications have greatly improved in recent years and a railroad to the city is now under construction.

The inhabitants of Urumchi are mainly of Uigur extraction and the city has been much exposed to Russian influence, especially after the Russian revolution of 1917 when it became a center for refugees. In recent years, Chinese influence has naturally tended to predominate. The city is an administrative and cultural center; it is the seat of Sinkiang Medical College and has institutes of Russian languages and a number of agricultural colleges.

Industrialization in and around Urumchi is proceeding rapidly. Coal and iron ore are mined and industries include the manufacture of cotton textiles, cement, electric light bulbs, flour and chemicals. There is also a small hydroelectric power station.

The Cities of Tibet

LHASA *(pop. 50,000)*

Lhasa, the capital of Tibet for many centuries, is situated in a valley of the Brahmaputra basin. It is on the right bank of the Kyi Chu River, about 25 miles to the north of the Brahmaputra, at an altitude of around 12,087 feet. The city is surrounded by a wide processional way enclosing a circle no more than one mile in diameter.

Lhasa is the center of religious and political life in Tibet and is an important Buddhist pilgrimage center. To the north rises a hill over 400 feet in height on which is situated the Potala, formerly the seat of the Dalai Lama.

The Potala is a monastery, a temple, a palace and a fortress. It has high, inward-sloping red walls and flat roofs with gilt canopies. Among the other buildings of the Potala complex are the Lu Kang, a circular temple on a lake, the Chakpori temple, and the temple of Jo Kang, which is traditionally said to be the center of Tibet and contains the throne of the Dalai Lama. Until the Chinese Communists' occupation of Tibet caused the Dalai Lama to flee to India, the whole of the Potala was occupied by hundreds of lamas, monks and beggars.

Formerly, Tibet's contacts with the outside world were limited to pilgrimages and religious festivals and a little trade in wool, skins and medicinal herbs. Since the military occupation by the Chinese the city has undergone drastic changes. The ancient religious character of Lhasa has been practically destroyed and industrialization has begun to take place. It may be said in favor of the Chinese, however, that they have improved some social services.

A Brief History

UNTIL THE SECOND HALF OF THE 19th century, China's economy was based on agriculture, the products of craftsmen and artisans and on extremely limited internal and foreign trade. The existence of a feudal social structure maintaining a culture which despised the applied sciences caused the restriction of scientific and technical progress. The rapidly growing population had little opportunity of acquiring capital, while the Manchu government instead of encouraging foreign trade often actively discouraged it. All these factors combined to curb the growth of a prosperous middle class —the strata of society in which social, industrial and economic revolutions originate.

The beginnings of modernization in China were due to foreign capital and initiative. By the Treaty of Nanking in 1842, following the Opium Wars, a number of foreign powers acquired favorable trading rights in China. This was followed by the establishment of a system of open ports which were, in effect, the territory of the country to which trade concessions had been granted. Foreign interests were further strengthened by the acquisition of zones of influence, leased territories and railway concessions.

China's first modern factory was a small textile mill erected in Shanghai in 1888. A few years earlier the first railroad had been built and the first coal mining on an industrial scale had begun near Tangshan in Hopeh. However, the activity of foreign contractors was chiefly limited to the construction of railroads, since these facilitated the import of foreign goods into China and the export of valuable raw materials. Chinese interests had little opportunity to share in the development. By the beginning of the 20th century, although some 6000 miles of railroad had been constructed, China's production of such raw materials as pig iron, coal and cotton was still comparatively low.

The foreign interventions, civil wars, revolutions and social disturbances which occurred during the last years of the Ch'ing dynasty and

A decorated boat is crowded with holidaymakers on the occasion of a festival.

Above: *The "Riviera district" of Tsingtao, a major commercial and industrial city of northern China. Because of its strategic location on the Yellow Sea, Tsingtao has been occupied several times by foreign powers. The Germans occupied the city in 1897 and held it until they were driven out by the Japanese in 1914. The Japanese occupied the city during the period 1914-22 and again in 1938-45. Tsingtao also served briefly as U.S. naval headquarters in the Pacific after World War II.*

Below: *A view of the Haichu bridge in the city of Canton. The bridge joins the two banks of the Chu, or Pearl, River. The old city, with its commercial center and one-time foreign concessions quarter, rises on the left bank of the Chu, while the new industrial zones and residential districts extend along the other bank (in the background). Thousands of people live on boats on the river itself.*

after the foundation of the Chinese Republic threw the country into chaos and caused widespread poverty. The threat of civil disturbance confirmed the speculative nature of foreign enterprises and resulted in the transference abroad of the greater part of the profits of their ventures, thus inhibiting development in spite of increased productivity.

By the 1930s, however, foreign investments had doubled. China's production of coal, cement, pig-iron and other materials could bear comparison with that of other industrialized countries. From 1931 onward, after their conquest of Manchuria, the Japanese were able to replace the old system of trade concessions with their own direct rule over much of China. It was under Japanese occupation, that the foundations of modern heavy industry in China were laid.

CIVIL WAR

After the defeat of Japan, China regained independence, and the remaining territorial privileges of foreign powers were almost all abolished. However, the following years saw a period of civil war attended by a grave economic crisis. By 1949, when the Chinese Communist People's Republic emerged as the government of most of China, inflation and war damage had set industry back almost 20 years; agriculture was at an even lower level.

The new government took drastic action to halt inflation and to restore the economy. Strict administration of all resources was initiated and an ambitious program of reconstruction began. Land reforms eliminated private property and the economic

POPULATION: PEOPLE'S REPUBLIC OF CHINA		
PROVINCES	**AREA** (sq. miles)	**POPULATION** (1957 census*)
Anhwei	54,015	**33,560,000**
Chekiang	39,305	**25,280,000**
Fukien	47,529	**14,650,000**
Heilungkiang	178,996	**14,860,000**
Honan	64,479	**48,670,000**
Hopeh	81,479	**44,720,000**
Hunan	81,274	**36,220,000**
Hupeh	72,394	**30,790,000**
Kansu	137,104	**12,800,000**
Kiangsi	63,629	**18,610,000**
Kiangsu	40,927	**45,230,000**
Kirin	72,201	**12,550,000**
Kwangtung	89,344	**37,960,000**
Kweichow	67,181	**16,890,000**
Liaoning	58,301	**24,090,000**
Shansi	60,656	**15,960,000**
Shantung	59,189	**54,030,000**
Shensi	75,598	**18,130,000**
Szechwan	219,691	**72,160,000**
Tsinghai	278,378	**2,050,000**
Yunnan	168,417	**19,100,000**
MUNICIPALITIES		
Peking	3,386	**4,010,000**
Shanghai	772	**6,900,000**
AUTONOMOUS REGIONS		
Inner Mongolia	454,633	**9,200,000**
Kwangsi-Chuang	85,096	**19,390,000**
Ningsia Hui	30,039	**1,810,000**
Sinkiang Uigur	635,829	**5,640,000**
Tibet	471,660	**1,270,000**
TOTAL	3,691,502	**646,530,000**

*estimate

Workers hoe a terraced field on a collective farm in Yunnan province. Terracing, irrigation and crop rotation help to make maximum use of China's limited arable land.

initiative was placed in the hands of the central administration by the nationalization of banks, railways, trading companies and industries.

THE COMMUNIST SYSTEM

The Five-Year-Plan of 1953, it was claimed by the Communists, succeeded in more than doubling output and greatly increasing agricultural production. The peasants were conscripted and organized into collectives, and industrial or trading concerns still in private hands became cooperative enterprises.

Further developments occurred in the years following the Five-Year-Plan. In 1958 the Communists claimed that steel production was 8,000,000 tons and in 1959 that it reached 13,350,000, a phenomenal increase. But these figures must be considered warily. Statistical surveys emanating from Communist China represent a manipulative skill which is not quite clear enough to disguise the propagandist initiative that may inspire them.

During this period, city and agrarian workers were organized into communes; production was increased and consumption strictly controlled.

Agriculture and Stockbreeding

China has a total area of approximately 3,691,502 square miles.

There are a number of characteristics which distinguish agriculture in China from that in other countries. The farming population is dense, between 3000 and 4000 people per square mile, and there is an average of more than one family to each acre of cultivated land. The necessity of supporting so vast a population on so limited an area, together with the ready availability

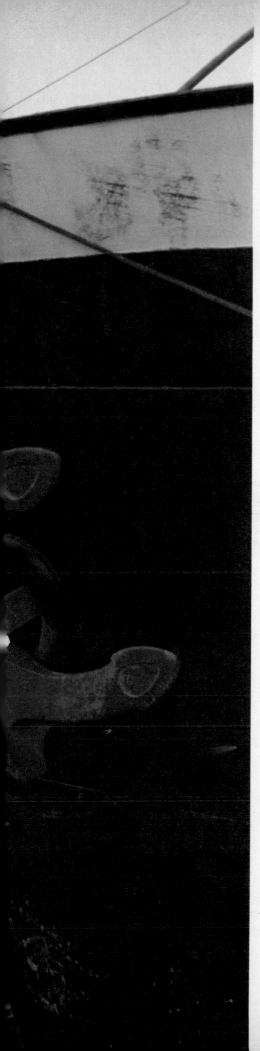

of labor, has caused very intense cultivation producing an output hardly sufficient to feed even the agricultural workers themselves.

Due to the unequal distribution of rain, for many centuries men have had to irrigate their land artificially by means of the greatest and most complex systems of irrigation and flood control of any in the world.

Since agriculture has, until modern times, been the basis of Chinese economic and social life, and since irrigation works have been the basis of agricultural prosperity, government irrigation schemes have been extended during the past ten years.

MODERN DEVELOPMENTS

A further feature of modern Chinese agriculture is its social organization. This is based on the large peasant collectives described as mutual-aid teams. These collectives are subdivided into groups all of which are centrally controlled.

Another characteristic, even with the increased industrialization of the last few years, is a scarcity of modern technical resources and equipment. While the Chinese aim at mechanizing agriculture, tractors and other motorized implements are in short supply and cultivation is largely carried on by manual labor and by draft animals. The use of chemical fertilizers is still very limited and much of the soil relies on fertilization by organic matter, animal, vegetable and human.

CEREAL CULTURE

Because of the great differences in geographical positions and therefore in climate between the various regions in China, the annual period of growth varies from little more than three months in some regions to a full year in others.

In Manchuria and in northern Mongolia there is only one fast growing harvest of spring wheat, while the island of Hainan has a twelve month growing season.

Rice, China's most important crop, is grown mainly in the area north of the Tsinling ranges and the Hwai River. Other crops, in order of importance, are cereals, pulses and tubers, oil producing seeds, textile crops, cane and sugar beet and tobacco. In addition, a considerable amount of land is set aside for raising fodder for livestock. Improved methods of cultivation have increased the yield of all crops during the last few years.

RICE

Rice occupies the largest area of cultivated land in China. It has a high yield and makes up about half the total cereal production. It is the most common crop in the irrigated areas south of the Hwai basin and the Yangtze, in the alluvial plains and on other heavy clay soils.

The chief rice producing provinces are Szechwan, Hunan, Kiangsu, Kwangtung, Chekiang, Kiangsi, Hupeh and Anhwei. In the more northerly provinces the rice is sown in summer and yields only one crop. In the south it is sown in spring and gives two crops. In some provinces a double crop is obtained by sowing wheat and rice in alternate rows, the wheat in winter and the rice in summer.

WHEAT

Wheat is grown mainly in the areas which have dark alluvial soil rich in calcium compounds. It is usually sown in winter except in the areas north of the Great Wall, where it is sown in spring. The province of Honan produces the most wheat, followed by Shantung, Hopeh, Anhwei, Kiangsu, Szechwan, Shansi, Heilungkiang and Shensi.

OTHER CEREALS

Other cereals grown in China are, in order of importance, corn, millet, sorghum, barley, oats, rye and buckwheat.

Corn is planted in summer in a moist belt extending from Heilungkiang across Hopeh, Honan, Shansi, Shensi, Szechwan, Kweichow and Kwangsi to Yunnan.

Millet and sorghum are summer crops which flourish on light soils rich in calcium compounds and will grow even in very dry conditions. For this reason they are mainly grown on the dry soils of the loess highlands and Manchuria. Shansi, Hopeh, Honan, Shantung, Mongolia and Kirin are the chief producers of millet. Sorghum is mainly grown in Manchuria, Hopeh, Shantung, Mongolia, Kansu, Hupeh and Szechwan.

Barley is the next most important crop. About half the total production

In the port of Shanghai, the bow of a large ocean-going steamer provides a contrast to the traditional Chinese junk in the background. The shallow draft of the junk makes it an ideal vessel for the navigation of China's rivers and coastal waters.

on light alluvial soils. Its principle center is Manchuria and it is also widely grown in Honan, Shantung, Anhwei, Kiangsu and Hopeh.

The middle Yangtze valley is the main center of sesame production, and sesame oil is the most highly valued product of the oil bearing seeds. The sunflower, a recent introduction, is grown for its seeds in Manchuria, northern China and Mongolia.

VEGETABLES

Groundnuts and rape, a species of turnip, are widely cultivated. The principal centers of groundnut production are Shantung, Hopeh, Honan, Kiangsu, Anhwei, Liaoning and Kwangtung. Rape, which has a lower yield than groundnuts, is cultivated in the central and southern provinces, in an area stretching from Szechwan to the Yangtze valley and to the provinces of the southwest.

Fresh vegetables are the main Chinese dietary accessories. They are cultivated in all parts of China in order to avoid extra cost and deterioration due to transport, around the larger cities.

Many varieties of vegetables are grown, the most important being common and Chinese celery (or cabbage), turnips, radishes and eggplant. There are also onions, garlic, spinach, beans, beet cucumbers, pumpkins, melons, watermelons, tomatoes, lettuce, carrots and cauliflower. In the northern provinces, greenhouses are used for winter cultivation and dried vegetables are used all over China.

SUGAR

The cultivation of sugar producing crops has been greatly increased in recent years. The most important is sugar cane, the principal production center of which is Kwangtung, followed by Szechwan, Kwangsi, Fukien and Yunnan. Sugar beet is cultivated mainly in the north, in Heilungkiang, Kirin and Mongolia.

INDUSTRIAL CROPS

Cotton, the most important of China's textile crops, flourishes best

is grown in Hopeh, Honan and Shantung. The rest is distributed over the loess highlands and in Manchuria, Szechwan, Tsinghai and Tibet. In Tibet it forms the basic diet of most of the population.

Oats are grown in Shansi, Shensi, Hopeh, Heilungkiang and Mongolia. Most rye is grown in Tsinghai and Tibet. Buckwheat is mainly grown in central China. In the oases of Sinkiang, rice, wheat and corn are all grown.

Cereals, especially rice, form the basic diet of the greater part of the Chinese population. Rice is usually steamed, while wheat, corn, millet and sorghum are ground and either steamed, baked or fried. They may also be made into noodles or used in soup. In general, rice is eaten mainly in central and southern China and wheat, corn, millet and sorghum in northern China.

Straw and the stalks of other cereals, which are generally uprooted rather than mown, are used for animal fodder, for fuel and for making paper.

PULSES AND TUBERS

Pulses and tubers are grown in the poorest hill and mountain regions in China. The pulses include a number of varieties of peas and beans, grown especially in the central regions and in the south and west. These are often ground into a paste and made into long, thin noodles and the young shoots are sometimes boiled.

Tubers include a number of varieties of potato and beet and other root vegetables. Sweet potatoes are grown in Shantung, Honan, Szechwan and the hilly regions of the south. The common potato is limited to northern Hopeh, Manchuria and Mongolia.

OIL PRODUCING SEEDS

The principal oil producing seed is soya, which is sown in summer in loose, alluvial soils rich in calcium compounds. The plains of the north are the main areas of production, the chief cotton producing provinces being Hopeh, Honan, Hupeh, Anhwei, Kiangsu, Shantung, Shensi, Chekiang, Szechwan, Shansi and Kansu. It is also cultivated in the valley of the Liao in Manchuria, in Sinkiang, in the oases of the Tarim basin and along the course of the Manass River.

Cotton is the basic clothing fabric. It is woven into single layers in the warmer regions and into multiple padded layers in the cold areas.

Other textile crops include jute, ramié, hemp and flax. Jute is the most important and is grown mainly in Chekiang, followed by Kiangsi, Kwangtung, Hunan, Kweichow and Szechwan. The production of ramié is concentrated in the middle Yangtze valley, Hunan, Kiangsi and Szechwan. Hemp is grown in the central provinces and as far north as Hopeh. Flax is grown mainly in the north, in Heilungkiang, Kirin, Mongolia, Hopeh, and northern Shansi and Shensi.

Cotton, hemp and flax produce oil bearing seeds as well as textile fibers. Cotton seed provides both edible oil and fuel for oil lamps. Hemp oil is produced for industrial use.

TOBACCO

Virginia-type tobacco is the kind most frequently grown in China. The main centers of production are Shantung and Honan, followed by Szechwan, Anhwei, Chekiang, Kiangsi, Yunnan, Kweichow and Liaoning.

TREE CULTURE

The cultivation of trees in China is generally less than the amount of wooded and forested areas in the country would suggest. In recent years, much more emphasis has been placed on the cultivation of cereals and cotton than on that of trees. Tree cultivation may be divided into the cultivation of trees providing food and the cultivation of trees yielding material for industrial use.

Pears are the most important fruit crop in China. They are mainly produced in northern China, in Liaoning, Shantung, Hunan and Hopeh.

Grapes are also a product of the northern provinces, being grown mainly in Kirin, Liaoning, Shantung, Hopeh, Shansi and Sinkiang. They

are used both for direct consumption, either fresh or dried, or for the production of wines and spirits.

Citrus fruits—oranges, lemons and grapefruit—are grown in the central and southern provinces. The chief centers of production are Szechwan, Chekiang, Kwangtung, Kwangsi, Kiangsi and Hunan.

A number of other fruit crops are cultivated in China, the areas of production depending upon climatic conditions. They include bananas, pineapples, chestnuts, walnuts, hazelnuts, peaches, apricots, plums, cherries, lychees, medlars, pomegranates, persimmons, figs and dates.

TEA

Tea, the Chinese national drink, is one of the best-known and most important products of the country. It is made from the leaves of a shrub which grows best on hillsides and the main centers of production are Fukien, Chekiang, Hunan, Hupeh, Kiangsi, Szechwan, Yunnan and southern Anhwei. The tea most popular in the West is produced in Fukien.

The unfermented leaves of the tea shrub produce green tea. Lightly fermented leaves produce the so-called *oolong*, the blend most favored in the West. Fully fermented leaves produce black tea. The Chinese drink only the first and third of these varieties. There are also short-leaved and long-leaved teas, and teas blended with flower petals to give them a pleasant odor.

TREE WAX

Tree wax, which Chinese peasants use for making candles, is collected from certain species of evergreen trees. A type of insect called *La-ch'ung*, which feeds on these trees, emits a whitish secretion which coats the branches. This deposit is scraped off, dried in the sun and then steamed over a pan of boiling water. The deposit solidifies after melting to form a white wax.

OTHER TREE PRODUCTS

The most important of the remaining trees is the mulberry, which is cultivated both for its fruit and to feed silk worms. Worms fed on mulberry leaves are the chief producers of silk cocoons in Kiangsu, Che-

Distribution of mineral deposits.

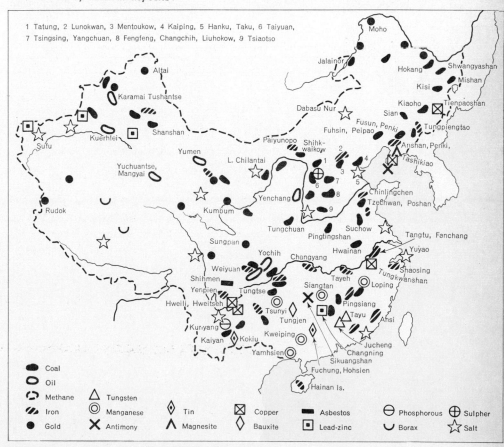

1 Tatung, 2 Lunokwan, 3 Mentoukow, 4 Kaiping, 5 Hanku, Taku, 6 Taiyuan, 7 Tsingsing, Yangchuan, 8 Fengfeng, Changchih, Liuhokow, 9 Tsiaotso

Coal
Oil
Methane
Iron
Gold
Tungsten
Manganese
Antimony
Tin
Magnesite
Copper
Bauxite
Asbestos
Lead-zinc
Phosphorous
Borax
Sulpher
Salt

SHEEP AND GOATS

Sheep and, less commonly, goats form the second largest group of domestic animals. They are found chiefly in areas of grass land, steppe and mountain; Sinkiang and Mongolia have the largest number. Sheep and goats are reared for meat, wool, hair and skins, and their milk is an important dietary item of the people of the autonomous regions of the west.

CATTLE

About a third of China's cattle are water buffalo, which predominate in the areas south of the Yangtze. Cows and yaks account for most of the remainder. The main center of cattle-rearing is Mongolia and yaks are raised mainly in Tibet and Tsinghai.

In agricultural areas, buffalo and cows are used almost exclusively as draft animals but in the great pasturelands of Mongolia, Tibet and Tsinghai cows are regarded primarily as producers of milk and butter.

EQUINE ANIMALS

More than half the equine animals of China are donkeys, which are used for farm work and transport. Horses and small ponies are found in lesser numbers and a small number of mules are used for transport in very mountainous regions.

Camels, traditionally used as beasts of burden in trading caravans, are chiefly found in Mongolia, Sinkiang, Kansu and Tsinghai. Other animals reared include the sika deer, whose powdered horns are thought to have medicinal qualities, and rabbits and other fur bearing animals, especially in Mongolia. Dogs and cats have practically died out in China, since they are of little economic value and the Communist government discourages the practice of keeping domestic pets.

FISHING AND FISH BREEDING

Fishing and fish breeding provide an important source of protein in

kiang, Anhwei, Szechwan, Kweichow, Kwangtung and Sinkiang. In some other centers of production the silkworms are fed on oak or camphor leaves.

Another tree is the tung tree, which produces a valuable oil. Its chief cultivation centers are Hunan, Hupeh, Szechwan, Kiangsi, Chekiang, Kweichow and Kwangsi.

LIVESTOCK-REARING

The most common domesticated animals in China are small animals that can be fed on agricultural waste.

Poultry and pigs are the most numerous. Hens are kept in dry regions and ducks in better watered areas. Turkeys and geese, which require a more abundant diet, are less plentiful.

PIGS

Pig-breeding is the most important branch of livestock rearing in China, which is thought to have more pigs than any other country. Pigs are reared by almost all peasant families and bristles are an important by-product.

the diet of China's population. About half the fish eaten in China are caught in salt water and the remainder are the product of fish breeding in inland water.

The chief centers of sea fishing are the larger bays of the coastal provinces and the areas around the offshore island. Seaweed and shellfish are also extensively cultivated and pearl oysters are bred where conditions are favorable.

Sea fish are either consumed while fresh in the areas where caught or are frozen or dried for transport to the interior. The most common varieties are mackerel, sole, cod, eel, cuttlefish, sea cucumber, crabs, prawns and lobsters.

Fish are also caught in the inland waters, particularly in the lakes of central China, but fish breeding is much more important in these areas. It has been developed in connection with the building of large reservoirs for irrigation purposes.

Apart from fish, mainly carp and crayfish, the lakes also provide edible algae, lotus roots and seeds and water chestnuts. Algae and other water plants are used for animal fodder and compost, while cane, reeds and grasses are used for basket weaving.

WOODS AND FORESTS

The total forested area of China is comparatively small and most forests exist in the border regions which have difficult access. More than half of China's forested area is concentrated in Manchuria and northeast Mongolia and other forest regions are found in Fukien, Yunnan, Szechwan, the region on the borders of Kwangtung, Kweichow, Szechwan and Hunan, the region between Szechwan, Shensi and Kansu, and in the Tien Shan mountains in Sinkiang Uigur.

Bamboo is one of the most important of China's timber resources and is found particularly in the areas to the south of the Hwai and Han rivers. It grows rapidly and combines

strength with elasticity and lightness. Bamboo canes are used for building huts, scaffolding, beds, stools, hampers and many other domestic articles. Bamboo shoots are an important dietary item.

In addition to natural forests, a number of reforestation areas and protective belts have been planted over the last few years. These are found particularly in areas where land is being reclaimed from the desert or where existing agricultural land is threatened by the encroachment of sand. Large green belt areas have also been planted around the larger cities.

Sources of Energy

According to figures issued in 1958, China's estimated reserves of minerals and natural energy are very great. They include huge deposits of coal and ferrous metals and other metallic and non-metallic minerals, and enormous reserves of hydroelectric power.

A great part of these resources lies in inaccessible areas which are distant from the places where they are needed. Thus, very great investment is needed before their potential can be properly exploited. Nevertheless, they provide a firm basis for industrial development.

COAL

Coal is the most important of China's natural resources, both because of its abundance and its many uses. The loess plateau is the site of one of the largest known coal deposits, and other important coal bearing areas are found in Szechwan, the highlands of Yunnan-Kweichow and Manchuria and in Shansi. Anthracite and bituminous coals for coke, steam and gas are found in all provinces in easily worked mines of varying potential. Lignite and peat are relatively scarce.

The amount of coal produced in 1960 was estimated at around 420,000,000 tons. The most produc-

Opencast coal workings in the Yangtze plain near Nanking, in the province of Kiangsu. Although this area has seen some industrial development in recent years, industry takes second place to agriculture, since this is the most fertile and densely populated part of China. During summer almost the whole province is under cultivation and the cities are populated more by agricultural workers than by industrial artisans.

The interior of a steel rolling mill at Anshan, the great industrial center of the Liaotung peninsula. Immediately after the Communist revolution of 1949, industrial production in this area dropped sharply. This was partly due to the destruction of the Manchurian blast furnaces by the Russians at the end of World War II and partly to a decline in foreign trade, especially with Japan, and a consequent lack of capital, attendant upon the accession of the Communist regime. However, progress has been made in increasing production in heavy industries.

tive mines were in Liaoning (Fushun, Fusin, Penki and Peipiao) and Shansi (Taiyuan, Tatung and Yangchuan). Other important mines, in order of importance, were those of Hopeh (Kailan and Tsingsing), Heilungkiang, Shantung (Tsaochwang and Fangtze), Honan, Szechwan (Yungchwan), Anhwei (Hwainan), Kirin (Kiacho), Kiangsi (Pingsiang), Hunan (Tzehing) and Yunnan (Kunyang).

HYDROELECTRIC POWER

While coal deposits are most common in the areas north of the Yellow River, the most important hydroelectric resources lie to the south. The basin of the Yangtze accounts for a large percentage of the total, followed by the basins of the Brahmaputra, the Salween, the Mekong, the Si and the smaller rivers of the southeast. The remaining hydroelectric resources are provided by the Yellow River, the Amur, the Hwai and smaller rivers to the north of the Yangtze.

Only a small proportion of China's total hydroelectric resources is now being exploited, though two of the largest electric power stations in the world are planned for erection in the narrow reaches of the Yangtze and the Matsang-Tsangpo Brahmaputra. The largest hydroelectric stations at present in operation are those of Shuifeng in Liaonong, Fengman in Kirin, and Sinan in Chekiang. Other important stations are at Chehsi in Hunan, Wanan in Kiangsi, and Kutien in Fukien.

OIL

Oil is not plentiful in China. The estimated reserves are small and the largest deposits are situated in regions which have poor communications and are distant from the centers of consumption. For these reasons, there has been a great development of the process of obtaining petroleum by distillation from bituminous shales and petroleum products

from the synthesis of coal.

The most important source of natural oil is the region of Yumen-Kiuchan in Kansu, which provides more than half of the nation's crude oil. Other important oilfields are found in Tsaidam in Tsinghai, Nanchung in Szechwan, and Yenchang in Shensi. Apart from the Yumen-Kiuchan field, communication routes from these areas are not good.

About half of the total output of oil obtained by the distillation of

shales and synthesis of coal is produced at Fushun in Liaoning. Other important centers of production are being built in a number of areas, including Hoku in Shansi and Mowming in Kwangtung. Refineries for petroleum products are found at Lanchow, the largest in China, built with the aid of Soviet capital and technicians, and at Fushun, Talien, Shanghai, Nanking, Yumen, Tsaidam, Chinhsien, Szeping, Kirin and Tatung. There are also a number of works for the production of methane and methyl alcohol.

NUCLEAR POWER

China has good prospects for the development of atomic energy. There are large deposits of fissile material in Sinkiang, Szechwan and Kwangsi, and nuclear research centers have been established at Peking and Wuhan.

Mineral Resources

IRON AND STEEL

China is rich in ferrous metals and in metals used in the production of steel alloys. The largest mines in China are found in Liaoning (Anshan and Penki), followed by Hopeh (Tangshan and Suanhwa), Shansi (Yangchuan and Changchih), Shantung (Tiehshan) and Mongolia.

Other mines in the north include those in Kirin (Tunghwa), Honan (Yiyang), Kansu (Tienshui) and Sinkiang Uigur (Urumchi). In the Yangtze valley are the mines of Szechwan (Weiyuan and Hweili), Hupeh (Tayeh and Yitu) and Anhwei (Tangtu). The most important mines in the southeast are those of the island of Hainan (Shihlu), followed by those of Yunnan (Imen), Kweichow (Shuicheng) and Fukien (Anki). Other small mines are found in almost all provinces.

The chief center of manganese production is Liaoning (Chinsi) and it is also mined in Kwangtung (Tsamkong and Hoppo), Kwangsi (Wuhsuan), Hunan (Siangtan), and in Kiangsi, Kweichow and Szechwan.

China is the world's largest producer of tungsten with mines in Liaoning (Antung), Hopeh (Chengteh), Kiangsi (Tayu), Hunan, Kwangtung and Sinkiang.

In addition to these minerals, molybdenum is mined in Sinkiang (Tsinghai), Liaoning, Hunan, Fukien, Chekiang, Yunnan and Kwangsi. Vanadium is mined in Hopeh (Chengteh).

On the basis of the resources detailed above, the iron and steel industry has been able to expand considerably. Figures issued for production show that pig iron amounted to 20,500,000 tons in 1959 and steel to 15,000 tons, in 1961. The industry is concentrated in about 20 factories of varying capacity. The largest is at Ansham in Liaoning and other important centers are Wuhan in Hopeh and Paotow in Mongolia.

Other important iron and steel works are situated in Liaoning (Penki, Fushun and Talien), Hopeh (Tangshan, Tientsin and Suanhwa), Shansi (Taiyuan and Yangchwan), Kiansu (Shanghai), Shantung (Tsinan), Hunan (Siangtang), Szechwan (Chungking), Kwangsi (Liuchow), and in Yunnan (Kungking).

OTHER METALLIC MINERALS

As well as tungsten, China holds a leading position in the world for the production of antimony and tin. The most important deposits of antimony are situated in Hunan (Sikwangshan), followed by Kwangtung (Yuyuan), Kwangsi (Hochih), Yunnan and Kweichow. Tin is found in Yunnan (Kokiu), and in lesser quantities in Kwangsi (Hohsien), Kiangsi (Tayu), Hunan and Kwangtung.

Considerable deposits of lead, zinc, copper and bauxite are distributed throughout China. They have not, as yet, been much exploited. Lead and zinc are found in Hunan (Shuikowshan), Szechwan (Hweili), Yunnan (Hweitseh), Liaoning, Fukien, Honan, Tsinkiang and Tsinghai.

Copper is found in Liaoning (Fuhsien and Chwangho), Kirin (Yenki), Hupeh (Tayeh), Szechwan (Kweili), Yunnan (Hweitseh), Sinkiang (Fushun and Fuhsien), Shantung (Poshan), Kweichow (Siuwen), Shansi and Anhwei.

Deposits of mercury exist in Hunan (Fenghwan) and Kweichow. Silver is found usually in the same areas as lead and zinc, while gold is mined in the Amur valley in Heilungkiang, and in Hopeh (Tsunhua), Sinkiang (the Altai mountains and Hotien), Szechwan (near Kantse), Shantung (Chaoyuan), Tibet (near Gartok), Kirin and Shensi.

NON-METALLIC MINERALS

China possesses a wealth of non-metallic minerals which are widely used by the chemical industries. Salt, most of which is extracted by the many salt-processing works, is among the most important. The salt not produced in coastal areas comes from salt springs in Szechwan (Tzekung) and Yunnan (Yenhing),

The location of major industries and industrial centers.

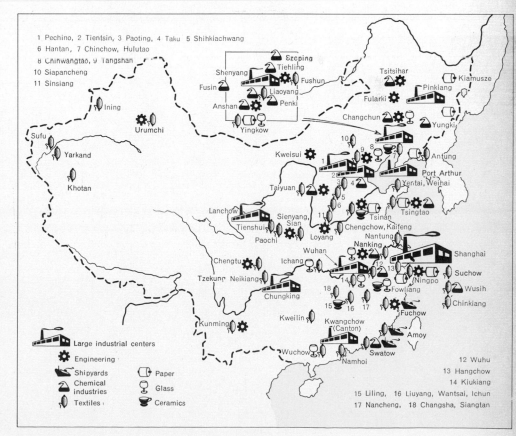

1 Pechino, 2 Tientsin, 3 Paoting, 4 Taku 5 Shihkiachwang
6 Hantan, 7 Chinchow, Hulutao
8 Chinwangtao, 9 Tangshan
10 Siapancheng
11 Sinsiang

Large industrial centers
Engineering
Shipyards
Chemical industries
Textiles
Paper
Glass
Ceramics

12 Wuhu
13 Hangchow
14 Kiukiang
15 Liling, 16 Liuyang, Wantsai, Ichun
17 Nancheng, 18 Changsha, Siangtan

A file of camels in the steppe land of Tibet. Camel caravans are the normal means of transport in the less mountainous parts of the Tibetan region, the two-humped Bactrian camel being the most common breed. Increased industrial and commercial development under the Chinese People's Republic is gradually leading to the construction of modern communication networks in the more remote parts of Chinese territory, as may be seen by the electricity pylon in the background of the picture.

salt lakes in Shensi (Tsingpien), Tsinghai, Mongolia, Tibet, Shansi, Ningsia and Kansu, and from numerous salt mines in Hupeh, Hunan and Sinkiang.

Deposits of rock phosphate and apatite, used in the preparation of artificial fertilizers, are found in Kweichow, Kiangsu and Hopeh. Natural nitrate quarries are found in Yunnan, Szechwan, Hunan, Honan and Kansu, and guano deposits are found in the small islands to the south of Hainan. Potassic salts occur in Tsaidam, Hunan and Tibet, and natural soda is found in many parts of Mongolia.

Pyrite, the raw material for the production of sulphuric acid, is found in Szechwan, Kwangsi, Kwangtung, Hunan, Kiangsi and Anhwei. Sulphur is produced in Shansi. Tibet possesses large reserves of borax and the Wuyi mountains of Chekiang are a source of fluorite.

The Chemical Industry

The wide variety of mineral resources, in addition to coal, electric power and oil, provides China with a basis on which to establish a flourishing chemical industry. Great progress has been made in this field over the last few years. Among other products, production figures show an increase for caustic soda, sodium carbonate, sulfuric acid, copper sulfate, methyl alcohol, insecticides, sulfanilamides and antibiotics. Other important products include synthetic rubber and fibers, plastics, dyes and pharmaceutical goods.

The main centers of the chemical industry are established mostly near the major sources of raw material, while consumer goods are manufactured in the cities and industrial areas.

Chalk, limestone, magnesite, alumite, clays, kaolin and siliceous sand (the kind used in the manufacture of ceramics) are found almost everywhere in China. There are large beds of chalk in Hupeh (Yingchang), Shansi and Kansu. Magnesite is found in Liaoning and alumite in Chekiang (Pingyang), Anhwei (Hofei) and Liaoning (Fengcheng).

CLAY AND CEMENT

Chinese kaolin, or china clay, is famous for its purity and has been used since very early times for the manufacture of the most delicate porcelain. It is found mainly in Kiangsi, Kwangtung, Fukien and Chekiang. The word *kaolin* comes from *kao*, high, and *ling*, a hill.

Cement and other building materials are produced in most provinces. Fireclay products are concentrated near the major iron and steel works. The glass industry is mainly centered on the coastal towns, such as Talien and Chinwangtao.

A number of other minerals important to the chemical, engineering and textile industries and to other crafts are found in deposits of varying sizes. These include emery in Chekiang; barite in Kwangsi, Shantung, Hopeh, Hunan and Kiangsi; graphite in Fukien, Honan, Hunan, Szechwan, Shantung, and Hopeh; asbestos in Liaoning, Hopeh, Mongolia, Shantung, Honan and Szechwan; mica in Szechwan, Yunnan and Mongolia; jade in Sinkiang, Yunnan and Manchuria; and precious stones in Yunnan, Sinkiang and Tibet.

The Engineering Industries

The engineering industries supply the essential tools for the industrialization of China. In the past few years, every effort has been made to increase the quantity and variety of transport facilities, industrial equipment, industrial machinery and mechanical apparatus of all kinds.

As a result, the range of products manufactured in modern China is now very wide. Among industries showing a considerable expansion are ship building, railroad rolling stock, industrial motor vehicles, tractors, aircraft, mining equipment, iron and steel, chemicals, cement, textiles, paper, timber, food, electrical equipment, diesel engines, ball bearings, radios, bicycles, sewing machines and clocks.

Food Industry

The production of food is the most widespread industry of China, as it is in other countries. Its nature is determined by the agricultural character of individual provinces and by the needs of the population.

The most important elements of the food industry are grain and rice mills. The former are concentrated in the grain producing areas to the north of the Yangtze River and the latter in the rice growing areas to the south.

Another very important process is the extraction of edible oil from oil-bearing seeds. Manchuria, Shantung, Kansu and Szechwan are the leading centers of production. The soap industry, which is related to the oil industry and to the meat industry, is distributed throughout the country.

The greatest development in food production has taken place in the sugar refining industry. This is based on sugar cane in central and southern China and sugar beet in Manchuria and Mongolia.

The canning industry has also developed considerably. There are many factories for the canning of fish in coastal areas. Beef is canned in Manchuria, Mongolia and Hopeh; pork in Liaoning, Hopeh, Shantung and Hupeh; and fruit in Kwangtung, Kwangsi and Fukien. Cheese is packed in Mongolia.

DRINK AND TOBACCO

There are a number of traditional Chinese drinks, some of which are peculiar to certain provinces. They are distilled from rice and other cereals and from tubers and have a high alcohol content. They are sometimes perfumed or sweetened. In the large cities, beer, introduced into Shantung by the Germans, is a popular drink. Wines and Western-type spirits are also produced.

The manufacture of tobacco was initiated by the British-American Tobacco Company, who introduced cigarettes into China at the end of the 19th century and promoted the growth of tobacco on an industrial scale. Cigarettes are the most popular form of smoking in the cities although the traditional long pipe is still smoked in some rural areas.

Textiles

COTTON

Cotton is by far the most important of the textile industries. It was already in an advanced state of development at the time of the Chinese Communist revolution. Expansion has been continued in recent years, especially in the inland regions of northern and central China. The main center of the cotton industry is Shanghai and the remaining mills are chiefly concentrated in Kiangsu, Honan, Shantung, Shensi, Hupeh, Hunan, Kansu and Sinkiang.

MIXED FABRICS

The production of silk, both natural and artificial, is also important. The industry has been considerably expanded as the result of a tendency to export less raw silk and to use rayon in mixed fabrics. Weaving is concentrated in the chief

The Ming River, a tributary of the Hwai River, which takes its name from the town of Mingkiang in southern Honan, through which it flows. The river rises in the Tungpai Shan range and flows southeastward through fertile alluvial plains to join the Hwai some 10 miles east of Mingkiang.

silk-producing areas of Kiangsu, Chekiang, Szechwan, Kwangtung, Shantung and Liaoning. Each area produces a different type of cloth, depending on the type of silk used and the methods of weaving and finishing.

Tough fibers such as jute, ramié, hemp and flax are used for industrial cloth and for furnishing and some clothing fabrics. The main centers of production are in Chekiang and Manchuria.

CAMEL HAIR AND WOOL

Traditionally, wool is important only in the sheep-rearing areas on China's borders. The industry is now being modernized and expanded but progress is limited by the shortage of high quality wool. An important branch of the industry is the manufacture of cashmere and camel's-hair garments.

Hand-woven carpets are another important product of the Chinese textile industry. The main centers of production are in Peking, Tientsin and Sinkiang.

Over the last few years, the textile industry has made great progress in the dyeing, finishing and design of fabrics. A further flourishing branch of the industry has been established for the mass production of household linen and industrial clothing.

Other Industries

The largest paper mills in China are found in Kiamusze, Nanping, Canton and Shanghai. Production is increasing rapidly, as is the production of rayon at Paotung, Antung, Peking and Shanghai.

The rubber industry is of growing importance, particularly for the manufacture of tires and footwear. Rubber-soled shoes are gradually replacing the traditional cloth shoes of northern China and straw sandals of the south.

The leather industry has always been limited by the relatively small amount of livestock and by the custom of eating buffalo and pig skins, together with the meat. Only in the northern provinces have skins, usually of sheep and goats, been plentiful.

Other manufactures, mainly centered around Shanghai, are fountain pens, vacuum bottles, which are used for hot boiled water drunk in the absence of fresh drinking water, and enamel utensils.

Transport and Communications

Navigable rivers have always been one of China's chief methods of communication and transport. Horses and donkeys have been used to draw carts on the northern plains, mules and yaks are used in mountainous areas and camels in the steppes and deserts. In all parts of China, human carriers were much used over short distances.

The transport system has been modernized in the present century by the construction of railways, the introduction of motor powered boats and the building of roads suitable for automobiles and trucks. Nevertheless, at the formation of the Chinese People's Republic modern means of communication were concentrated in the areas of Manchuria, Kiangsu, Hopeh, Shantung and the Canton delta.

ROADS

At present there are road networks covering almost every part of the country. About half the total mileage, estimated at 275,000 miles in 1960, consists of paved roads, the remainder being broad wagon-tracks with dirt surfaces. In 1959 it was estimated that the total number of China's motor vehicles was 210,000 almost all of them belonging to public concerns. The number of wheeled vehicles of all kinds was estimated at over 1,000,000.

INLAND WATERWAYS AND SEAPORTS

The inland waterways of China have an estimated mileage of 70,000 miles, about a third of which is navigable by powered craft. The most important river ports are Nanking, Wuhan and Chungking on the Yangtze River, Canton and Wuchow on the Si River, Tientsin on the Hai River and Harbin on the Sungari.

The most important seaports include Talien, Tsingtao and Shanghai, all of which do a considerable international trade. Other important ports of China's coastline, from north to south, are Antung, Chinwangtao, Sinhailien, Wenchow, Foochow, Amoy and Swatow.

In 1962 it was estimated that the total tonnage of craft suitable for both river and coastal traffic was 522,500 tons. In addition there were estimated to be about 300,000 junks, propelled by sails or oars, with a total tonnage of around 4,000,000 tons.

RAILROADS

The 8750 miles of railroad in actual use in 1951 had increased to an estimated 18,641 miles in 1959. Most of this total was accounted for by single lines, though progress in double tracking was being made on the main lines, such as the Peking-Harbin, Peking-Canton, and Suchow-Lanchow lines.

Railroads are the most important means of transport in China. Not only do they carry a large proportion of the total freight of passenger traffic but also they carry loads for longer distances. Total rolling stock in 1959 was estimated at 4700 locomotives, 128,000 freight cars and 4800 passenger cars.

Air services have increased considerably over the last few years and in 1958 it was estimated that China's

The Chinese woman setting off for work on her bicycle is a symbol of the progress of women's emancipation in modern China, as is the propaganda poster behind her.

air routes covered 20,000 miles. The strength of China's air fleet, both civil and military, is not known.

Commerce

With improvements in transportation and communications China's internal and external trade has increased greatly. The greatest increases have taken place in the fields of fuels, raw materials, industrial machinery and agricultural equipment, and there has also been an increase in trade between the industrial centers and the rural areas.

Most of the consumer trade, both in urban and rural areas, is carried out through the state controlled trading companies. Most basic goods, such as cereals, oil and cotton cloth are strictly rationed and prices are fixed in every kind of shop, whether state owned or run by a cooperative.

Foreign trade is entirely controlled by the state and is carried on through a number of specially formed trading companies. China's economic policy is directed toward the maximum of self-sufficiency and only goods which cannot be produced in the country are imported, mainly raw materials and machinery needed for further industrialization.

China's exports consist chiefly of raw and processed agricultural products, mining products and a wide range of manufactured goods. In the past, the bulk of China's foreign trade was with Great Britain, Japan and the United States of America. Since the establishment of the Chinese People's Republic, however, political considerations have dictated that the bulk of China's foreign

trade should be with the Communist countries of Europe and the uncommitted nations of Africa and Asia.

Foreign trade is mainly conducted by sea and to a lesser extent by road and rail across China's frontiers. There are other contacts with foreign countries. Former Chinese emigrants are allowed to send money to their relatives in China and there are credit plans with the U.S.S.R. under which China receives assistance in economic development. Foreign ships are often leased to make up for deficiencies in China's merchant navy. Furthermore, China has progressed sufficiently to be able to offer commercial credits to African and Asian countries, partly to encourage trade and partly for political reasons.

A Chinese girl wears a red scarf to add color to the blue denims which have become a semi-official uniform for the Chinese working class.

MARXISM AND ANCIENT FAMILY TRADITIONS

THROUGHOUT HISTORY, CHINA HAS been a country which, in its culture and customs, was alien to the peoples of the West. Few travelers penetrated beyond the coastal towns where Western traders set up commercial outposts; the travelers who penetrated the interior did so by conforming to the Chinese way of life. Foreign peoples were distrusted; foreign ways were excluded.

China, today, remains cut off from the West for political reasons, and the Marxists who conquered the mainland in 1949 are dedicated to the destruction of historical Chinese tradition. The country has become a vast political laboratory, under a dictatorship dedicated to changing it into a world industrial and political power and to the creation of a new culture permeated by Marxism. In the communes and factories, the people are conditioned by constant propaganda to become "workers," in Communist terms. The family unit, which was the basis of Chinese society throughout history, is being replaced by the commune.

However, the context of ancient China still is apparent. Women no longer bind their feet, men no longer plait their hair into pigtails, but smoke stacks and oil derricks surround many ancient pagodas. Modern industrial innovations change the ancient traditional way of life. But despite the massive industrial regimentation of the people by the Communist government and the consequent re-adjustments of social customs, this way of life continues in many parts of the country. Chinese traditional customs relate to a specific attitude towards life and nature which in places resists the changes made by the Marxists.

Technical knowledge has brought benefits to the Chinese, but because these benefits are common to America and Europe, it seems more interesting and informative to describe the older aspects of Chinese life that survive.

Marriage

The marriage tie was strong in China because the family unit was considered the foundation of society. The father held the traditional position of authority in the family. He was entitled to veneration from his wife and children and absolute obedience from all members of the family.

When death came to him he lived on in the family memory and his children continued to follow his teachings and honor him.

Elder brothers had authority over their younger brothers until they had become established as heads of their own families.

Family succession had to be preserved unbroken. Ancestors must not be forgotten and thus deprived of the due respect of their descendants. The dead were not taken lightly in China; their wishes were binding even after they had died.

TRIBUTE TO THE DEAD

In an old tale, *Lu-Kiao-Li*, the story is told of a father who wished to find a husband for his daughter. The 19th-century translator, Abel Remusat, wrote in his preface:

"It is curious that men who while alive show no great interest in their fate after death, and have no concept of a future life, should exert themselves so greatly to influence events after they die. There is perhaps not one Chinese in a thousand who knows or even cares whether a soul will survive his body's decay; yet there also is none who would not be horrified by the thought of not receiving the posthumous honors, especially those tributes which his son or the nephew pays at fixed times during each year; such tributes are made before a tablet on which the dead man's name is inscribed.

"The comfort of survival with the context of the 'family mind' colors the whole traditional culture of the Chinese; it is the principal motivating force in the most important actions of a man's life. Hence the great aversion to celibacy and the dread of dying without male descendants."

This belief in the perpetuation of life through the family partly explains the importance which the Chinese attached to marriage. A wedding feast had to be conducted most luxuriously and with great ceremony and ostentation. It is recorded that at one time special laws were passed to limit the exuberance of the celebrations; as a result, rules established by ancient custom were often neglected, and rules distinguishing the rank of the guests sometimes ignored. The ceremonies were so lavish that they could only be afforded by a privileged class.

MARRIAGES WERE MADE BY PARENTS

In a traditional Chinese marriage, the couple to be married had to conduct themselves in a reserved manner.

The marriage was arranged by the parents or nearest relatives without reference to the wishes of the couple, who were not allowed to meet before the marriage. But in some cases, they saw portraits or heard descriptions of each other. If the young man, after meeting his bride, considered himself to have been falsely informed as to the lady's qualities he could obtain a divorce.

THE HUSBAND PAID

The parents of the girl did not provide a dowry, and gave no presents to the bride. Instead, relatives of the bridegroom arranged the match through the women of the family, and settled the amount of money to be paid.

This money was used to provide clothing and adornment for the bride on her wedding day. Thus, in practice, the groom paid the dowry. This type of negotiation, which was conducted with great diplomacy and thrift, was common among people of the poorer classes.

Mandarins and rich landowners were so lavish that in the wedding celebrations alone they spent more than the entire dowry. On the other hand, poor people who did not have enough money to pay a dowry, often

Springtime in Liangshan, eastern Szechwan. Three women in traditional dress stand in a field of flowering rape listening to a peasant playing upon a stringed instrument. The chief agricultural produce of this area is cereals, rice, sugar cane, sweet potatoes and beans; Liangshan is also a center for the export of tung oil and medicinal plants.

waited at the doors of foundlings' institutes until a girl was handed over to them.

After a marriage had been arranged, the bride's family prepared for the wedding day. The calendar was carefully studied in order to find a propitious date for the wedding.

Relations between the two families were maintained meanwhile, by an exchange of gifts between bride and groom. Suitable, gifts were rings, necklaces and other ornaments. Letters, often long and elaborate, were exchanged between the couple, taking the place of the forbidden personal contact.

TORCHES IN DAYLIGHT

If the bride came from a wealthy family, she would go to the house of the bridegroom on her wedding day in a locked litter, seated on a throne. She was surrounded by silk curtains, and carried by at least twelve bearers wearing the livery of her family. To add to the brilliance of the proceedings, her relatives formed a procession on horseback behind her.

Eventually, the litter, followed by the procession, arrived before the house.

The bridegroom, standing in the doorway, was handed a key by a woman chosen by the relatives or by the oldest servant. He then went to the sedan chair, unlocked it and welcomed the young girl, leading her by the hand into a sumptously decorated room.

The celebrations were long and magnificent, and it was traditional for men and women to remain in separate groups.

THE REFINED CONCUBINE

According to ancient Chinese laws a man could only have one wife. But in practice, polygamy was legal from very early times. A man might have as many concubines as he could afford to keep. Their children were considered legitimate offspring, and divided the inheritance with the children of the regular marriage. A later Chinese civil code, however, distinguished legitimate children from those born to concubines.

The concubine was usually a slave, although some were free. Special institutions existed (those in Yang-chow and Suicheng were famous) to instruct such girls in music and singing; they thus were educated for a refined environment. A traveler of the 15th century, the Florentine Lorenzo Magalotti, confirms some facts about concubines which still were true until fairly recent years.

FREE CONCUBINES AND SLAVES

"It should be known," he says, "that the Chinese, assuming they have a wife, may have as many concubines as they wish. These are of two sorts; free and slaves." The free ones were illegitimate daughters of noblemen or gentlemen. They, to lighten the burden of a large family, placed their daughters as concubines, receiving for them a small dowry. This was not returned if the girl was later rejected. After a separation, children of the union remained with the father if he accepted them. If not, they followed the mother, with an allowance for their keep.

The slave concubines came from peasant families. Peasants sometimes got rid of offspring by killing them if they were deformed at birth, and selling others, the boys as servants and the girls as concubines. Their price was about $15.

Concubines were under the authority of the first wife, and sometimes had to do heavy work.

GROUNDS FOR DIVORCES

Marriages could only be dissolved by mutual consent, but concubines were simply rejected and sent back to their homes.

The wife's consent obtained, the husband could divorce her for abandoning the conjugal home, for being quarrelsome to the extent of

Nursery schools and kindergartens are an important feature of modern Chinese life, since they free mothers for industrial or agricultural work. In addition, they are an aspect of the breakdown of the family system under the Communist regime. The introduction of communal apartment blocks, attendant upon the movement of the population to industrial areas and the consequent weakening of family ties with the introduction of community living, has considerably weakened the traditional authority of both men over women and parents over their children.

A woman with her child in Peking, the ancient capital of China. Peking consists of an Inner and an Outer City, both ringed by walls. Within the Inner City stands the Forbidden City, formerly the site of the imperial palaces, but now the cultural center of Peking; the ancient palaces have been converted to museums housing works of artistic or historical importance. A number of parks, such as the Sun Yat-sen Park, have been laid out within the city, and one of the chief centers of social life is the Working People's Palace of Culture.

which they lived and burned themselves alive, having locked all the doors so that no one could come to their aid. A few days later, however, the husband returned and when he saw that all the concubines were dead, he built a new house and found new companions."

Position of Women in the Family

However distinguished a Chinese wife's family, she was not permitted to leave her apartment, which was situated in the most secluded part of the house. The only company she was allowed was that of servants and children. Her occupations were domestic or in the arts of painting, music and poetry recitation.

Travelers, up to recent times, related that few upper-class women were to be seen in the streets or in shops, except in Peking, before

A happy group of Chinese children in the care of an older girl. Provision for day-nurseries has been made in modern China, allowing an increasing number of women to be employed in industry.

striking him, for gossiping spitefully, for adultery or for sterility. He could obtain a divorce if he thought he had been defrauded by the marriage contract. The wife could also be sent home if she lacked respect for her husband's parents, stole, or was afflicted with an incurable disease.

A woman could escape these penalties if she wore mourning for three years for her husband's parents, if she married him when he was poor, or if she had no relatives.

A wife could ask for a divorce but only with her husband's consent, if she was beaten, if she was deceived by the marriage contract, or if her husband became infected by leprosy.

THE WIDOWS KILLED THEMSELVES

In ancient China, it was customary for wives to kill themselves on the death of their husbands.

In a drama, *Sacrifice on the Yangtze*, written during the time of the Three Kingdoms in the 3rd century A.D., this custom is illustrated.

Souen, third wife of the king of Ch'u when her husband dies, sacrifices to the gods, then drowns herself; the dragon of the Yangtze River then proclaims her a virtuous wife.

HUNG IN A SCARLET NOOSE

L. C. Arlington, a traveler in China, mentions suicides. "I remember," wrote Arlington, "the case of a young woman engaged since childhood to a man who died a few days before the wedding. The girl informed her friends that she considered herself a widow, and that she was joining her promised husband in the grave. She therefore had set up, in the principal street of the district, a platform surmounted by a canopy, from which was suspended a scarlet noose which she put round her neck. Then, covering her face with her hands, she leapt from a stool, not forgetting to salute her helpers when her body was dangling in the air."

WIDOWS SET FIRE TO HOME

Another suicide is described as follows: "One day, the death was announced in Peking of a man who had seven concubines and many children. When they heard the news, the women set fire to the house in

women became emancipated. Mongolian or Chinese females of humble birth were more often seen in the outside world, and had almost as much freedom as European women.

The women in modern Chinese cities are much different. They wear blue overalls or brief jackets in traditional floral designs, and trousers. They work in offices or on farms. For centuries Chinese women obeyed decrees which relegated them to obscurity in the home and in society, and yet some became ardent revolutionaries.

HUSBANDS AND WIVES

Inside the house, the wife's apartment was separated by a wall from that of her husband, and the communicating door was always locked. Husband and wife did not go to each other's apartment freely. According to the ritual books of etiquette which governed Chinese daily life, the slightest feminine impertinence was sufficient to warrant a request for divorce.

Before the republic was founded in 1912, as has been noted, the husband had full authority. He divided his attention between the women of his household. These usually were the first wife, secondary wives (concubines) and his mother.

THE FIRST WIFE

Children who were deprived of their mother through death or divorce were entrusted to a stepmother. The first wife in a household had to regulate the relations between the concubines and the husband. When one of the concubines had a son, the first wife also received some of the credit and enjoyed added prestige. There is a play called *The Third Concubine and her Adopted Son*, which praises the third concubine of a merchant, Hsueh Kuang, because she educated the children of the first wife, and was the only one to remain faithful after the death of the merchant, when the other wives took to a life of pleasure.

WARRING WIVES

A house in which there were several concubines was often the scene of quarrels, complaints, petty jealousies and spite, and there were continual

A Chinese boy reads to a group of younger children.

feuds. A modern novel, *Rickshaw Boy*, by Lao She, depicts the turbulent life of an official whose two wives do not get along together, and argue and contradict each other in front of the servants. But some students of Chinese society have said that concubinage contributed toward the solidarity of family life by preventing the husband from being bored, and ensuring that there would be children.

The marriage law passed on May 1, 1950, which is now in force, forbids concubinage, bigamy, childhood engagements and the killing of newborn babies and gives married women, like men, freedom in the choice of a job outside the home.

FILIAL PIETY AND THE EMPEROR

The strongest of the traditional influences on family life was, as has been noted, that of filial piety, and this concept constituted a serious obstacle to reform, since it applied not only to reverence for parents and ancestors, but also to many other relationships. It affected relationships between inferior and superior, and between the citizen and the state.

Confucius (551-479 B.C.) the most influential Chinese philosopher, formulated and preached these obligations as the primary social principles and raised them to the status of an official cult. According to his teaching, these were obligations which every Chinese should follow.

Duties toward parents were many and included serving them, honoring them when alive, burying them after death and preserving their memories by prescribed sacrifices. During their lifetime, one should refrain from causing them sorrow, esteem and be warm and affectionate toward them. Duties toward descendants consisted in the obligation to produce children, so that customs would be handed down and the family name be known to future generations.

This was laudable enough, but when the duties of filial piety were extended to the emperor the way was opened to state corruption. Veneration of the emperor was an expanded reflection of the veneration the individual gave his parents, since the sovereign was considered the father *and* mother of the people.

All his representatives therefore, were symbols of his power.

A book entitled *The Canon of Filial Piety*, written by Tsenz-tzu (3rd Century B.C.), a disciple of Confucius, states: "In our general behavior, not to be orderly is to lack filial piety; in service to our sovereign, not to be faithful is to lack filial piety; in the execution of the duties of a magistrate, not to be attentive is to lack filial piety; in wars and in battle, not to be courageous is to lack filial piety. These duties are all part of being a pious son."

This preaching was partly responsible for certain defects in Chinese society, such as a general apathy, a rigid traditionalism which ignored all attempts at reform.

INFANTICIDE

The Chinese practiced the custom of destroying children whom they could not afford to keep. This was widespread in ancient times when new-born babies, male or female (but particularly female), were likely to cause financial difficulties in poor families. Many regions had few men and numerous women, so that in some cases a daughter could not escape a degrading life if her family was not in a position to support her. Abandoning her was a solution to these problems.

Another factor contributing to the practice of infanticide was superstition. For example, if a birth was difficult and the new-born baby had endangered the life of the mother, it was feared that the anger of the powers of darkness had been aroused.

Deformed babies were killed, in the belief that the deformity brought with it an evil spirit hostile to the family. The fact that new-born babies could so readily be put to death is explained by the concept of the child as the property of the father and therefore completely at his disposal.

Evil spirits were placated by burying a baby in the foundations of a new house. If a disaster occurred, such as a river bursting its banks and flooding a village, new-born babies often were not saved but were left to die among the ruins.

Infanticide was very widely practiced in south China, especially in the districts of Canton, Amoy,

Hsinghwa, Tsungming and Hang-chow, and in the province of Hunan. Parents used various ways of getting rid of unwanted children, such as suffocation, or abandonment to wild beasts or just leaving them in the city streets. This custom was not practiced by the rich, who tried to persuade the poor to take a more humane attitude. But their financial help, often given most generously, combined with other philanthropic actions, such as institutions for abandoned infants provided by Buddhist nuns, could not totally allay this evil which persisted until after the establishment of the republic in 1912.

In an effort to abolish this attitude, a text book used in Chinese schools contained the following passage, "The child is not the 'creature' of his parents, and those who believe so are wrong. It is therefore forbidden to throw new-born babies into water, and to abandon them in the streets. The child, although born to the parents, is a member of society and a citizen of the state."

The new republican spirit, to a great extent, weakened such inhuman customs. By insisting on rights for women and freedom in marriage, it practically destroyed the traditional concepts. But the process is slow, especially in country districts. The population seems to be compliant but many peasants are opposed to change.

The Family in Modern China

Life in China, today, has changed a great deal. Toward the end of the 19th century important intellectual movements started among students and professors in the universities and among writers and politicians.

These formed a basis for the long struggle against established concepts, paving the way for a more modern type of society. The most militant and popular ideas were those expressed in a progressive Peking review, *New Youth*, which attacked the basic concepts of traditional Chinese society.

The reformers considered the traditional view of the family incompatible with freedom. They were against a system in which the husband was honored as a dictator while wives were regarded as slaves and the children absolutely bound by too many rules. The idea grew, based on contemporary Western thought, that marriage should be founded on mutual love and respect. Women should be emancipated, and no longer tied by tradition to domestic occupations.

ABOLITION OF FAMILY UNIT

Children born in a marriage based on love and mutual respect should be brought up with affection. They should be taught the elements of hygiene and intelligently prepared for life in the world. The concept of the family as a complete, self-contained unit should be abolished and replaced by the concept of national unity.

The legislation of the Chinese Republic was profoundly influenced by these ideas, and in 1926, at the Kuomintang Congress, progressive groups decided to enroll women in their campaign for social reforms.

Criticism of the ancient concept of the family can be summed up in the views of a scholar, K'ang-Yu-wei, who headed the reformist movement during the late 19th century and influenced the opinions of *New Youth*. "Filial piety as we know it," wrote the philosopher, "is not a natural phenomenom. Birds and animals care for their young but do not expect a reward; love does not ask to be repaid." He continued that an obligation of mutual assistance between members of a familiy was a habit peculiar to man.

The patriarchal system, he thought, was reactionary and was an obstacle to national liberation. Under this

The new laws passed by the Communist regime regarding such aspects of social life as women's emancipation and marriage have not done away with the Chinese tradition of family affection, as may be seen in this illustration of a young couple with their child. One of the most important statutes affecting family life was the Marriage Law of 1950 which, among other provisions, banned the arrangement of marriages by parents or matchmakers, the exaction of dowries, bigamy, concubinage, child betrothal and interference with the remarriage of widows. It also provided for the equal social and financial status of husband and wife and made provision for illegitimate children, step-children and the offspring of divorced couples.

A woman transplanting rice in the fields of Yunnan. Rice is the leading summer crop of the region, together with other cereals, while oilseeds and opium are harvested in winter. Women now take their place beside men in agriculture.

system, at its best, a man looked after his own children but neglected his fellow countrymen, working solely in the interest of maintaining a united family.

WESTERN INFLUENCES

Other sociologists accused the traditional family system of making citizens too docile and conformist, lacking the initiative to institute social reforms. Western propaganda contributed toward the struggle against the more inhuman traditional aspects of Chinese society. The Western influence was spread by novels, stories and philosophical, sociological and political writings. Among the most influential Western authors were John Stuart Mill, Anatole France, Macaulay, John Dewey, George Bernard Shaw, Dickens and Ibsen. The concepts of Marxism reinforced the reformers' views of the family, but in practice gave the Communist Party the father's place as sole authority.

A new Civil Code was formulated in 1931, after years of study of the problem, which attempted to reorganize the family system.

NEW FAMILY CODE

This code, though respecting some Chinese family traditions, was strongly influenced by Western ideas.

Husbands must earn the respect of their families, and could not demand it as their right. Women were permitted to choose their own husbands, the laws regarding heredity conferred equal rights on sons and daughters, and the law protected the private property of the married woman. The widow's livelihood was assured in cases when the children inherit.

Concubinage lost its semi-legal status. Both partners had equal rights to divorce.

The legal position of children was improved by the new code: fathers could no longer kill them with impunity, and if the parents abused their authority they were restrained by Family Councils. Boys might leave their parents on attaining their majority and they had rights of ownership from an early age.

CHOOSING ONE'S OWN PARTNER

Marriages in modern China, except in backward country areas, are no longer arranged by the families of the bride and groom. Young people, factory workers and students, meet freely at their work, and choose their own partners.

Certain specifically European customs have been adopted, for example, the publication of announcements of marriages in the newspapers.

DINNER AND FESTIVE DRESS

Until a few years ago wedding ceremonies were similar to those of ancient times, but in big cities customs are now less elaborate. A young couple may invite their friends to dinner and, at the end of the party, announce themselves man and wife. According to the new law, public declaration constitutes a legal marriage. There is no excessive formality about the ceremony, apart from the wearing of festive dress by the young couple.

The status of illegitimate children has been changed and provision is made for their support.

Children still feel obliged to support their parents: but there is no longer an obligation to support more distant relatives.

The laws of the new code indicated social progress, but it must not be thought that the country had changed completely.

Peasants in Hupeh, central China, with a water buffalo, the most common draft animal of the area. Hupeh consists mainly of a well-watered alluvial plain favorable to agriculture. The main crops of the area are rice, cereals and cotton.

In 1935, a French author, Jean Escarra, wrote: "These laws are not suitable for present conditions, except with reference to certain families living in large cities open to international commerce. In the interior, the majority of the peasants are unaware of these laws and will continue to be so for a long time yet."

WOMEN AND CHILDREN BENEFIT

In the People's Republic of China, in 1950, the government issued new laws concerning the familiy.

A decree published by the first session of the Central Educational Committee of the republic stated: "In feudal times the family was a barbaric and inhuman institution. Women were oppressed and children neglected. But the new society acknowledges equality between men and women, while the status of children is given new importance."

The general view of past customs, as expressed, is propagandist in the Marxist way. But there is no doubt that conditions for women and children are improved by new ways.

Marriages have now to be registered in the records of the local administrative unit. The new code adheres to the traditional prohibition of marriages between relatives up to the fifth degree of relationship. Divorce can be obtained by mutual consent, as before, or at the request of only one of the parties, but this, too, must be registered with the local administration.

Divorced women and their chil-

The offices of the Ministry of Construction in Peking. All the major organs of state power are centered in Peking, including the National People's Congress, which is responsible for the election of the Chairman of the Chinese People's Republic, the President of the Supreme People's Court and other major officials.

dren are protected by the law, women having the right to keep the children, while the husband is bound to provide for them. He must also provide for his divorced wife until she remarries, but two-thirds of his income is the maximum amount he can be made to pay. This is paid either in a lump sum or in installments.

THE EMPEROR

THE EMPEROR WAS KNOWN AS THE *Son of Heaven;* it was believed that his rule was sanctioned by Heaven. Heaven was supposed to be his father, his mother being the Earth.

His palaces had such names as *Palace of the Court, Hall of Gold, Court of Cinnabar, Forbidden Palace,* and *Celestial Court.*

An emperor's person was sacred and inviolable. In practice, his power was absolute, although philosophers ruled that this should not always be the case. In the *Book of Annals,* a compendium of Chinese wisdom, it is written: "The mandate of Heaven which grants sovereignty to one man does not give it him forever: it is obtained by maintaining justice and the rule of good, but it is lost if injustice and evil are practiced."

Another philosopher commented as follows: "The prince's fortune depends on Heaven, and the will of Heaven resides in the people: if the prince obtains the affection and love of the people, the Almighty One will look on him with favor and will safeguard his throne, but if he loses the affection of his people He will be wrathful and the kingdom will be taken away from him."

THE EMPEROR'S FAMILY

Confucius explained the meaning of "father and mother" when talking of the emperor: "Whatever the people love must be loved; whatever the people hate must be hated: this is what being the father and mother of the people means."

The emperor bequeathed his fortune to his first-born, but chose his successor as emperor from the most suitable of his sons. The emperor's relations belonged to a privileged class exempt from most laws; and they came under the jurisdiction of a minister of the Imperial Household. They were divided into two groups: the Imperial House, which

The façade of the modern building which houses the Polytechnic Institute of Shanghai. The city is situated on the Whangpoo River some 50 miles from the southeast coast of China and is one of the country's most important commercial and cultural centers. It is the seat of a university and technical institutes .

consisted of the closer relations; and the *Tribe of Gold*, which included all, even the most distant, relations of the emperor.

THE TRIBE OF GOLD

The special minister in charge of the emperor's household kept records of the *Tribe of Gold;* he registered all births of children of royal blood and adoptions; these had to be proclaimed in public. He registered marriages, deaths, promotions, and demotions, as well as honors conferred on the emperor's family, and every ten years his records were engraved on marble. The register dealing with the next-of-kin was known as the Yellow Register, while the one listing the emperor's collateral family was called the Red Register.

The emperor's relatives held titles similar to those held by European royalty, such as prince, duke, high marshal, marshal, etc. Princes did not receive their titles at birth, as in Europe, but at an age when they were considered capable of understanding the duties of their offices.

IMPERIAL CRIMINALS

All these relatives were supervised by a special minister, who acted as judge if they committed offences. If the misdemeanor was serious, the minister had power to order imprisonment and to remove the culprit from office, but extremely grave crimes had to be dealt with by the emperor himself. Privilege gave way

before guilt, at least in theory, provided the emperor was fair-minded; the guilty party might then be stripped of every badge of office, including membership in the mandarin class.

Members of the royal family close to the emperor wore yellow or gold sashes, while others wore red. All received annual allowances of silver and rice from the public treasury, though if grave offence had been committed these allowances were reduced to subsistence level.

Titles conferred on women were of two kinds: in the first class was the title of princess, given to the emperor's daughters; the second class, comprising five titles, was bestowed on daughters of high officials of the imperial family and of the emperor's more distant relatives.

PALACES AND COURTIERS

The emperors of old were magnificent sovereigns, living lives of dazzling luxury at their colorful courts.

Those of the Han dynasty (202 B.C.- 220 A.D.) lived in northern China with their capital at either Loyang or Nanking. Their palace was big enough to house ten thousand people, among them many extravagantly dressed girls, astrologers, divines and soothsayers.

SHEEP-DRAWN CARRIAGES

An emperor's staff included a troop of beautiful women who rode

at his side like a royal cavalry. Another group of women entertained him at table, playing musical instruments. A member of the previous Ch'in dynasty (221 -206 B.C.) had troops of women soldiers, but preferred sheep to horses; he liked to drive about his vast gardens with his womenfolk, in carriages drawn by sheep.

This emperor, Hui-ti (210-207 B.C.), had an ambitious "second empress," who persuaded him to expel the first empress, poison her son, and all who opposed her aspirations.

One of the Ming emperors had thirteen princes of the royal family put to death as part of his name-day celebrations.

Emperor Chung Tsung, a member of the T'ang dynasty (618-907 A.D.), amused himself by pretending that his courtiers were shopkeepers. He made them open shops, and then, followed by his friends, went round his "market" buying, haggling, and exchanging insults.

ONE HUNDRED AND TEN SOLDIERS

The imperial way of life was luxurious, as we have seen. A traveler who attended a sumptuous reception given in honor of Dutch and Tatar emissaries in 1656, tells, in his description of the imperial court at Peking, how the throne room, more than one hundred paces in circumference, was lined by guards dressed

A Chinese family wearing garments made from heavily padded layers of cotton. Clothes of this type are typical of the colder regions of China.

in cloaks of crimson satin. The throne itself was flanked by 110 soldiers, each carrying an ensign of the same color as his cloak, and all wearing black hats with yellow plumes.

Beside the throne stood twenty-two officers, carrying rich yellow shields, or "suns"; behind them stood ten more, carrying gilded shields of the same shape, and finally six other officials carrying shields resembling "full moons." Behind the officers stood sixteen guards armed with half-pikes or spears covered with silken ribbons of different colors. They were followed by thirty-six more guards, each bearing a banner decorated with a dragon or other beast.

Surrounding these soldiers were richly adorned courtiers, dressed in silk cloth of identical color and cut; this uniform gave an impressive effect to the scene. In front of the steps leading to the throne were six white horses with richly decorated saddlecloths and bridles adorned with pearls, rubies and other precious stones.

THE THRONE

The throne, raised above floor level, was covered with sable skins on which the emperor sat cross-legged. It was reached by two flights of six steps adorned with ivory. The floor and walls of the hall were hung with tapestries and pictures. Ministers, kings, vassals and princes were all prostrate before the throne,

A decorated shopfront in the old quarter of Shanghai. Most shops and indeed all commercial enterprises are now run either by the state or by workers' cooperatives, though it is believed that a number of illegal private businesses are still in existence, especially in Shanghai. The city formerly had an evil reputation for organized vice and lawlessness, but the Communist regime claims to have stamped out these abuses completely. In the last few years, night-clubs have been closed, the race-track and dog-racing stadium have been converted into a recreation park and museum, and thousands of criminals of all kinds have been sent to state reformatories.

their faces touching the ground. There was music, and bells were rung. The throne, the kings and princes all glittered with precious stones, gold-embroidered cloth, and blue satin costumes decorated with dragons and serpents.

This was of course an official audience designed to impress foreign visitors, but court life, even in day-to-day affairs, was magnificent. In early times the emperor wore yellow, a color reserved for him and his highest dignitaries. His litter was borne by from eight to thirty-six men, compared with a maximum of eight bearers for higher mandarins and four for lower mandarins. The sunshade was a symbol of the emperor's rank, being yellow in color and made of silk.

THE EMPEROR'S SINS

The emperor's costume was magnificent. Pearls were used as buttons; there were jewel-encrusted dragon motifs on his silks; the simplest of his necklaces consisted of more than a hundred pearls, intermingled with rubies, lapis lazuli, and yellow amber; his sashes were ringed in gold and studded with rubies, sapphires, and pearls.

An act of antonement made by an emperor who wished to publicly confess his sins and reconstruct his empire on different lines gives a general picture of the excesses of imperial life.

Such an emperor might be atoning for having built palaces of excessive magnificence, and incurring other pointless building expenses, or having loved too many women, having eaten too much, or having enjoyed too much the flattery of courtiers.

THE EMPEROR'S WIVES

One emperor, Liu An, who died in 122 B.C., forbade his ministers to discuss affairs of state with him, so as to leave him free for pleasure.

More recently, during the Ch'ing dynasty (1644-1912), the emperor's life was hedged about by many rules of protocol, which, though irksome, gave him a quasi-divine position. He could not touch the ground, for instance, and had to travel by litter or on horseback; the road before him was sprinkled with specially cleaned yellow sand. Even at the end of the 19th century, the emperor had so many wives that their exact number was unknown. They were divided into various grades. The empress belonged to the first grade,

Two men play checkers in a public park while a third looks on. Contemplative games such as this, together with chess, dominoes and cards, have always been very popular in China. The present regime, however, encourages creative, communal recreation as part of its political program. Workers are organized into groups for meetings, discussions and sessions of mutual criticism.

there were nine wives in the second grade, twenty-seven in the third, and finally a fourth grade made up of concubines.

Every three years, the emperor chose concubines from among the twelve- to sixteen-year-old daughters of his officials. It was possible for a woman to rise from the lowest rank and eventually become empress and there was much competition for this position. Wives were waited on by eunuchs who were extremely influential in politics as a result of their power over women in the harem. Any daughters born to these women were taken away, and good marriages arranged for them. The emperor chose his heir from among his sons.

THE EUNUCHS

Chinese history is full of popular revolts and court conspiracies inspired by eunuchs, who first were harem guards, then rose to high public office.

Their history is one of intrigue and cruelty. The tradition of entrust-

ing women and domestic duties to eunuchs dates from the Chou dynasty. The many eunuchs available for such tasks were provided by the Five Punishments set out by law, one of which was castration. The emperors, requiring manpower for building palaces, tombs and monuments, conscripted castrated convicts to work for them.

THE EMPEROR'S WAY WITH CRITICS

During the Han dynasty (202 B.C.-220 A.D.), the eunuchs' power and authority grew until they almost completely controlled the country. The office of magristates could be bought and sold; the Tao-tze sect, which eunuchs then controlled, became excessively powerful and disorder increased. Scholars did not hide their displeasure, and left the court. In the 2nd century A.D. one, Li Ying, led a critical faction which asked the emperor to abolish the eunuchs' privileges and reduce the size of the harem—the emperor had almost 1000 women. The emperor replied by halving the size of his

A pleasure boat at Hangchow, the capital of the province of Chekiang. Hangchow, a commercial and cultural center, is situated in picturesque surroundings at the southern terminus of the Grand Canal on the shores of West Lake. It is surrounded by high, wooded hills on which there are a number of monasteries and shrines dating from as early as the 10th century. Rivers and canals have always played an important part in Chinese life, and there is still a considerable boat-dwelling population.

harem. He also had Li Ying and his faction executed.

THE EMPEROR, THE EUNUCHS AND THE YELLOW TURBANS

The next emperor, whose name was Ling-Ti, also favored eunuchs. So great was the discontent he created in the provinces, that the *Yellow Turbans,* small rebel bands of peasants (for whom yellow symbolized the earth) led by three brothers called Chang, made prolonged attacks against the Imperial Army, beginning in 184 A.D. Imperial troops finally destroyed them.

The Han dynasty was nearing its end, and there were more conspiracies and attempts to overthrow the eunuchs. But during the reign of Wen-Tsung (809-840 A.D.) the eunuchs were victorious and had their enemies put to death; during the T'ang dynasty they were still in a powerful position and continued triumphant under the Ming dynasty (1368-1644 A.D.), which could not curb them. Emperor Cheng-Tsu (early 15th century) deliberately raised them to greater glory and restored all privileges that his predecessors had attempted to curtail. The political importance of the eunuchs was not so much due to their ability as politicians as to their flair for intrigue.

Under the Manchus their power declined but it had a brief resurgence when the Dowager Empress Tzu-hsi controlled the government. In 1912 eunuchs disappeared with the establishment of republican China.

EDUCATION

IN THE PAST, CHINESE CHILDREN in the family circle were taught by the wife, the boys until they were seven, and the girls until marriage.

Girls did not receive academic education; only girls of the upper classes received even a minimal schooling. It was considered enough that they should know how to behave with modesty, to submit to their husbands, and to practice the arts of embroidery, music and painting. Active qualities were discouraged.

While education of young children was entrusted to the wife, it was supervised by the father. The law conferred great authority on him, and he was responsible for crimes committed by his sons.

At the age of seven, boys were separated from their sisters. From this age, boys were instructed in literature, and taught to read and write. At ten, they went to school; from thirteen to fifteen they were taught the arts, particularly music and physical exercises and archery.

At twenty they should have earned the equivalent of college graduation and the right to wear silk clothes, furs and other finery. Until the age of twenty, even a rich young man wore only cotton clothes, as an inducement to humility.

In wealthy families tutors educated the sons. They were respected by their pupils and held in great esteem. Some of them occupied public positions, and they were well paid.

The emperors were patrons of the arts, but no state schools were founded.

Examination Systems

After this initial period of instruction, there were several further stages of education. A system of examination was established during the reigns of the T'ang and Northern Sung dynasties (618-1126 A.D.), and it continued until the fall of the Manchu dynasty in 1912. The degrees were, *hsiu-ts'ai* (the equivalent of a Bachelor of Arts degree), *chu-jen* (equivalent to an M.A.) and *chin-shih* (Doctor of Literature). Scholars who obtained the *hsiu-ts'ai* had to be re-examined every three years in order to keep the degree.

The career of a scholar with a *chin-shih* degree continued until eventually the dignity of membership in the Han-lin Academy was reached. The Han-lin Academy was founded in 754 and it was based on Confucian precepts. It had charge of all the royal literary work and the composition of state documents. Members of the Han-lin Academy and holders of lesser degrees were offered important positions in the civil service. Wealth and status were assured to them. In theory, the system of literary examinations was democratic, because all, except slaves, could enter. In practice, however, only those who could afford a private education were able to compete.

Power of the Mandarins

The system of examinations was essential for those who wished to enter the civil service. If they succeeded they became mandarins. As such, they were divided into two classes: mandarins of letters and mandarins of arms. They limited the power of the emperor, because they could intervene in his councils, almost without fear of suppression.

The mandarins of letters filled the positions of city governors, magistrates, and police chiefs.

Mandarins were graded in nine

categories. They were treated with great respect by the people. If they were judges, the ordinary people knelt before them and they always appeared in public on decorated litters each borne by four men, followed by a magnificent escort, and flanked by officials. A servant carried a parasol to shade the mandarin from the sun. Another went ahead to warn of his master's approach by striking a copper bowl; a crowd would always gather, bowing low.

SPECIAL MANDARINS

The most learned scholars belonged to a special tribunal, the Tribunal of History. This tribunal elected mandarins to the highest grade, and recorded the history of the empire. Another of its duties

was to supervise the education of the heir to the throne.

The grades of mandarins were distinguished by the kind of button worn on the headdress.

Mandarins were enjoined to strict impartiality. One of their rules was: "Even where a man of virtue and ability has been your enemy he should be promoted; if a man of blemished reputation has been your friend, he should be discarded."

These precepts were not always followed, and at times there were many corrupt mandarins. On the other hand, Chinese society enabled

talented individuals of humble origin to gain top positions in government by study and application.

In some cases death caused bereaved officials to resign their posts. A mandarin would resign on the death of his father, mother, or paternal grand-parents, when mourning had to be observed for a period of three years. To conceal or deny such deaths in public in order to retain one's position was a crime.

GUILTY MANDARINS

Mandarins were allowed to retire when their parents reached the age

A view of modern administrative buildings in Peking. Formal, functional buildings of this kind, much influenced by Russian official architecture, have arisen in Peking beside the splendid palaces of the former imperial court. The demands of economy have led to the development of an austere, drab style. Recently, experiments have been made with multi-colored, tiled buildings based on traditional designs, but these have been criticized on ideological grounds as representing a return to opulent decadence out of keeping with the policies of the government.

of seventy, and they could not be forced to remain in office. They were not permitted to marry into families of the lower classes.

A list of imperial mandarins was published every four years, bringing up to date civil service postings.

The rules mentioned give only the broadest outlines of mandarin protocol; each grade had its own detailed rules. One important regulation was that any mandarin found guilty of treason, pillage or extortion was disgraced and his badges of office were removed; these penalties also involved his descendants.

MANDARINS OF WAR

For a career in the armed forces, examinations were unnecessary; instead, the aspirants to a military career practiced horsemanship and exercized physically. They eventually became mandarins of arms. Although mandarins of arms controlled military affairs, a grade of mandarins of letters was entrusted with the inspection of troops.

Mandarins of arms, as has been noted, were not academics, but men who had gained their position by showing courage and skill in battle. They had laws and tribunals of their own, of which the most important of the latter was at Peking. They were divided into categories such as mandarins of the rear guard, mandarins of the right wing, mandarins of the battle corps, and mandarins of the vanguard. These offices entailed wide powers over the armies. The war mandarins were subject to a supreme war tribunal.

The emperor was careful not to give them too much power, and instituted a new grade of mandarin of letters, the Superintendent of Arms. This official was supervised by two other inspectors; all three were subject to a higher court.

There exists a detailed description by William Alexander of a military mandarin who accompanied a British delegation to Canton. Alexander writes:

"In reward for services rendered in the wars in Tibet, he wore a peacock's feather in his hat as a special sign of his sovereign's favor, besides a ball of red coral to mark his standing. He wore the normal dress of his office, that is, a short but wide coat of fine cotton, and over it another coat, embroidered in silk. From his belt there hung his handkerchief, knife, chopsticks in a case, and several tobacco pouches. His thumbs were adorned with two large agate rings, which he used to draw his bow. The tips of the arrows that filled his quiver were of varied shape, some grooved, some diamond-shaped, etc. His boots were of satin, with thick paper soles, the normal footwear of mandarins and Chinese of quality."

Women's Education

Women's education was limited to a few indoor occupations and no place was given to developing individual initiative. There have, however, been exceptions. One was Pan Chao (50-112 A.D.), sister of a historian, Pan Ku. She was married at the age of fourteen to a mandarin, Tsao Shou; when he died she went to live with her brother and collaborated with him on a work commissioned by the emperor.

Pan Ku allowed his sister a free hand and did not hesitate to praise her publicly. When he died, Pan Chao completed his work, eventually becoming the empress' teacher.

THE PERFECT WOMAN

Pan Chao wrote a book, *Lessons for Women* (106 A.D.), which gives a clear idea of the relationship between husband and wife. "We occupy the lowest position in the human race," she wrote, "we are the weak part of mankind, and to us belong and must belong the least important tasks: this truth must penetrate our beings so that it influences all our behavior and becomes the fount of our happiness."

Views of this kind show that Pan Chao did not advocate the emancipation of women, but accepted with humility their state of weakness and subjection. She wrote: "In old times, when a baby girl was born, it was three days before anyone took any notice of her; she was left lying on the ground on some old rag, near the mother. It was only on the third

Lamas in a Tibetan monastery sit cross-legged to recite the sacred scriptures. Lamaism evolved from a late Indian form of Buddhism introduced into Tibet and Mongolia by Padmasambhava, an Indian Tantric scholar, in the 8th century A.D. The teachings of Padmasambhava were combined with the indigenous Shamanishi faith. A rather incongruous note is struck in this illustration by what appears to be a portrait of Mao Tse-tung in the left background.

day that anyone thought about the newborn babe."

Pan Chao went on to advise married women: they should respect their husbands if they wished to be respected; they should discipline their faults and should cultivate virtue, and gentleness in speech, person and deeds.

WIVES AND BUTTERFLIES

To sum up the views of Pan Chao: "If a woman has married according to her wishes, it should be for life. If she has married against her wishes, it should be for life." It is not surprising that this writer was successful in a society dominated by men. In short, Pan Chao confirmed through her maxims the lowly position of women.

Among the occupations Chinese ladies were encouraged to follow was that of painting. A favorite subject for their painting was butterflies, which in China are particularly beautiful. The ladies used to keep caterpillars in large boxes, in two layers, until they became chrysalises. When the butterfly emerged from the chrysalis, it was set free in a greenhouse filled with flowers. Ladies then had their models within easy view.

Education under the Communists

Today, in China, education is essentially Marxist in its aims and objectives. The government department which administers schools policy is controlled by the commissars in charge of Communist Party propaganda. Mao Tse-tung has stated that the objective of education is to make "a socialist minded worker."

Between 1953 and 1957 the Chinese government claims that the number of students in all types of schools increased from 54,000,000 to 71,000,000.

At present the figure given is 100,000,000, which includes 1,470,000 in universities and technical colleges.

Technical education is closely linked with production; professors and students run their own manufacturing plants; those who are preparing for a career in agriculture run their own farms.

Progressive indoctrination in Marxist philosophy is carried on in all levels of schooling and the twin principles which guide the whole system are Marxism and technical efficiency.

In short, the Chinese Communist school aims at replacing the old type of academic mandarin with an en-

Lamas in the monastery of Yuan-chao in the Wutai Shan mountains, northeast Shansi province, seated in a circle for a discussion. The Wutai Shan range, which rises to a height of 9974 feet, is sacred to the Mongols and the mountains are the site of a number of monasteries which are centers of pilgrimage.

tirely new kind of educated Chinese, a Marxist technocrat who will contribute, not to his own family, but to the commune, which is the new unit in the vast machine which the Communists envisage as the Chinese republic of the future.

THE LAW

UNDER THE EMPIRE THE RIGHTS OF the citizen were safeguarded by a complex but cautious legal system.

The death sentence had to be approved by the Supreme Court. Other courts, including the criminal courts, Courts of the Imperial Censors, Courts of Appeal, Courts of the three judicial powers, and the High Tribunal protected the law and the rights of criminals; these checked the functioning in lower courts, and made certain that sentences were properly carried out. There were occasions when, despite these pre-

cautions, the work of the courts was hampered by corruption, but in general Chinese legal institutions represented strong methods of keeping the peace.

Punishments

Sentences were always severe, and often cruel. During the Ch'in dynasty punishment was ferocious, but under the following Han dynasty penalties were more moderate. A further relaxation took place under the Wei and Tsin, but during the Sui and T'ang dynasties laws again grew savage.

The Chinese legal code listed ten capital offences: civil revolt, desertion of one's native land, killing one's father, murder of a family or of several members of the same family, sacrilege, lack of filial piety, family discord, civil insubordination, assassination and incest.

According to tradition, under the Yu, the earliest Chinese dynasty, which reigned some time before 2000 B.C., there were five established punishments: branding on the forehead, amputation of the nose, amputation of the legs at the knees or of the kneecap itself, castration and death.

These major penalties could be commuted to exile; beating and fines were normal penalties for minor crimes.

The five punishments were carried out in country market places, or at the imperial court. The emperor himself was in theory subject to the same laws as his subjects.

In later times, punishment was extended to descendants of criminals, though this was later repealed.

Other major penalties were laid down in 1039 B.C. by Emperor Chao Wang; these form part of the Chou constitution, which influenced the judicial system until 1911.

These included whipping, slavery with forced labor, branding on the forehead, shaving of the head and compulsory service as porter or watchman, cutting off the nose or feet and castration for service as a eunuch in the imperial palace. Criminals were executed by beheading or quartering, or sometimes by being torn apart by horses or chariots. Bodies of executed criminals were exposed in public for three days as a warning to the people.

Mitigation was allowed to those who killed the murderer of a father or brother, and for those who slew brigands who attacked villages. Children under seven and old people over ninety were exempted from punishment, while women were exempt from branding on the forehead and amputation of the feet.

In 912 B.C. the five punishments were still enforced, but in cases where there was doubt these were remitted. A system of paying fines was instituted, which lasted until the end of Ch'ing dynasty in 1912.

A HEADLESS GHOST

From 746 B.C. onward, brothers, wife, sons and parents of the accused were sentenced with him. In 361 B.C. it was ordained that anyone reporting a criminal should be rewarded, while anyone harboring him was sentenced to death and his goods confiscated. Idlers and vagabonds were sentenced to slavery. Ostentation was forbidden, unless it was justified by services to the state.

Strangulation and beheading were penalties for certain crimes. Strangulation was considered a mitigation of the death sentence. Beheading, on the other hand, mutilated the body. This was a disaster for the true believer, as he had to enter the next life a decapitated ghost.

In many parts of China there was a superstitious concept of life after death; it was thought of as a vague shadow-world in which life continued in almost the same way as on earth. A headless spirit would therefore suffer; having no mouth, he would be unable to eat; his body would be repugnant to women and he would not be able to see. Therefore, whenever possible, Chinese criminals would choose to be strangled rather than beheaded.

The belief that the body should enter the grave whole was one of the main obstacles to progress in surgery, because it prevented anatomical research. This belief was so strong that the family of a beheaded criminal would sew the corpse's head back onto the trunk before burial.

THE YOKE

The pillory or *cangue* was a square wooden yoke which rested on the shoulders, with a hole for the head. It weighed about twenty-five pounds, and had notices pasted to it giving the length of the sentence, and name of the criminal. Its purpose was to expose criminals to the ridicule and contempt of the public.

It was a form of torture, exhausting its wearer, who could neither sleep nor feed himself. Sometimes it was imposed for life, and usually caused the criminal's death.

BRANDING

Branding, as a punishment, originated in early times. Its purpose was similar to modern finger-printing in that it helped to identify criminals. Thieves were branded on the left forearm for a first offense; on both arms for a second offense; and if caught a third time, their punishment was strangulation. Different brand marks were used, depending on whether the crime had been committed against the govern-

A polychrome statue of the war god Kuan Yu, one of the many fearsome deities of the pantheon of the old Celestial Empire, in Loyang, northwest Honan. Loyang is the earliest recorded center of Chinese settlement, in 1900 B.C., and was the capital of the Chou dynasty (770-255 B.C.) and the Eastern Han dynasty (25-220 A.D.).

ment or against religion. Military deserters were branded on the face.

The section of the law dealing with branding was as follows: "All condemned thieves are, in ordinary cases, branded with characters designed to be a lesson to themselves and a warning to others. It is essential that marks remain unerased, both where permission is given to return home immediately after corporal punishment is given, and where permanent exile is decreed. If persons are found guilty of erasing marks to make them illegible, they shall be punished with sixty blows, and branded again with the same characters."

VENGEANCE BY SELF-SLAUGHTER

Suicide was common in China, the more popular methods being by swallowing opium, phosphorus or arsenic, which were preferred by men; a knotted cord round the neck or a plunge into a river were considered more dramatic, and were preferred by women.

The Chinese, who were anxious to be buried and honored with sacrifices as was their due, often saw suicide as an easy way of solving their personal problems and embarrassing those they disliked.

The law punished anyone who caused a suicide, directly or indirectly. For this reason, a Chinese eager for revenge would commit suicide outside, and sometimes inside, his adversary's home, knowing that the law would avenge him.

Although the law punished anyone who drove another to suicide, it was lenient toward a man who threatened suicide for noble motives.

In the ordinary course of events, anyone who threatened to hang or poison himself gained his objective. If a debtor was being pressed for money, he had only to warn his creditor that he was planning suicide for his debt to be extended on advantageous terms. A creditor knew that if he was accused of causing a suicide, he might have to pay a heavy fine and be reduced to poverty. Difficulties in presenting a defense, and the uncertainties of legal procedure, which was long and drawn out, made it ill-advised to embark on lawsuits of any kind.

There were many motives for suicide, some as a result of duty or obligation and others caused by threats, or through remorse for lack of filial piety. Suicide of disgraced officials was common.

UPPER-CLASS SUICIDE

Suicide out of a sense of duty was usually confined to people in high positions. When, for instance, a ruler or military leader died, or where an important problem could not be solved, suicides were common in official circles. In the feudal era a struggle for the succession among the sons of the dead emperor might be ended by the suicide of the legitimate heir, who, by taking his life, cut short a dispute centered round himself.

Suicide was committed when honor was at stake. If, for example, a minister was slandered in the presence of his sovereign, or if a supporter of one claimant to the throne found another elected, pride dictated that he should take his own life. Defeated soldiers, civil servants deprived of their posts and students failing in their examinations would often commit suicide.

BEATING

Under the Manchu legal code, the *bastinado*, a punishment in which the criminal was beaten on the soles of his feet with bamboo rods, was important. Beating to death was a punishment for parricide, high treason, and crimes of violence. Anybody could be beaten or executed, including high dignitaries.

The Manchu code, drawn up about the middle of the 18th century and based on laws already in existence, was considered "if not the most just and equable, at least the most intelligible, uniform and best suited to the mental standard of the people for whom it was made."

The Manchu code strengthened

A bronze statue of Confucius, the great Chinese philosopher who is traditionally supposed to have lived between 551 and 479 B.C. Many legends have sprung up concerning this great sage, whose Chinese name is Kung Fu-tzu and who is thought to have been a member of an impoverished aristocratic family. He dedicated his life to resolving the spiritual and mental troubles of his time and his teachings, less a religion than a moral and ethical system, were spread by his many devoted disciples.

A statue before a mural in the Tungyne temple at Sian. The mural dates from the 17th century, either at the end of the Ming period or the beginning of the Ch'ing period. Chinese artists, traditonally, have been very successful in their treatment of landscapes; it is possible that this may be due in part to the widespread teachings of Ch'an (Zen) Buddhism.

the principle of communal responsibility or "guilt by implication." This theory held a person responsible for the actions of others; it could establish a chain of guilt involving a whole family or village.

FOR THREE GENERATIONS

Within a family, the head of the household was responsible for crimes committed by other members, including slaves, servants, and adopted children; but if he was extremely aged (over eighty), or incapable through illness, his responsibility passed to his next of kin. When high treason had been committed, family responsibility spanned three generations, and included relations living in different households.

Closely connected with this was the theory of neighborly responsi-

bility. This theory stated that a neighbor who witnessed a crime committed next door was partly responsible. At an earlier period, the population was divided into groups made up of five families, and each group was encouraged to spy and inform on other groups. Villages and even towns were sometimes held responsible for crimes committed by their inhabitants. Whole cities were, under the practice of this theory, demolished and rebuilt. Implacable upholders of the law insisted that if a crime was constantly repeated in the same place, the whole town should be razed to the ground and rebuilt on another site. The principal aim of this code, therefore, was to spread criminal responsibility as widely as possible, exempting no social class, so that the people would take responsibility for discouraging crime.

The Rights of the Dead

An interesting feature of the legal code was the blood feud. For a long time, Chinese administered their own justice, especially in areas where imperial authority was ineffective

and family life was the mainstay of society. Long drawn-out feuds developed in many localities.

The main purpose of blood feuds was to pacify the soul of the slain, who would suffer eternally if the murderer were not brought to justice. This superstition, which involved the living with the imagined rights of the dead, may not be totally forgotten today.

According to it, for example, a drowning man should not be saved. It was believed that the spirit of a person drowned previously at that spot was attempting to drown the man, to gain possession of his spirit. To save the drowning man would be an act of hostility toward the dead, so he was left to drown. This superstition was so deep-rooted that tribunals in the main cities tried

for many years to eradicate it by promising rewards to anyone who saved a drowning man.

The Power of the Seal

Every Chinese had his own seal, which was used as a signature in legal agreements and documents. Seals were regarded as a means of identification and a mark of personal authority. The emperor, his concubines, officials and dignitaries had several seals, each used for a different purpose, such as ceremonial seals, seals for decrees, decorations and stamps. Private seals were generally worn in a little bag around the neck. But official seals for special occasions were placed under guard, and used only with suitable ceremonies of great solemnity.

Seals were of differing shape and size, and made of different materials, which included jade, gold, silver, jasper, copper and wood for officials. In shape, they were square or oblong, and had figures such as dragons, tigers, unicorns or tortoises

A detail of the architecture of the Summer Palace at Peking. Although the present structure is comparatively modern it remains an example of traditional Chinese architecture; for, until very recently, basic planning and constructional methods had remained unchanged for centuries. Traditional Chinese architectural form was based on religious and philosophical concepts, particularly on the belief that the proportions of a building should conform to the natural laws of proportion observed in nature. The most usual building material was timber.

engraved on them. On one side, they had Manchu characters, on the other Chinese characters. Private persons' seals were made of jade, quartz, wood, ivory, metal, horn or other substances.

THE EMPEROR'S SEAL

The emperor's seal was used to give authority and authenticity to his declarations. When ordering a religious procession he used a red seal. Except for those of officials, concubines (whose seals were always gold), empresses and princes, seals were passed from father to son, and were recast from time to time in a mint called *The Great Ministry of the Rites*. Special seals were made under the emperor's direct supervision.

THE BANDIT'S SEAL

Officials' seals of office were transmitted with the office. The ceremony in which an outgoing functionary handed over his seal to his successor was a complicated one; the seal was wrapped in red paper, the official signed his name on it, and shut it in a box covered with yellow paper, yellow being the imperial color. It was taken in an ornately decorated litter to the house of the newcomer, who, dressed in ceremonial garments, received it, inspected it and accompanied it back to the official residence where other ceremonies took place. Finally, the seal was printed on a large sheet of red paper, which was hung on the east door of the official residence.

Ceremonial visits were then made to the new offical, who sat on a throne and was addressed as "His Excellency." Every year all seals were locked up for a month, and similar ceremonies took place.

The seal was a necessity in official transactions, and in trade. Seals were used by priests, soldiers, and even by bandits, who on occasion drew up agreed ransoms and pledges, signing the papers with their personal stamp. Severe penalties were imposed on anyone losing an imperial or official seal, or using the wrong kind of seal. Counterfeiters of seals were condemned to death.

The Law and Authority

Chinese law gives a clear picture of traditional relationships governing the arts, crafts, and the people themselves.

A Chinese proverb states that man has three benefactors: father, em-

An image of the Buddha in the Pavilion of Heavenly Perfume, a part of the Summer Palace at Peking. The complex of buildings which make up the Summer Palace are situated in northwest Peking within the quarter known as the Forbidden City.

peror and master. The first gives him life, the second order and prosperity within society, while the third teaches him his living. Father, emperor and master thus enjoyed a legal position upheld with severity.

MASTER CRAFTSMEN AND SCHOOLTEACHERS

Masters of arts and crafts maintained a life-long connection with their pupils; even when the period of tuition was over, special laws governing their relationship retained their force.

Relations between schoolteachers and pupils were even closer, being considered on a par with the relationship between uncle and nephew. The relationship was protected in the same way as family ties, and persisted throughout life.

These laws did not prevent quarreling, fighting and murder among priests, both Buddhist and Taoist, scholars, disciples and pupils.

If, for example, a student of letters was killed by his master, the latter's punishment was one hundred strokes and three years' exile. If the criminal was a priest or a master craftsman, the punishment was strangulation "after the assizes." The sentence was the same for premeditated murder and for homicide where no motive could be established. Teachers of literature enjoyed greater leniency and greater prestige in the courts.

PUPILS AND SLAVES

A pupil who killed or injured a master of letters was sentenced as if he had killed or wounded an older relative. In the case of a Buddhist or Taoist novice or pupil who killed a priest, the penalty was the same as for a man who had murdered the head of his family.

If a slave assaulted or insulted a magistrate, his master would receive fifty strokes, because he was considered responsible for the actions of his slaves, who were his property.

WIVES AND CONCUBINES

In spite of the precepts laid down by Pan Chao, women were not always obedient and gentle, so that in Chinese law provision was made for crimes committed by women. A principal wife who killed her husband unintentionally, for instance impulsively in a quarrel, was strangled or beheaded. If the murder was premeditated, she would be slowly tortured to death. A second wife, if found guilty of wounding or killing her husband, would receive a similar sentence. A husband, however, would get off extremely lightly for killing his wife in a domestic quarrel, though in this case, the magistrate would find out whether blows has been struck with the flat or edge of the hand. If a husband merely hurt his wife by striking her with the edge of his hand, she could make a charge, and divorce was allowed, as the effect of such a blow might be lethal.

The Chinese family system often encouraged quarrels among the women, the first wife quarreling with the second, with other concubines, and each with the other's parents. There were further causes for dispute, caused by elaborate rules of precedence among the women of the household.

WAR AND THE ARMY

IN THE PAST, UNTIL EUROPEAN AND American traders, followed by military detachments, penetrated China, warfare in the country had much in common with the so-called ages of

The Jopao pagoda on Mt. Puto, Chekiang province, which is situated on an island of the Chusan Archipelago in the East China Sea. The island is sacred to the Buddhists and has many temples and monasteries. The Buddhist pagoda form is based on the Indian stupa, *and like its Indian counterpart it has symbolic significance as an architectural expression of the composition of the universe.*

chivalry in Europe. The war mandarins had much in common with European knights and condottieri: warfare to them was a way of life and, despite the appalling hardships it brought to the common people, a sport. The opposing generals had more in common with each other than they had with the men they led into battle. The rituals of Chinese chivalry were as romantic as those described in Sir Thomas Malory's *Morte d'Arthur* (1469-1470) and to the contemporary Western mind were quite as absurd. The blood sports of nobility of the period brought only tragedy and suffering to the poor, who were, however, inured to this way of life.

The Chinese Soldier

Military records tell us not only about the generals of the armies of the past but also about their men. Chinese soldiers were not trained in the same way as Western armies.

Their exercises were not "well regulated, but consisted of ragged marching"; they marched past, and re-formed in a confused and noisy fashion to the sound of horns and bugles. War mandarins in charge of troop inspection were often slipshod or inattentive in spite of their ability as strategists. Chinese soldiers in the past were less aggresive than their Mongol opponents.

ON THE ATTACK

Mongols were noted for their violent attacks, but in defense they lacked patience and stamina.

An emperor said: "The Mongols are good soldiers when fighting bad soldiers, but bad soldiers when against good troops." The best Chinese soldiers came from the northern provinces, and took their profession seriously. Others were grateful for their pay, but in spite of the fact that they were enrolled in the army for life, lived with their families. They did not put on their uniform unless the alarm was sounded, a revolt broke out, or a mandarin arrived for a parade.

Weapons and Iron Helmets

The sword was worn at the right with the point facing forward. It was drawn from the scabbard using the right hand from behind, though according to some travelers it hung on the left side and was drawn by passing the hand behind the back, a difficult movement if the enemy was at hand. Other weapons included bow, spear and, latterly, rifle and cannon.

Lamaist monks in a monastery at Yung-ho in the province of Shansi perform a traditional dance. Lamaism contains many superstitious and magical elements based on pre-Buddhist beliefs, and dances and rituals play an important part in its observances. The Communist regime does not profess militant atheism but in practice it pursues a policy of state control of religion.

Herdsmen with their cattle on a broad expanse of pasture land in the eastern border region of Inner Mongolia. Conditions in this area are favorable to stock rearing, an occupation in which most of the population are engaged. The region is famous for its small but hardy horses. It also has a wider variety of wild animals than any other part of China, among them tigers, wolves and many kinds of deer.

A polychrome figure of a demon in the temple of Kuan Yu at Loyang. Representations of evil spirits like this one are common in ancient temples. Loyang was the capital of the Chou dynasty and the Eastern Han dynasty but suffered a decline from the 13th century onward. Most Chinese sculptors of antiquity were, like the artists of pre-Renaissance Europe, anonymous craftsmen belonging to professional guilds.

Mongol horsemen wore iron helmets in the shape of inverted funnels. Officers had decorated helmets, gold, red or blue uniforms, and black boots. There were also crossbowmen, and troops known as "war tigers," and "terror squads;" indeed there was a certain similarity between these soldiers in their yellow uniforms striped in brown and real tigers. Their headdress, pulled down to cover the whole head, displayed a tiger's head with ears.

SCIMITARS, SHIELDS AND DRUMS

These troops were armed with scimitars and used tightly woven shields painted with awe-inspiring animals, including dragons. Chinese cavalrymen wore arm and thigh coverings decorated with dragons, mountains and flowers; crossbowmen, too, were armored.

Fusiliers carried pouches containing two kinds of powder of different strength. When their powder ran out they fought with battle-axes, as a system of refurbishing supplies had not been worked out.

Signals consisted of drum, trumpet, and a sonorous wooden wind instrument shaped like a fish, which, was placed in front of the commander-in-chief's tent. A horn, made from a shell, was used to sound the retreat; each unit possessed one of these.

HOOKS ON THEIR CHARIOT WHEELS

Armies of the feudal period were raised by the local warlord who armed his followers with swords and shields from his private armory. Levies were raised only in special circumstances. Armies were composed in the main of peasants, mercenaries and convicts, liberated for the purpose.

The officers were noblemen, whose chariots were drawn by four horses. Each of these chariots drew a large framework set on two wheels; this had hooks which were used to grapple the enemy, unseat him, and slay him as he lay on the ground.

Each chariot had a team of three men: a lancer, an archer and the helmsman, all sheltering behind large shields. Everything about the chariot denoted membership of a privileged class, from ivory decorations and paintings on the shields to precious ornamentation on the armor and horses' harnesses.

BLOODSHED BEFORE THE BATTLE

Battle was joined in a leisurely fashion. An army encamped around a hostile city, for instance, would await the right day, spying out the land, arranging with the enemy such details as a suitable date for their encounter. They occupied their time in taking oaths, listening to their generals' exhortations and attending prayers.

When fighting broke out, the two opposed camps usually knew whether they were involved in a war to the death, or whether the encounter was to be little more than a joust, where the object was to win great prestige. When the battle was against a real enemy, an invader, a threatening ruler, or a despised barbarian, cruelty was rife. Battle began with several of the best soldiers, selected from the ranks of freed convicts, cutting each others' throats with great cries, so that their souls should mingle with and terrify the enemy ranks.

Chinese Chivalry

Chariots then appeared, rapid sorties were made into enemy lines, and personal challenges, expressed with courtesy and regard for convention, were made and accepted. It was considered meritorious to spare a vanquished enemy's life on the battlefield, and admirable to expose oneself to danger or to fight bravely on behalf of one's superior officer.

A good soldier refused to retreat if the flag was unfurled. The main aim of the encounter was to bring the enemy into disrepute, and the battle itself was accompanied by insults, oaths and curses to prove a warrior's nobility, ambition and loyalty. The physical annihilation of the enemy was considered unnecessary; it was sufficient to demoralize him.

THE GENERAL'S DRUM

Victory belonged to the general whose personal honor was vindicated in the battle. The general took re-responsibility for the battle. His strength of character, his qualities, and his dedication to the conventions were of great importance. A defeated general was considered worthy of his command if after the battle he could say of himself: "They have overthrown me on the sheath of my bow, I have spat blood, but my drum never ceased beating."

The general was always close to his drum and banner (his command was revoked if the banner was destroyed), though it was hardly ever carried on to the field of battle itself.

WAR, A WAY OF LIFE

A victorious general would assume an air of modesty, and if the vanquished leader declared that he could not continue the struggle and offered a challenge for some time in the future, he would accept.

Peace was followed by the victor's triumphal march, but savage measures were not taken against the vanquished. This was because experience had taught the war lords that vassals of the winning side, enriched by their victory, might well form rival groups and attempt to gain supremacy over their lord. In such an emergency, a magnanimous victor might rely on the support of his former foes.

For the aristocrat, war was not a means of material aggrandizement —he distributed booty to his troops —but rather a way of confirming the loyalty and material ardor of his men. It was a game.

WAR BECOMES MORE SAVAGE

The great feudal rivalries of China led to the creation of countries within the country proper; these vast provinces gave rise to a flourishing interest and trade in war.

Thus ended the feudal period, in which military matters were dominated by what might be termed a "sporting" attitude to questions of war. Princes began to keep their spoils, including any land they conquered.

War became more savage; wars of conquest were carried on from province to province and the south fought against the north, and east against west. The purpose now was to destroy the enemy; the development of weapons made great progress, and military science was studied. Only strong men joined the army, and champions of physical prowess were specially trained for battle.

LAWS OF WAR

Older, more chivalrous feudal laws were discarded. War ceased to be a sport and became a business. This did not prevent philosophers from discussing the art of war, nor writers from composing works full of moral reflections and teachings on the subject, as far back as the 6th century. The best-known of all books on

A detail of the roof of a Chinese temple, decorated with intricately carved figures of dragons and supernatural beings. The traditional Chinese temple, of which roofs like the one in this illustration are an important feature, consists of three identical buildings on each of three sides of a courtyard which is entered through a gate on the fourth side. It is built on a framework of wooden columns and beams.

warfare was *Military Laws and Regulations,* which instructed warriors, and described how to begin a campaign. This book examined in detail the technical problems of an army, including supplies, exploitation of captive populations, ways of employing prisoners, of handling troops, methods of attack and engaging and disengaging the enemy, sieges and road blocks. They added moral reflections on victory, defeat and the ambitions of the officer class.

Here is an example of the type of moral maxim found in the work: "To wage war is generally speaking evil in itself. Necessity should be the only reason for doing so. Conflict, of whatever kind, is always disastrous, even for the victor. It should only be allowed to break out if no other solution is possible."

Gunpowder

The Chinese probably were the first people to invent gunpowder. The country was the source of early rumors of pipes burning with thunder and flame, fire spewed out at the enemy, ships encompassed by lightening and thunderbolts, flaming lances, and a host of mystifying details which can be explained only by the existence of muskets and cannon.

Whoever the inventor, gunpowder was known to Chinese before the 14th century, when it was first introduced into Europe.

The flaming lance of old imperial times can be described in some detail as it was still used in some areas only a few decades ago. A simple tube partly filled with powder,

An ornamental garden in Soochow. The Chinese are traditionally expert landscape gardeners and excel at using water, vegetation and buildings to produce charming, imaginative effects. Soochow, an ancient walled town dating back to 1000 B.C., is situated in a district of hills and lakes traversed by a number of canals.

it was, in effect, a rudimentary rifle.

As early as 1200 A.D., in their battles against Mongol and Chinese troops, the Chin in the Hunan region used long iron tubes that "thundered" when packed with gunpowder. Nothing is known of the destructive capacity of these primitive cannon.

At the end of the 11th century, during the reign of one of the Sung emperors, "arrows of fire" were used during a naval battle between Chinese and Mongols. These destroyed many ships, though it is not clear whether the weapons were cannon or other weapons similar in design. The Mongol troops also had wooden cannon,

made of bamboo bark bound together with rope.

FIREWORKS HAD PRIORITY

Father Mailla, a missionary, states that this bamboo weapon gave the Chinese an idea for a cannon made of iron, though it was not developed for many years. In 1577 small field guns were on show in China. These were observed by a Spanish missionary, Father Heralde, and were rudimentary in construction and of limited efficiency. This missionary also saw several mortars at Nanking, but states that the Chinese were rather ignorant of their principles. To sum up, it is safe to say that while fire-arms and gunpowder were known to the Chinese at an early date, they were not fully exploited. The Chinese preferred to keep their gunpowder for firework displays.

RELIGION

Cult of Ancestors

CHINA IN PRIMITIVE TIMES HAD neither religion, temples nor priests.

Primitive Chinese society was matriarchal. Women ruled the family. In country districts there were special feasts, in which women played an important part, to celebrate new births and invoke rainfall. It was believed that the transience of nature and refreshing clarity of water were feminine qualities and women's prayers would therefore become effective.

Later, women ceased to be objects of veneration in daily life and in religious myths.

Prayers were directed towards the emperor, called the *Son of Heaven*. It became his responsibility as representative of the people and head of the state, to make sacrifices to the Supreme Being, and to take the lead in worship.

The sacrifices, which were not officially recognized for some time, consisted of offerings of food and the slaughtering of animals on certain days. These offerings were made to either the divinity or the ancestors who, according to ancient beliefs, watched over their descendants as guardians and advisers.

There were periods when human sacrifices were made and there are records of many victims being sacrificed in honor of dead emperors, or

of genii or legendary protectors of districts.

The cult of ancestors, common to subjects and emperors, developed gradually over the centuries into a religion, but it was a religion without revelation. Sacrifices and prayers were addressed to ancestors before any important action was taken.

There have been many folk cults, producing many unformulated varieties of idolatry, but Chinese society has always had a common philosophical base, which is ethical rather than religious.

The Chinese God

The guiding principle for Western peoples who wish to understand the Chinese is that the vast mass of the people and the rulers have never been religious in the theological sense. Lao-tzu counselled a philosophy of quiet goodness. Confucianism, fundamentally, is an ethical and philosophical system which has indelibly marked Chinese culture.

The Chinese practice in a vague, unimpassioned way a complexity of religious rites, believing them to be, in themselves, worthy; but the effective Chinese God always has been the family, and through the family the ancestors which fathered and mothered it. Confucius taught that veneration for the family was the first principle of good living. The early Jesuit missionaries understood this and were aware that if China was going to be converted to Christianity, the process would involve many centuries of patient work. Christian missionaries made relatively few converts among the vast population of China, while the doctrines of the Buddha were modified in the Chinese way, each taking second place to the permanent religion of adoring the ancestor.

THE EMPEROR'S SEVEN ALTARS

The emperor had seven altars to his ancestors, a vassal ruler five, and so on in descending order through the ranks of society. Sacrifices were made before the tablets in the room of the ancestors. There were periodic rites which were performed by the whole family in the temple. Incense was burned every day, and offerings of food were made twice a month, at each altar. This devotion was stimulated by a profound faith in the power of the dead to assist the living and by fear of the ancestors' curses, should they fail in attention.

Lao-tzu

Lao-tzu a semi-legendary figure, is said to have been born in the kingdom of Chou, a feudal state, in the 7th century B.C. (the modern Honan), about fifty years before Confucius was born. There is a legend which attributes to Lao-tzu a previous incarnation, in 1321 B.C. in the State of Ch'u, where he was said to have been born with white hair and the features of an old man. The name Lao-tzu, in fact, means "Old Master." There are many tales about the birth and childhood of the philosopher who is said to have been the son of a peasant. His most important teaching is in a book known as *Tao-te-Ching* (The Book of Supreme Reason and Virtue).

According to Taoism, there are two levels of human nature, the material and the spiritual. The spiritual nature should be cultivated and it is therefore necessary for man to free himself from the demands of the body. He should dedicate himself to a life of meditation, which develops the values of the spirit. Tao is Supreme Reason, and all material things are merely an extension of Tao. These, the *li*, return to their origin, the Supreme Being, to be reunited, and enlightened with the great superior intelligence. Those who have the good fortune to achieve enlightenment during this life, will not experience a further incarnation. If they have behaved with humility and goodness they will merit reunion with the Universe.

It has been said that the doctrine of Lao-tzu resembles primitive Christianity. This is partly true, as the writings of the Chinese philosopher express love of mankind, a gentle attitude toward the forgiving of misdeeds and urge a mystical existence.

The doctrine of Lao-tzu also preaches simplicity of life, affirming, as the 18th- century French philosopher Jean Jacques Rousseau did, that man is born pure and society corrupts him.

Lao-tzu taught that enlightened regimes shun violence and that governments which need the support of armies are doomed to be short-lived. His doctrine was corrupted and distorted by later Taoists. Taoism became divided into orthodox Taoism, which was mystical and contemplative, and a corrupted form, closely connected with magic and superstitious practices. Taoism was very influential in China, but declined with the advent of Buddhism and the official support given to Confucianism.

Confucius

Confucian doctrine supported and clarified traditional beliefs. Confucius preached filial piety and strongly supported the cult of ancestors. He said it was necessary to account to ancestors for happenings on earth, and that special family rites should be observed. He preached respect for governments, so that the state would be solidly founded. Lao-tzu had faith in human nature and believed it unchangeable, although capable of improvement through contemplation. But Confucius stated that it should be cultivated, developed and refined by study, by direct experience and by travel. Both philosophers, however, favored love, respect for neigbors, and the peacefulness of contemplation.

KING WITHOUT A KINGDOM

Traditionally, Confucius was born into a noble family in the state of Lu during the Chou dynasty, in 551 B.C. Confucius' father, governor of a small town, had ten sons by his first wife, and after her death he remarried, at the age of seventy years. His second wife, the mother of Confucius, was a young girl, from the Yen family.

The birth of Confucius is surrounded by legends. According to these, a spirit known as Chilin, popular in Chinese mythology and

Funerary wreaths on sale in the streets of a Chinese city. According to the ancient folk traditions of China, death was a summons from Yen-lo Wang, an aspect of the Buddha, the king of the Underworld, who sent a messenger for the soul of the dying person. A special ceremony was performed after a death in the hope of recalling the soul of the deceased to the body.

associated with good tidings, appeared in the garden of Confucius' home just before his birth. This spirit belched up a large piece of jade on which was written: "A child pure as the crystal wave will be born with the decline of the Chou; he will be a king without a kingdom."

The life of Confucius was in many ways different from that of Lao-tzu. It is said that he showed virtues at a very early age.

JUNIOR MANDARIN

As a boy he amused himself by imitating religious and social ceremonies, for which he acquired great veneration. At the age of seven, he began his education and distinguished himself by diligence, modesty and gentleness.

His education finished, he accepted a junior mandarinate in agriculture, and devoted himself scrupulously to this work. He mastered all its inherent problems, trying to resolve them with an equity which earned him the sympathy of the farmers and the public.

At nineteen, he married and had a son, and at twenty he was asked to join the government and was given responsibility for agrarian reforms. After holding several public offices, always showing singular skill, as when he persuaded the peasantry that the dead should not be left without burial, he retired and devoted himself to study.

MEETING WITH LAO-TZU

While still a civil servant, he is said to have met Lao-tzu in the capital, where the Taoist philosopher was employed as a librarian. They are said to have respected each other's intellects, but did not agree, Lao-tzu disapproving of the emphasis placed by Confucius on tradition and ritual; he admonished him for wearing bright clothes and leading a gay life.

Confucius continued his career happily, became governor of a town and the minister responsible for criminals.

Eventually, envy of his good fortune and talents won him many enemies. The sovereign of Lu withdrew his patronage and Confucius was forced to wander first through the state of Wei, and later in the state of Sung, finally retiring into the country near Ch'en. He died in 479 B.C.

His collected works are known as the "Classics" in Chinese literature.

A young Chinese woman in traditional dress. In ancient China dress was a mark of rank and fashions were slow to change; the main sources of the few developments in Chinese dress were the accessions of foreign dynasties. The basis of Chinese dress over the last few centuries was the chang-fu, *a plain, long robe introduced by the Ch'ing dynasty.*

The aim of Confucius' doctrine was to teach man to achieve perfection through the practice of virtue and the acceptance of traditional standards. The government should be shown the best means of avoiding injustices in the social system. This involved every man's playing a strictly defined part in society.

Confucius made self-perfection obligatory for all citizens, rich or poor, weak or strong, as the only way to attain moral standing. This is achieved by knowing one's duty. Duty, in the Confucian sense, consisted of studying suitable works, thus cultivating the intelligence and gaining moral perfection, and raising oneself above the level of poverty and indifference. Confucianism shuns all superstitious practices and magic rites. It spread slowly, often meeting with hostile influences, but eventually became extremely widespread.

Buddhism

Buddhism originally reached China during the 1st century A.D. and in the Chinese way was soon given native formulations.

The Mahayana school was dominant; Buddhist priests of this

A competition in poetry between an old and a young man in a Chinese village. Poetical contests of this kind, in which the audience adjudicates on the merits of the contestants' work, are an ancient custom which is encouraged by the present regime. The Chinese Communist leader Mao Tse-tung is himself an accomplished poet and his Talks at the Yenan Forum on Art and Literature, *delivered in 1942, have had a considerable effect on modern Chinese writing.*

Girl students sketching on the outskirts of Peking. In secondary education great emphasis is placed on practical work; students often divide their hours of study between their classrooms and the factories, laboratories or other organizations in which they will eventually be employed.

group taught that Gautama, the founder of Buddhism, was merely one of many incarnations of the Buddha, that he was pleased by prayers and exhortations which took the form of praise and nothing gave him greater pleasure than gifts. The tastes of Gautama, in his Chinese guise, bore a marked resemblance to those of the emperor and the mandarin civil servants.

The Buddhist heaven also resembled the social lives of the imperial organization of China. The gods lived in great mansions like imperial palaces and kept court surrounded by lesser deities.

Buddhist religious communities were peopled exclusively by monks who were purely ritualists; their lives were given over to the presentation of ceremonies in which sacrifices for ancestors and festivals associated with parenthood and the family played a major part.

The religion, to a great extent, remained static until the competition of new ideas from the West and restrictions placed upon it under the republic inspired a re-examination of its tenets by the Buddhist clergy. The Chinese Buddhist society which was founded in Chungking in 1937 had 4,500,000 members.

Competition had brought an intellectual and religious revival and between 1920 and 1950 many Buddhist texts were republished.

Monks and their Ways

In China, in the past, perhaps due to the absence of a dogmatic theological religion, the practices of the clergy were not uniform. Monks of each sect lived in monasteries, and were divided into lay brothers and priests.

Taoist monks altered the original preaching of Lao-tzu, interpreting it as a doctrine of a universal creative force, and associating it with extravagant magical and superstitious practices.

From the proceeds of prayers, ostentatious penitences, divinations, and magical practices, they managed to live comfortably, obtaining convents and gifts.

They had their own funds and administration, but were recognized and controlled by the imperial government. Under special laws relating to priests, they had authority over those who aspired to become monks. These could not be accepted in a monastery more than one at a time and were placed under the disciplinary rule of their general superiors in the district, the sub-prefecture or the local authority.

Anyone who broke the law was referred by the superior of the monastery to the civil authorities, and a superior who neglected this duty was punished by eighty strokes with a bamboo cane.

MONKS WITH WIVES

Monks took vows of celibacy, but in practice these received only token observation; many monks had one or more wives. This is particularly true of Taoist monks. Sometimes, in order to marry, they pretended to be asking for a wife for a relation, and would then take possession of the lady themselves. Some Taoist priests continued to frequent their parents' houses, make sacrifices or offerings to their ancestors and wear mourning for deceased relatives. In short they remained in normal society instead of withdrawing from the world and devoting themselves exclusively to their religious functions. As has been noted, the social structure of China based on the family and ancestor worship made the Chinese less susceptible than other peoples to theological differences and more tolerant of human weaknesses in their priests.

Among the practices of Chinese monks was shaving the heads of novices. This was a solemn ceremony of initiation.

Another was the practice of branding, particularly among Taoist monks. Brands were small and round, and there were three, nine, twelve or eighteen, according to rank. Their purpose was to constantly remind the monks of their vows and devotions. Branding also made monks easily recognizable, since the marks were indelible. Branding was carried out by an expert who stamped a black circle on the shaved head of a novice, on top of which a sticky paste made of medlars was smeared. A stick of incense about one inch long was placed on top of this and set alight so that the paste boiled and dripped down the forehead until the paste was burnt to ashes.

This ceremony was accompanied by rhythmical drumbeats, high-pitched chanting, bells and bass drums. The novice, arms raised, prayed while one of his companions massaged his temples with his thumbs, to ease the pain.

A scab, formed by the branding and mixed with ash from the medlar paste and incense, remained on the head afterward and then fell off. Hair never reappeared on the branded skin, and the monk carried an indelible sign of his calling.

TEMPLES AND PAGODAS

Pagodas, which are Chinese temples, were first built during the Six Dynasties period (220-589 A.D.) and were based on the Indian Buddhist stupas, shrines built like pyramids. Most pagodas were built in mountainous areas sometimes surrounded by canals, woods, and gardens. At one time they were visited by pilgrims and processions from distant provinces. This custom was particularly agreeable to women since it was their only opportunity to leave their homes.

There were many pagodas, and despite their Indian origins they were among the most characteristic buildings of China.

ANIMALS IN THE CLOISTERS

The pagodas, multi-storied, tower-like buildings, formed the central feature of Buddhist temples and monasteries. The monasteries con-

Schoolchildren in Lhasa sketch the Potala, the great palace of the Dalai Lama situated on a rock outcrop outside the city. The Potala, which contains more than 1000 rooms, is a colorful building; it has gold roofs and a white and red façade, the middle portion being colored crimson, a color symbolic of sanctity.

sisted of courts surrounded by cells for the monks, buildings in which domestic animals were kept, cloisters paved with square, polished stones, halls, pavilions, and long loggias ornamented with stone or bronze statues. The cells had no windows and received light from the doorways.

The roofs glittered with brilliantly glazed yellow and green tiles and were adorned at the extremities with dragons of the same colors. The pagoda was always the most out-standing feature in the surrounding countryside. Pagodas varied in size according to the size and wealth of the monastery, and the material with which they were built; most were built of fairly small bricks and they had wooden columns.

Inside the pagodas were images

A Tibetan holy man holds a parchment inscribed with a religious text.

representing gods or supernatural beings. Many of these gods had their origins in mere folklore. They were often depicted in warlike attitudes with drawn swords or brandishing spears. Sometimes they were seated with crossed legs, sometimes lying down. These supernatural beings were also represented in paintings or sculptures in clay and porcelain, and were covered with gold leaf and brilliantly varnished. Most pagodas had many images of this type.

RED WAS A SACRED COLOR

In the middle of the chamber there would be an altar on which stood a very large idol; the temple was named after this idol, which was surrounded by several smaller idols. The altar was red (a sacred color) and at the sides there was a bowl for offerings and two incense burners.

In front of the idol stood vases containing perfumes; and candles and aromatic resins burned all the time, forming a dense cloud of incense.

Country folk had a simpler cult with a few small temples in the fields or erected at the entrances of villages. These temples contained images of propitious spirits or stones bearing the name of the tutelary spirit.

Wherever there were dangers to be met with on roads, the Chinese erected a small pagoda so that the traveler could seek the protection of its deity.

Idols and Dragons

The idols varied in size and style, depicting different gods in the hierarchy.

Many were grotesque, though some Buddhist idols were extremely beautiful and severe. Around them centered many superstitious practices and beliefs.

They were made mainly of lacquered wood or porcelain, but they existed in all sculpture materials including wood and stone.

Dragons were the symbol of heaven for the Chinese; they played an important part in religion and were portrayed wherever possible — on hangings, embroidered on clothes, and in books and pictures. There were dragons of all sorts, some with one head, some with two or more heads or with tongues of fire. There were earth dragons and lake dragons, good dragons and bad, often accompanied by other monsters.

Dragons were usually bearers of happiness, and had a festive significance; hence their popularity and the devotion they received from a population who wished for happiness. The arms and insignia of the emperor also bore a dragon.

There were different classes of gods. The most powerful, Po, derived from Buddha and belonged to the aristocracy, with the philosophers Confucius and Lao-tzu; then came those of the second grade such as the War God, who is said to have been born from a flower; then those of the third grade, the genii, divided into those of water, earth and fire.

Chinese idols were sometimes made to look ugly because their worshippers were supposed to be afraid and tremble before them; ugliness and deformity were conventional symbols of awe and majesty. If a god failed to carry out promises which he had made, according to interpretation of omens, there was widespread anger against him. When this occurred, it was likely to provoke rebellion and sacrilege. New gods and new magical powers were sought, and the slothful idol was shattered and replaced by others.

THE FAT GOD

The God of Immortality was represented by a fat, grotesque idol. His name was Kin-gan and he wore a crown and was dressed in gold. Mandarins used to make vows before his shrine to follow faithfully the obligations of their calling.

Another grotesque god was Quant-cong, who was smaller but had an enormous belly and muscles and was always portrayed accompanied by a robust servant. He was believed to have invented articles useful to man. There were other idols with sixteen arms, holding swords, flowers, or pieces of fruit, perhaps as symbols of nature; they were known as *Pu-tsei*.

Men and women who had been celebrated in their lifetimes could become gods; for instance, a sorceress known as Neoma was deified with a fan in her hand. A famous alchemist, Hujumsin, was made a god. He was said to have found the philosophers' stone and used it to free people from a wicked dragon, fighting it and tying it to a column. These images were mainly worshiped in Buddhist temples.

Islam

Islam, according to the Communists, had 10,000,000 adherents scattered throughout China, but earlier sources estimated 15,000,000.

The Islamic faith penetrated China slowly and a *Life of Mohammed* was not written in the Chinese language until 1712, nearly a thousand years after the first Islamic community was established in the country.

The Chinese Moslems segregated themselves from the remainder of the community and preserved, with great tenacity, their social customs. They set up their own enclaves. They wore turbans and held fast to their own food laws. The men were permitted to marry non-Moslem wives but the women were restricted to Moslem husbands. They used Arabic and Persian in their ritual and when greeting each other, and to them as to Moslems the world over, Mecca was the center of their religious life.

There is evidence that this relatively tiny segment of the Chinese population retains its religious ardor, for hundreds of Chinese Moslems still make a pilgrimage to Mecca each year.

Christianity

The story of Christian missionary activity in China is largely confined to coastal areas, but Matteo Ricci, the Jesuit scholar, penetrated the interior in the 16th century and indeed became a court favorite and a mandarin, due largely to his respect and affection for the Chinese and their scholarship, to his own knowledge of mathematics and astronomy and his ability to mend clocks, which the emperor found both pleasant and useful. However, disagreements with other Catholic missionaries lead to the suspension of the Jesuit mission and, as has been noted, missionary activity in the following centuries was confined largely to the coast.

Both Protestant and Catholic missionaries, teaching Western ways, influenced the rise of the Chinese republic by their introduction of European and American social values. These missionaries contributed much to the development of social welfare.

FOLK CULTS

Witches, Death and Dreams

CHINESE SUPERSTITIOUS BELIEFS WERE expressed in many different ways. Magic was an important element of Chinese tradition from the most remote times and, indeed, linked as it was with ancestor worship, it

Members of various Chinese national minorities in traditional dress at Peking airport. The Chinese Communist government has pursued a policy of "local nationalism" in regard to the many national minority groups, whose needs are considered by the Peking National Minorities Institute. Concessions to national pride have included the return of the ashes of Genghis Khan, removed by the Kuomintang government in 1939, to the Mongols in 1949. Except in Tibet, where repressive measures have been taken, this policy has so far proved successful.

influenced Taoism, Buddhism and Confucianism.

Magicians, or shamans as they are sometimes called, and witches were important people. *The Ritual of the Chou,* compiled about the beginning of the 1st century A.D., speaks of them as people possessed by the souls of ancestors.

Witches also had an official position which was a matter of policy, since emperors in ancient China knew that by recognizing them they could placate the people, who were extremely superstitious. To supress them, or discourage belief in them, would have been almost impossible.

THE WITCH AND THE PEOPLE'S WILL

In about 850 B.C., during the reign of Li Wang, people were dissatisfied with the government and resisted the emperor.

He, however, summoned a famous witch from the state of Wei, which was well known for producing women with supernatural powers. He kept her near his throne, charging her to make known to him all those she deemed his enemies and slanderers.

This resulted in mass slaughter, since anyone indicated by the witch was executed immediately, without trial, and thus, opposition to the emperor was fiercely suppressed by a rule of fear.

The ruler of the state of Chao suggested to Li Wang that it was not politic to build a dam against the will of the people. He said it was not merely a matter of damming a river; if the will of the people was ignored, their resentment would eventually break out in open revolt, like water bursting through a dam. The emperor ignored his advice, and eventually the population rebelled, and the emperor was forced to flee.

The Emperor Wu-ti (140 B.C.) was also under the influence of witches. One day he dreamed that he was being thrashed by many cudgels. He had his dream interpreted by his magicians, and on the strength of their advice he put to death many of his subjects who were found guilty of witchcraft.

THE EFFIGY WAS TORTURED

In ancient China, witches made effigies of anyone they wished to destroy, and the spirits of darkness were invoked. These effigies were tortured and buried, and the witches awaited results.

Another method was to make an image representing the Spirit of Revenge, arm it with a sabre and a spear, and make offerings to it in an attempt to rouse its anger, which would then be directed against the enemy.

RECALLING THE DEAD

A further function of Chinese magic was to forecast future events. Witches claimed that they could influence nature and recall the spirits of the dead. This last function was performed by suspending a writing-brush so that it touched a sheet of paper or a tablet covered with a thin layer of sand or ash. When the necessary invocations had been made, the writing-brush was supposed to reply by writing a sentence in the sand. If the spirit, when summoned, did not write anything, it was thought that reply was forbidden for reasons of piety or discretion.

It is possible that some of these superstitions still survive in China, as similar ones survive in Europe.

A GOD DOWN-GRADED

In their efforts to obtain rain, Chinese peasants used ritual sacrifices, fasting and public vows. Drought was a national disaster, sufficiently serious to warrant the participation of the emperor in the rites. On such occasions he went to a temple to intercede with the gods and, if all efforts failed, the gods incurred the wrath of emperor and people.

When a divinity did not heed the prayers of its worshipers, it was treated harshly; not only that, but if it continued to be ineffectual, it was abandoned.

Once, during the reign of the T'angs (618-906 A.D.), when the country was devastated by famine, the god known as the "Father of the Crops" was considered to have shown himself powerless and was downgraded in a formal ceremony.

There are many examples in Chinese history of folk gods being demoted to a lower position in the hierarchy. In the 10th century B.C. during the reign of Emperor T'ai Tsu, the emperor was visiting the temples when, among the idols, he caught sight of an image of a warrior, Pai-ch'i, who had been head of the state and later recognized as a divinity. As soon as the emperor saw the image, he pointed his finger at it, a gesture of contempt in China, and ordered that it should no longer be housed in the temple. This

A Chinese girl and thousands of her fellow students crowd a sports stadium. The Chinese government has instituted a vast national sports program as a means of developing and maintaining physical fitness among China's millions of students and workers.

was because Pai-ch'i, during one of his campaigns, had committed the cowardly action of killing all his prisoners.

CRYSTAL VASE, CLAY DRAGON

At one time, to induce rainfall, peasants put in a crystal vase a piece of metal which, according to tradition, had fallen out of the sky. The vase was carried in procession to Peking, to the accompaniment of shouts of joy, and was placed in the temple. The day of the ceremony was fixed by a proclamation from the emperor, who came in person to worship the fetish and pray for water for the crops.

Other fetishes which were believed to have the power of producing rain

included a clay dragon, made by the prefect of a district of Peking in 774 B.C. The people used to pray to this object for rain, assisted by a troop of magicians dancing before the image. But on one occasion their efforts were unsuccessful and the emperor ordered the dragon to be destroyed. Then the emperor prayed and fasted until the rain at last came.

THE INNOCENT BROUGHT RAIN

On another later occasion, an emperor prayed for two days and two nights on a mat in the open air, in front of the Altar of Mountains and Rivers. When his prayers were not answered, and it appeared that he had failed to intercede with the gods, it occurred to him to find out whether

there were any prisoners in jail, who had been wrongly accused. Some innocent prisoners were found, and as soon as they were released rain fell in torrents.

In some regions, a frog was placed in a crystal vase and worshiped by the people until the rain came.

Eclipses

During eclipses of the sun or the moon there were special rituals to be observed. Gongs were beaten in the streets, and there were fireworks and shouting to frighten away the monster who was trying to swallow the sun or moon and hide them from the earth.

At the same time, the news of the eclipse was officially conveyed to the government and the emperor by the Great Department of Rites. The workers in the capital and the provinces were also informed, and they in turn passed the news to the rural areas.

In primitive China, the movements of the heavens, dates of eclipses, and variations of the calendar were calculated with reasonable accuracy.

People surrounded this science with superstitious beliefs and believed that the stars showed interest in the earth and its inhabitants by means of phenomena such as eclipses. In this way, Heaven expressed its opinion about men's actions, especially political decisions.

The eclipses of the sun were regarded as warnings of disaster, admonishing the emperor to correct his faults and policies. For this reason, a solar eclipse was important politically and was received by the court with special ceremonies in which learned and important people took part.

According to the sacred book, *Chou-king*, during the legendary period of Chinese history the official court astronomers Hi and Ho failed to predict a solar eclipse that was due to happen on a certain day in 2155 B.C., during the reign of the Emperor Chung Kang, and did not warn the government. This is how the sacred book tells the story:

"At that time Hi and Ho were leading a life of debauchery, neglecting their duties, dedicating themselves to wine and behaving in a manner contrary to the correct conduct of magistrates. From the very beginning they caused confusion in the astronomical calendar and acted in a way unworthy of their learning."

Eclipses were in primitive times

A Chinese gardener at work. Flowers have always played an important symbolic part in Chinese mythology; the art of gardening was formerly one of the traditional pursuits of the leisured classes. Even in modern China, flowers are lovingly cultivated, though most available land is of necessity given over to the growing of crops. It is the custom for most families to grow their own vegetables.

accompanied by the following procedure: a blind musician would beat a drum, mandarins offered gifts, especially pieces of silk, to the heavenly spirits, the emperor and high court dignitaries fasted and dressed simply without orders or ornaments; these were solemn and elaborate ceremonies.

When the solar eclipse happened without warning, confusion and panic possessed the court. The mandarins tried to perform the sacrifices but few were successful; the dignitaries who were supposed to hurry to the palace with bows and arrows to defend the emperor from the wrath of the sun, failed to turn up. People could not understand this heavenly phenomenon which had occurred without official warning, and struck with fear, they fell into disorder.

Hi and Ho, the two dissolute astronomers, were sentenced to death, although until then a mistake or carelessness in the matter of heavenly studies was punished with a fine, a reprimand or reduction in rank.

Hi and Ho, however, were also princes, and they escaped to their fortified territories where they defended themselves against the imperial troops.

RED CANDLES FOR THE SUN AND MOON

Under normal circumstances, once everyone had been warned of the danger to the sun or moon, the officials proceeded to perform the prescribed rites. Upon a small square table they placed another narrower rectangular table of equal length, and upon this, two candelabras bearing lighted red candles, and a small urn full of ashes in which lighted sticks of incense burned. Behind the candles and the incense was a small shrine, open at the sides and containing a tablet, inscribed with characters meaning "the disc of the sun (or moon) has reassumed a circular shape." This tablet was covered by a second one, the text of which described the peak of the eclipse, and a third indicating the beginning of the eclipse.

The altar was placed in the court of honor of the temple, facing in the direction of the sun or moon. The priest in charge of the ceremony, with his retinue wearing black cloaks, made genuflections to the altar, while twelve priests, bonzes (monks) and Taoists, advanced, reciting prayers and beating a gong. During different phases of the eclipse, the tablets bearing the inscriptions were

The tricycle-rickshaw, as shown in this illustration, has replaced the hand-drawn rickshaw and the even more ancient sedan chair since 1949. For centuries, manual labor was the main means of transportation in many parts of China, since most roads were unsuitable for wheeled traffic. In the 20th century, however, carts, bicycles, automobiles and trucks have begun to replace human porters.

uncovered, telling the crowd what point had been reached. At each successive phase there were renewed genuflections, prayers, songs and soundings of the gong. This sequence continued until the eclipse ended. In Peking, the ceremony was conducted by the emperor, in person, who was thought to be able to communicate directly with the gods.

The belief in the God of the Hearth had a large following. He was believed to live in the kitchen, where an image representing him was kept beside the hearth, and was responsible for the well-being of the family, watching over them and the events, good or bad, which occurred to them.

Some people ignored his presence,

but others, more cautious, offered him honey, sweetmeats, molasses and cakes, so that, when he visited the Supreme Being, his palate would be sticky and he would stammer. The God of the Hearth made this journey in three days, during the twelfth moon. When he was gone, members of the family removed his image from the hearth and on his return they put another one there. In the interval during his absence there was great celebration and gaiety in the streets.

The Death Cult

The death cult was so strong in China that dying was an elaborate social affair. To pass on peacefully was impossible. When the end was

one himself, increasing the thickness with varnish, pitch and bitumen; this was applied inside as well as outside, to minimize the damage inflicted by soil and moisture.

The interior base of a coffin was covered with lime; pillows were added to support the head, while the space around and above the body was stuffed with wadding to prevent possible shock. Those rich enough provided several caskets, one inside another; the outside casket was inlaid with pearls and other jewels.

PERFUMES AND CANDLES

Great ceremonies were involved. These included greetings before the bier, deep bows in which the forehead touched the ground several times, perfumes, candles placed all round the funeral room and on the tables and much lamenting.

When the time came for the last farewell, the eldest son made the responses, accompanied by his brothers who stood with him behind a curtain, near the body. The women of the family were also in the room, and special mourning-women who were hired to wail. After this ceremony, visitors went into another part of the house where more distant relatives and close family friends entertained them with tea, fruit and sweetmeats.

Notices announcing funerals were sent out in advance. The funeral started from the bereaved family's home where relations and friends dressed in mourning were assembled. The funeral procession was accompanied by cardboard figures of men, women and animals to give the appearance of a great crowd of mourners. In double file, men carrying banners and incense burners, dirge-singers and musicians walked. Then under a violet silk canopy, the corners of which were embroidered in white silk came the bier; immediately behind it was the eldest son, leaning on a stick, his body bowed, his head covered by a sack. Last came relatives, friends, daughters, concubines, wives and servants.

THE ELDEST SON

After the burial, sons, relatives and friends dispersed to neighboring rooms specially provided for funeral

near or seemed to be near, friends, relatives and servants removed the sick person from his bed and placed him on a table, his head on a cloth pillow shaped like a cock. The cock emblem was thought to scare away evil spirits. The dying person was dressed in special clothes, men in coat, hat and shoes, the women with veils over their heads. Other garments were replaced by wadding or other soft material which was later used to pad the coffin. Furs were forbidden because it was believed that thus attired the dead person might be reborn as an animal.

When death came, the person's name was shouted from the rooftop, in the hope that the spirit, just beginning its journey, might stop and return to the body.

BISCUITS WERE BURNED

Before putting on their mourning clothes, the relatives of the dead person continued the search for the spirit which had left the body, to make sure that no resurrection was possible. When night arrived, they went to the temple, each bearing a lighted torch. There they prayed that the spirit might make a safe journey. They stuck a coin to a wall of the temple by means of a stick of incense, and each cried out in a

loud voice asking whether the spirit had reached the temple.

The following evening, after another visit to the temple, they tested, with the same stick of incense, the walls of the dead person's home, which were covered with mourning cards. If the incense stick adhered to the walls when the same question again was asked in a loud voice, it was believed that the spirit had returned from the temple, and was at home preparing for the longer journey into eternity.

At this point, in front of the door of the house, a paper bag of special biscuits was burned to make the path of the dead easier. These customs were known as the "spirit carriage" and included other rites.

CONFUCIAN PRECEPT

"Pay to the dead," says Confucius, "the same respect they would enjoy if they were still alive and present." Funeral rites were the most important of all ancient Chinese ceremonies.

MAKING COFFINS

Coffins were made of extremely hard and solid wood to withstand the ravages of time. Anyone too poor to buy a coffin in a suitable wood went to great lengths to make celebrations and there settled down to a magnificent meal, after which ritual thanks were given to the eldest son.

The grandeur and duration of the respects varied according to the rank of the deceased. When he was not only rich but a member of the government of the empire, the grief was greater and more prolonged; the tombs of such people were thronged with mourners for as much as two months. In this way the eldest son was assured of the profound grief caused by his father's death.

WHITE FOR MOURNING

White clothing was worn to indicate mourning, three years for a father or mother, and one year for a brother or wife. For her husband, a wife wore mourning for three years. On the death of a father, his sons wore clothes of coarse material, tied with a cord at the waist. When one year passed, their grief was mitigated, so they were permitted to wear clothes of finer cloth. By the end of the third year a return to silk clothing was permitted.

THE ROOM OF THE ANCESTORS

Mourning customs included strict rules regarding diet. A special ritual was followed by close relatives of the rich going into the city; they must travel in enclosed sedan chairs covered in white to denote mourning.

There were additional, stricter rules, for those who kept the body of a deceased relative in their own house for several years. They were obliged to sleep every night on reed mats beside the bier.

The room of the ancestors in a Chinese household was a basic element of the cult.

This room was a vast hall which accomodated many official helpers and relations, who could enter regardless of rank, age being the only criterion of precedence. The oldest member of a family always received the most respect.

FOOD AND WINE FOR THE TOMB

The room of the ancestors had no ornaments, but its walls were lined with the portraits of the most illustrious ancestors, and there were rows of tablets inscribed with the names of members of the family, with their dates of birth and death, and description of their occupations and careers.

The room of the ancestors was also used for banquets given in honor of ancestors, but this practice was limited to the very wealthy. The ceremonies which took place in the room were not regarded as a substitute for the custom of visiting the tomb twice a year.

These visits were a tradition that was strictly respected and on such

A street scene in Shanghai. Manually drawn rickshaws like those seen here, together with sedan chairs, were prohibited in 1949. The most common form of personal transport in modern Chinese cities is now the bicycle or the tricycle-rickshaw. Automobiles are still in short supply in China.

occasions wine and food were taken to the tomb.

This ritual was observed by the Chinese until recently and it constituted an essential part of their traditions of family life.

Death of the Emperor

The funeral of an emperor was attended by many thousands of people. These were not simply curious, or exceptionally faithful subjects. All present actually took some part in the rites. The entire country went into mourning.

Royal funerals were arranged with great dramatic effects. The corpse was accompanied to the tomb with models of horses, carriages, and human figures, such as courtiers; in early times these were made of paper, later they were carved from wood or modeled in terra cotta. The horses and other images were burned when the imperial remains were entombed.

This usage developed from the custom of sacrificing live persons to the illustrious dead. Such ceremonies first took place in the 7th century B.C.

The sepulchers of emperors, like those of other eminent personages, such as ministers, princes, holy men or men famous for their learning and preaching, were protected by bodyguards.

The law forbade "cattle-grazing, wood-chopping or plowing" in fields containing all burial mounds, and in neighboring fields.

To violate a tomb or interfere with human remains outraged the people and earned severe punishments.

The respect felt by the Chinese for the dead was so great, that even recently, a doctor could not easily carry out an autopsy.

STRANGULATION THE PENALTY

Once deposited in the earth, a coffin must not be touched unless for urgent reason. Anyone who opened a tomb and revealed the coffin was punished by strangulation. There were minor penalties for other offences in connection with the sepulcher or the corpse; the violation of urns containing the bones of the dead was also punished.

Legislation connected with desecration of tombs provided for many possible offenses. Examples of offenses were, the stealing of bricks or stones from the tomb, the removal of the coffin with "insufficient reason," the mutilation of the coffin or its destruction or damage by water.

If, under such circumstances, the corpse only lost its hair, the penalty was comparatively light. If it was damaged by a fire lit by hunters, if a burial mound was flattened for cultivation, if a corpse was discovered and the discovery not announced to the magistrates or if a body was stolen, heavy penalties were prescribed.

DEATH FOR SACRILEGE

Relationship between the corpse and its profaners was also considered, and the punishment varied accordingly.

It was a serious crime to fell and steal trees which grew around a cemetery. Other laws stated that civilian and military officials and their retinues in charge of the imperial cemetery must, when approaching it, dismount from their horses at a distance of a hundred paces. Anyone who violated this rule was guilty of lack of respect and was punished with a hundred strokes.

Removal of the cypresses growing in the central enclosure of the imperial cemetery constituted sacrilege; the principal offender in any such case was condemned to death. The

Gardens by a lake in Peking. The development of modern Peking has presented an architectural problem, caused by the demands for space for modern administrative buildings and dwellings in an ancient and crowded city. An uneasy compromise between the skyscrapers of the West and the traditional low buildings of China has been reached by the erection of five-story blocks in dull colors and neutral styles. Provision has been made, however, for well-planned public parks and gardens.

A new bridge in Foshan, in the province of Heilungkiang, built to a traditional design. Foshan, situated on the right bank of the Amur River, was once a marshy, unhealthy area. In recent years, drainage projects and new buildings have changed the ancient city to a thriving modern community.

case, however, had to be first submitted to the emperor. Accomplices were condemned to exile in remote areas of the empire.

WOODEN COLLARS FOR IMPIOUS SONS

If a son or a nephew cut down trees from the burial ground of his father or ancestor, he was punished by a hundred strokes or was forced to spend three months with his neck and hands encased in a heavy wooden collar, called a cangue.

If the trees were valuable, this, too, was taken into account and an additional penalty for theft was inflicted.

Dreams

According to Chinese superstition, a spirit left a man while he was sleeping, and entered a sphere in which supernatural elements were revealed. On the authority of these dreams, the feelings and actions of the dreamer were interpreted.

This theory is illustrated in a story dated 679 B.C. At Ch'eng, in full daylight, two large serpents were seen fighting at the gates of the city, one defending the entrance and the other trying to force his way in. The defender was killed and the aggressor entered the city and disappeared.

Six years later, the ruler of Ch'eng was attacked and killed by a rival. The ruler of Lu asked a certain Shenssu whether the dream portended this event, to which the reply was: "Say rather that as such an event was expected and feared by many people, the waiting and the fear produced the two monsters and their fight."

In other words, human anxieties had materialized in the shape of monsters. Thus, in some ways, a Chinese superstition foreshadowed the findings of modern psychologists.

FESTIVALS

Marriage, Lanterns and Love

FESTIVALS IN PRIMITIVE CHINA WERE linked to the changing seasons and alternating gaiety and sadness of life. As in all primitive societies festivals were associated with the land and farming. These festivals varied with different social structures and climate and were given form by the characteristics of the various parts of the country.

In the fall and winter peasants remained at home, but in spring and summer they worked and enjoyed themselves outdoors. Their living pattern therefore, completely changed twice every year. These changes inspired the open-air festivals.

WHITE FROST AND WEDDINGS

The most important festivals took place in spring, but there were festivals in the fall.

Festivals followed the seasonal rhythms of peasant life, such as those celebrating the completion of work in the fields, and return to the village. There was a link between marriage and festivals, especially in spring and fall, when many marriages were celebrated.

"When the white frost comes woman's work is done, and marriage can be arranged" says a proverb. Another says: "When the ice melts work in the fields starts, mulberry leaves are gathered, and wedding rites are completed."

Festivals included oaths, sacrifices to the soil and offerings to ancestors and household gods. Some developed into orgies, great quantities of food and drink were consumed, and there was much dancing, music, flags, and masks. The main aim of the celebration was to bring together normally isolated family groups and facilitate marriages and business deals.

The ancient festivals developed more formal religious characteristics at a later stage, and were conducted in a more solemn atmosphere.

NATURAL WONDERS

All festivals were characterized by a feeling of brotherhood between men, and a closeness between man and his environment.

Peasants receive instruction in the new, written language by reading letters painted on a wall which they pass during the course of their work. A new alphabet based on Latin characters was introduced in 1957 and it was found that after mastering this the peasants, who before has been mainly illiterate, were also capable of mastering Chinese characters. A great drive against illiteracy was decreed by the All-China Conference on Education for Peasants and Workers in September 1950.

Women of Uigur nationality learn to read during a break from their labor. The Uigurs, who are mainly concentrated in Sinkiang province, are Moslems of the Sunni sect. They live in large family groups, usually occupied in agricultural work. They are not strict in observing the rites of the Moslem faith and retain many folk beliefs in their worship, notably the ancestor cult.

Popular superstitions held rivers, forests and rocks in great respect. As one ancient text says : "Mountains, forests, rivers, valleys, wells and hills have the power to make clouds, rain and wind, and produce wonders. In everything they are said to be secret powers." This is a philosophy which is still attractive.

Flowers, particularly orchids, were important in festivals. Girls addressed each other in verse holding bunches of flowers. Flowers were used to symbolize every phase of life.

FESTIVALS FOR LOVERS

Important festivals were at harvest time, when women displayed clothes they had spent the winter weaving and dyeing.

Girls and boys had mock battles with flowers, and there were singing competitions, jousts, wrestling and games. Similar festivals were held in south China until quite recently.

A succession of dances, ballads and games gradually overcame the timidity of the young folk. The festival atmosphere favored business deals, and men and women exchanged gifts as a basis for future marriage settlements.

The festivals that occurred at the opening and close of the season were the most important. The winter made agricultural work impossible, and people kept indoors, renewing their strength for the coming year and cementing their contacts and friendships.

FESTIVAL OF THE OLD

Some festivals held during the winter had a stimulating effect on the community; they were accompanied by dancing, displays of magic, and wine. Peasants wore cat and leopard skins, danced, ate and enjoyed the fruits of successful harvests.

With the advent of Confucianism, a more austere spirit in social relationships developed and the older festivals became increasingly formal. Other ceremonies developed to fill the gap caused by the loss of primitive festivals. One ceremony, presided over by elders dressed in mourning, symbolized the "leading of winter to its end," a festival of the old to celebrate the end of the dead season.

FESTIVAL OF THE SOIL

There were other ancient festivals many of which survived almost unchanged. The Festival of the Soil, for instance, was celebrated by all classes, from the emperor and his princes to the poorest peasants. This festival was religious in inspiration. The emperor and his courtiers fasted for three days, and wore clothes as simple as their subjects. The emperor then went unescorted and without ostentatious pomp, to the site of the ceremony.

In the temple, sacrifice was offered, after which the emperor went to a specially set aside part of the temple precincts. Here the full symbolism of the ceremony became apparent. The emperor seized a plow drawn by a pair of oxen with gilded horns, and plowed several furrows, which were then sown. Later, the corn grown in the imperial furrows was harvested and stored for sacred purposes.

BOY WITH ONE SHOE

In towns and villages, the highest official, for instance the governor, appeared decked in flowers on a litter, preceded by soldiers and musicians, and accompanied by flags and banners decorated with portraits of worthy local farmers. This procession went through streets decorated with arches, lanterns, and tapestries, followed by all the peasants, to the east gate of the town. This gate was used because it faced the rising sun, and thus symbolized spring.

The center-piece of the procession was a huge earthenware buffalo, its horns painted gold. A boy wearing

The fishing boats of a village on the east coast of China have obviously just landed a catch of cuttlefish, which are being sorted for drying in the sun. Fish provide an important source of protein in the Chinese diet and are likely to increase in importance with the development of better transport facilities. Most sea fish are dried and salted because of the lack of refrigeration facilities. Fish breeding is an important pursuit in fresh water lakes and ponds, especially in silk producing areas where the fish are fed on silk-worm waste.

only one shoe to symbolize the humble toil and wisdom of the countryside, led this effigy, carrying a rod to drive it. Behind the boy peasants marched, some playing musical instruments, others carrying agricultural implements; after the peasants came masked figures, and lastly, players miming scenes.

The procession returned by the same route from the east gate to the point of departure. The buffalo was stripped of its decorations, and its belly opened to reveal smaller clay buffaloes, which were kept to commemorate the festival. Finally, the governor made a speech in praise of farming.

Festival of the New Year

Another important festival was that of the New Year celebrated in late January and February. The whole empire took part in this festival, all work ceased, official seals were laid aside, and people gave themselves over to games and celebrations. Temples were crowded, and religious ceremonies were carried out with great pomp.

Father Grosier, a missionary student of China, describes the scene: "The humbler mandarins do homage to their seniors, children to their parents and servants to their masters. In the evening all families are reunited and have a solemn meal together at which the compliments of the season are exchanged." During the days following the festival the scene was less peaceful; the atmosphere became gayer and livelier, and games, plays and feasts were held.

Festival of Lanterns

The Festival of Lanterns is the noisiest and most colorful in Chinese city life. It begins in February and its date of origin and exact significance are unknown. One legend relating to its beginnings tells of a much-loved mandarin who lost his daughter who was drowned while walking on a river bank. All through the night by the light of hundreds of lanterns, her father, his friends and the peasants joined in the search for the drowned girl. In memory of the tragedy, and in gratitude to all who aided him, the good mandarin had hundreds of multicolored lanterns lit each year by the river bank and the custom took hold and gradually spread throughout China.

In imperial times, the Festival of Lanterns lasted for three days. In the capital, it began with the sound of cannon, bells, cymbals, trumpets, and other musical instruments. Throughout China, there were millions of bonfires. Lanterns were lit along rivers, on the seashore, in harbors, on mountain tops, at roadsides, at palace windows, and at hovel doors. The richer Chinese decorated their lanterns splendidly.

There was great variety in the shapes of lanterns; some were so large that they seemed like ballrooms, dining rooms, bedrooms or theaters. Such elaborate lanterns were extremely expensive.

ALL KINDS OF LANTERNS

A missionary traveler in China tells how lanterns "were contrived so that shadows in the likeness of

Children in a Chinese village wear the traditional large, straw hats as protection against both sun and rain. Child welfare programs are an important aspect of modern China, the main efforts being directed against the high rate of infant mortality. County health centers have been set up in rural areas, public hygiene and street cleaning have been improved and measures have been taken to stamp out such pests as rats, mosquitoes, flies and sparrows.

Mongolian women preparing small pies of booth, a mixture of mutton and beef. The Chinese are fond of highly-flavored foods and fruit, the most popular among the latter being peaches, pears, mangoes, lychees and persimmons. Cakes of flaky pastry and tarts and soups flavored with almond paste are also popular delicacies.

soldiers, actors, and other characters appeared, with movements in harmony and words spoken by their manipulator." These lanterns were a precursor of the movies, operating on the same principle of moving pictures, light and shade.

Father Grosier wrote: "Besides lanterns which are shaped like real rooms, there are countless others remarkable for their elegance and ornamental richness. Most are hexagonal in shape, consisting of panels one foot high and six inches wide, framed by strips of wood that are painted, varnished, or gilded. The panel itself is made of delicate and transparent silk, on which are painted flowers, rocks, animals, and sometimes human figures. The colors used in these pictures are vivid, and are lent brilliance by the lights inside the lantern. The six corners are usually surmounted with carved and gilded figures. Multicolored satin streamers hang on all sides.

"There are lanterns of different shape: triangular, square, cylindrical, glove and pyramid-shaped. They may be made of silk, gauze, horn, mother-of-pearl, glass, transparent oyster shell or thin paper."

During the festival shops were closed and streets were crowded by processions followed by bands of musicians. The womenfolk were treated with indulgence for the occasion. Women of middle rank were allowed out of their homes riding on decorated donkeys, others in two-wheeled chaises, followed by mounted women playing on musical instruments and singing.

DOCTORS, BABIES AND POETS

An almanac dated 1850 lists many other festivals, the majority dedicated to the glorification and birth of some noted figure, such as Confucius.

In one festival the God of Medicine was honored, and two popular doctors would be granted divine status.

Anyone wishing for children offered sacrifice at the Festival of the Mother of Babes during May. In May, too, was the Festival of the Queen of Heaven, patron of sailors.

Writers and poets had their own deity, the God of Literature, whose feast was in March; there was a propitiatory ceremony, consisting of placing two figures of children behind the doors of houses.

The dead were remembered much as they are in America and Europe, by friends and relatives visiting their tombs at the time of the festivals in remembrance of them. But at such times the Chinese placed food and drink on the burial mounds. This ceremony was repeated four months later, when children would fly long-tailed kites in honor of their departed ancestors.

GODS JOINED IN THE FESTIVAL

There were festivals in honor of the Patroness of the Blind, known to the Chinese as the "Holy Mother with sparkling eyes of fire," and in honor of the Nine Stars of the Plow, which descended to earth once every year to receive homage. There was a Festival of the Mulberry Leaves, when the empress plucked mulberry leaves from the trees.

The Bird of Man was celebrated as was the God of Splendor and Plenty; and many other festivals were celebrated, in boats, in the countryside, with games and open-air plays.

In September, after the harvest, there was a further important festival expressing gratitude for the fertility of the soil and its produce; this lasted sixteen days, during which temples

DANCE OF FERTILITY

The Dance of the Pheasant, popular in the past among country people, was performed at the beginning of spring. Dances such as this were symbolic, and linked with fertility cults. According to Marcel Granet (1884-1940) a founder of the Institute of Chinese Studies at the Sorbonne, Paris, writing in his book *Chinese Civilization*, these dances preceded love-making; the women were dressed brightly, like pheasants, and made the overtures, singing to the men.

Later, the men also dressed like pheasants, took up their roles, and the significance of the dance gradually changed, so that it finally became a dance symbolizing nature, and through nature, the power of thunder which returns each spring after its winter exile. At this point the peasants, male and female, sang and beat their "wings" in imitation of thunder.

THE PHEASANT AND THE STONE GIRL

In myth, thunder was represented as a male pheasant. In the Tsin region a male pheasant alighting on a sacred stone at night during a thunderstorm was made an object of worship. According to the legend the sacred stone was a girl transformed into a stone; this attracted the pheasant because during her life the girl had been the companion of a young man. When she was turned to stone, he became a god in the shape of the pheasant. Anyone able to seize the young man as he returned for his companion would be elected king.

The pheasant also figured in Chinese dancing as a symbol of Yu-wan, traditional founder of the Chinese Empire. The dancer used stones he clapped together like castanets. In one part of China, in feudal times, girls and boys would wade across streams to attract thunder by using primitive castanets. At the same time they performed a graceful dance during which, by raising and lowering their shoulders, they imitated the pheasant flapping

were crowded, and banquets, dancing and theatrical performances were held. At this time, the gods were supposed to come to earth.

Dancers and Dragon Heads

The Chinese had many dances, both military and religious in inspiration, which had been performed since ancient times. They took place in towns and on hills, at festival time, at religious ceremonies and at shrines. Dancers carried shields, pikes, axes, and banners surmounted by dragons' heads from which hung silk ribbons.

Typical dances were the Dance of Arms, named after the battle-axe and shield which was carried; the Dance of the Standard, which was performed during a feast held to propitiate the soil; the Dance of Plumes, in which a banner was crowned by five plumes; and the Dance of the Ox, in which an ox's

tail was placed at the top of the standard.

Festival dancing sometimes took place in temples, accompanied by singing and music, and the re-enacting of past conflicts commemorating the deeds of the ancestors. Dancers would face each point of the compass with loud cries, and finally, still singing and playing, form themselves in a line.

A Chinese treatise on dancing speaks of a dance which represented the conquest of China by Wu (141-87 B.C.) who defeated the country's enemies and set boundaries to the state, governed wisely with the help of two good ministers and stabilized the empire.

Such dances were originally didactic and aimed at exhorting spectators to worthy actions. Boys between thirteen and fifteen years old were trained to do dances of this kind. They belonged to the richer classes, and were destined for military training.

his wings; then they stood upright on one leg in imitation of a pheasant. Later, in sacred places, the dance ended with a sacrifice.

TIGHT-ROPE DANCERS

There were also remarkable tight-rope dances, many games of skill and acrobatic feats. Men balanced on steel wires or on hanging ladders, gave collective acrobatic displays of strength and suppleness. Similar performances survive and may be seen in Communist China today.

COURTESY

THE CHINESE PEOPLE WERE COURteous, but not so much out of altruistic motives as out of obedience to principles clearly laid down by Confucian writers. There were 800 of these principles, and all were learned by heart by people who were particular about etiquette.

In minor matters or matters of great importance, the neglect of prescribed forms and age-old conventions could be disastrous. Great dignitaries, for example, were for long afraid of the executioner, not so much because he would kill them but because he could abase and make them objects of contempt. When a sentence of death was imposed on such a minister, the emperor accorded him the privilege of killing himself to avoid the shame of the gallows.

Likewise, a magistrate was permitted to die wearing his audience gowns. If a servant thought he was about to be dismissed he anticipated his dismissal by handing in his notice voluntarily. These cases were all governed by formal courtesy and etiquette. In all ranks of society, the Chinese were preoccupied with personal prestige and decorum, and would commit suicide if they felt disgraced.

Rules for the conduct of everyday life were many, laying down correct behavior toward equals, relatives, servants, and masters, a suitable attitude of the people toward the emperor and the correct approach of the emperor to the divinity.

STUPID AND HONORABLE

When people were introduced for the first time, it was necessary to ask: "What is your honorable name?" and the reply, apart from giving the name, had to include polite questions about the interrogator's sons. If a wife was mentioned in conversation, she was referred to by her husband as "the stupid one of the family,"

A restaurant in a small town in the province of Kwangtung. The emphasis placed on public health is evident in the face mask worn by the young waitress. Malnutrition is much less common in China than formerly, since improved communications mean that extra supplies can be quickly supplied to areas suffering from shortages. For most people, however, the diet is monotonous; there is generally enough rice for all, but meat is in short supply.

but his interlocutor would call her the "honorable lady."

In feudal times, everyone, with the exception of the emperor, followed the custom of denigrating his own character, in obedience to principles of good education. Thus, "I, a wicked man," or "our abject village" were phrases which revealed the gentle breeding of a man speaking of himself or his home.

LETTER ON RED PAPER

Anyone who wished to visit a friend had to send a servant several hours in advance, to deliver a letter on red paper requesting the pleasure of making a visit.

The letter would read something like this: "Your disciple, (or your younger brother) has come to bow down his head to the ground and to offer you his respects."

This sentence would be written in large characters to convey an impression of good education combined with a sense of personal dignity, but the characters gradually decreased in size as the author's desire to appear humble diminished. If a man was called upon without having first re-

The gateway to a temple in Chungking, in the province of Szechwan. The ornate decorations that characterize Chinese temple architecture, a form of great antiquity, are much in evidence in this illustration. Chungking contains a number of fine examples of traditional Chinese architecture; it is a most ancient city, having first achieved importance under the Chou rulers in 1100 B.C.

ceived a letter, he could send a servant out to his visitor begging him to wait; or could put on his best clothes and go to the door of the house saying "I beg you to enter." The main gate was opened (it would have been indelicate to invite the guest to enter through a side door) and the guest would enter on horseback or in a sedan chair. He would then proceed to a room set aside for visitors where seats had already been placed in two parallel lines. Bows were exchanged at the entrance, while the visitor was seated on the south side of the room. In southern provinces this side was considered more noble, though in the north the contrary was true. Small rugs were brought up to cover the seats. There was prolonged ceremonial before anyone sat down, with reciprocal offers for the best seat, a pretence at removing dust, genuflections on the part of the guest and the host, until everyone was comfortable by the time tea was brought in porcelain cups. This elaborate and leisurely ceremony is no longer observed today, although much of the spirit of courtesy survives.

Etiquette

When speaking to an emperor, it was necessary to use words specially chosen from the sayings of a court poet or from sacred texts, after first prostrating oneself before the monarch, the fount of all good and all affection.

Mandarins who represented the sovereign were bound by special formalities. "Whenever a member of the public meets a mandarin, he immediately halts, standing with his arms by his sides and his head slightly bowed, and carefully refrains from greeting him. When the need occurs to speak to a mandarin of high rank or present an appeal to him, it is necessary to kneel and bow low, indicating by this posture a desire to make a request. If the supplicant is a person of note, the mandarin will ask him to rise and he should then stand a short distance away and deliver his speech from a standing position. When one is speaking to anyone who occupies a public position, propriety demands that one should shield one's mouth with one's hand and bow respectfully."

There is still a certain amount of ceremony and formality in the Chinese character and society, in

These ornamental pavilions are typical of the tower-like structure which is a favorite motif in Chinese architectural form. The bright colors of traditional Chinese buildings have a symbolic importance. The Li Chi, *a work of etiquette written under the Chou dynasty (1122-222 B.C.), states that pillars in the emperor's apartments should be red; for the feudal princes they should be black, high officials, blue-green, and other members of the upper classes, yellow.*

spite of the social revolution.

If two Chinese of equal rank met, they had to bow to each other, and shake hands with their left hands. Respect was shown by a person of lower rank to his superior by joining his hands in front and raising them several times to his mouth, while pronouncing words of greeting.

Mandarins obstinately sought to avoid each other; when they did not succeed, the mandarin of lower rank had to get out of his sedan chair or dismount from his horse and bow deeply. If two mandarins of equal status met on foot the interchange was prolonged, since the first to take his leave lacked courtesy toward the other.

GIFTS AND MUSIC

Anyone visiting a governor had to bring rich gifts, and a long, varnished box decorated with gold flowers and divided into eight or twelve compartments containing sweetmeats. These visits necessitated much ceremonial. If a governor distinguished himself in the administration of justice and was generally attentive to the public

good, scholars, and important men would order a coat to be made of small squares of satin, symbolizing the people governed, and would present this to him on his birthday, to the accompaniment of music, singing and dancing. The governor had to feign indifference to the gift, and declare that it must have been given to him by mistake; when he finally accepted it, he did not wear it, but kept it at home among his more precious belongings.

Tea was obligatory on all occasions, but it was not drunk as it is in the West today. The ancient Chinese placed the tea-leaves in a porcelain cup, poured boiling water over them, covered the cup and placed it in a copper bowl before offering it to the guest, who removed it with both hands and tasted it. Instead of a teaspoon, the lid of the cup was used for stirring.

LETTER-WRITING

Letter-writing in ancient China was a complicated process, governed by the status of the writer and that of

Chinese horsemen in the costume of warriors of antiquity. Until the 13th century, cavalry was the major weapon of offense in battles fought on the great plains. In 1232 A.D., however, history records that the Chinese defending Kaifeng in Honan against the Mongol horsemen used weapons described as "arrows of flying fire," probably a kind of rocket. In the same battle, the defenders are said to have dropped a type of bomb from the walls.

A party of travelers in the Himalayas, in southwest China, near the borders of Pakistan, India, Nepal and Bhutan. The Himalayas, formed by modifications of the earth's crust during the Tertiary period, reach an altitude of 29,028 feet in Mt. Everest, known to Chinese as Chomolungma, the highest mountain in the world.

the person to whom he wrote. White paper was used for a person in a high position and the sheet was folded ten or twelve times, the writing starting in the second fold and the signature placed on the last. Everything was pre-ordained, including the characters themselves, the expressions and the exact distance between the lines.

Ceremonial Bowing

A deep bow, in which the subject or guest had to touch the ground with his forehead, had to be made before the emperor during audiences. This bow had to be repeated three times, not only before the emperor himself but also before letters, decrees and other symbols of his power. When vassal rulers were favored with communications from the emperor, they had to receive them in a kneeling position.

The ceremony of bowing dates back to ancient times, bows being addressed to people worthy of special regard.

There were many different types of bows: for example a deep bow made with hands clasped in front, a bow made with knee bent in a genuflection, a bow made entirely from a kneeling position, and the *kowtow* which involved kneeling and touching the ground with the forehead. This last was required in the emperor's audience chamber.

There were other bows, reserved for the gods, which involved kneeling down three times then touching the ground with the forehead three times.

Gods were divided into a hierarchy, and requirements of different gods consequently varied.

PETER THE GREAT'S AMBASSADOR

Subjects, of course, bowed before their emperor voluntarily, but ambassadors of foreign states, concerned with maintaining the dignity of their countries, did not agree so readily to prostrating themselves; the Chinese, however, insisted that traditional ceremony be observed. Discord arose between people of intelligence who desired to avoid appearing ridiculous, but usually compromise arrangements pleasing to both sides were reached.

The ambassador of Tsar Peter the Great, Ismaloff, visited the court of Emperor Kang in 1719. When the moment came for making his *kowtow* the ambassador delayed, and the emperor, with great diplomacy ordered his prime minister to *kowtow* before Peter's letter, which Ismaloff was carrying. After this, the diplomat reciprocated the homage rendered to his sovereign and bowed before the Chinese sovereign.

NO KOWTOW, NO AUDIENCE

Ambassadors who refused to *kowtow* returned to their countries without obtaining what they wanted. In 1793, when Lord McCartney, an envoy from Great Britain, faced the formality of the emperor's court, instead of prostrating himself, he knelt on one knee only. Because of this, he had to depart without proper consultation with the emperor. A similar case occurred when a Russian diplomatic mission was frustrated because its head, Count Golovin, refused to *kowtow*.

In June 1873, representatives of foreign governments asked for an audience with Emperor T'ung-Shih, who had just attained his majority and taken over the government. They obtained an audience, and were excused from performing the *kowtow*. But when the audience took place, and they were satisfied that they had defeated protocol, they found that the emperor was receiving them in a chamber destined for messengers of subject states.

Lord Amherst, the British ambassador, arrived at the imperial palace at 5 a.m. on the Aug. 20, 1816, after a long journey without rest. At the palace, he found an assembly of princes and courtiers in formal attire, who had counted on the new ambassador's weariness to induce him to *kowtow* without dispute. They jostled him and pulled at his jacket in an endeavor to make him do so. But the ambassador refused, making his tiredness and lack of suitable attire the pretext. Because of this, he had to leave the court.

The Chinese loved luxury and made such a great show of it that the law of the *Ta Ch'ing Lu*, the Manchu penal code, sought to modify their excesses. The magnificence of houses belonging to high officials, was limited by law. These houses were noted for richly decorated beams, splendid colorings, huge rooms and the lavish use of precious metals and decorative rings inlaid in the doors. Glazed tiles and very large bricks were reserved for the emperor's buildings. Hangings and tapestries were elegant, made of damask and pure gold embroidery; these were used by high magistrates but forbidden to people of middle and lower rank.

NATIONAL DRESS

THE DRESS OF THE GENERAL PUBLIC was limited to coarse silk; peasant women could wear gold earrings and one other ornament on their heads but they could use as many kingfisher feathers as they wanted.

Umbrellas and parasols were symbols of rank. For lower ranks they were made of varnished paper and for aristocrats, silk.

Officials had specially distinguished umbrellas, ornamented in silver or red (silver for the first and second grades) while the silk of which umbrellas were made was yellow for the first four grades and blue for the others.

There were other distinctions and gradations in clothing and in possessions. For example, tombs of high officials were larger and had more grandiose monuments than those permitted to lower-ranking people.

On the question of decorations, the yellow tunic was the highest distinction conferred by the emperor, and a sable tunic with tails was another mark of distinction. It was considered a great honor to have one's own distinctive horse bridles (an honor conceded only to princes) or to wear peacock feathers. Another distinction was the Order of the Dragon, which was divided into four classes: red, blue, black and yellow dragons.

The dragon was a symbol of prosperity and often appeared in heraldry. It was also a symbol of the emperor, who was called "the true dragon"; "the seat of the dragon" was his throne, and "the clothes of the dragon" were his ceremonial robes.

TROUSERS AND TUNICS

Since ancient times the Chinese have paid little attention to new fashions in clothing, preferring to wear the same type of garments for

An illustration from an illuminated manuscript, probably of Western execution, dating from the 14th century, showing Kublai Khan, the ruler of China (1280-94), supervising the construction of a road. As well as refurbishing the imperial roads, Kublai Khan was responsible for the rebuilding of Peking, the construction of the Grand Canal and the establishment of an efficient postal service.

generations. Clothes, with the exception of ceremonial robes, were generally modest and sober.

Both sexes wear broad trousers made of linen, silk or satin embroidered with cotton or raw silk, or, in the north, edged with fur. Men have always worn a long jacket, closed at the left side by four or five buttons made of gold, silver or some other metal, depending on their position. Their hands are almost entirely covered by long sleeves. On top of this jacket they wore another which reached the calf, with sleeves reaching the elbow. A white taffeta vest beneath both jackets, heavy shoes or boots and silk socks completed the costume.

In ancient China streets were colorful with many different styles of dress, showing the lively and gay temperament of the citizens. Much of the color was provided by the bright shades of silk clothes.

Empress Sin-Lin-Chin, wife of the legendary Emperor Huang-ti, is credited with perfecting a technique of manufacturing and painting silk.

Before silk was discovered, people are said to have dressed in skins. The empress, however, used woven materials and silk which then became popular with rich and poor, and all ranks of society. Woven materials were made into garments with very full sleeves reaching to the ground. Silk clothes were produced in turquoise, yellow, and many other colors. They were ornamented with feathers, flowers, ears of corn and paintings. Such clothes were, of course, for formal occasions.

Poor people wore heavier cloth in summer and skins in winter. In time, new materials came into use, including brightly colored brocades, wool and cotton. All clothes indicated, by their style and ornamentation, the social status of the wearer.

Ancient ceremonial robes are memorable for their splendor. Ceremonial costumes had sun, moon, stars, dragons and pheasants painted on them. Underneath was embroidered, in five colors, a vase used for ceremonies in the room of the ancestors, an aquatic herb, fire, white rice, a hatchet and the letter *fu*. These were symbols of virtue.

Ceremonial caps, with ribbons and balls of cotton at the sides, were worn. Caps of all types, each with a different meaning, were popular in China. Some caps covered the entire forehead and fell over the brow.

Although foreign invaders, such as the Mongols and Manchus, influenced them to some extent, clothes changed little except for the public robes of emperors and high officials. The Manchus favored brocades, long jackets, symbolic designs, ermine linings to keep out the cold, ermine sleeves and sable collars, as well as satin shoes.

Women dressed in a similar way to their husbands; the wife of a mandarin, for example, dressed according to her husband's rank.

The Pigtail

Today the pigtail has disappeared, but until a few decades ago it was still being worn. The Manchus, who themselves wore pigtails, after conquering the Chinese forced the men to shave their heads and wear pigtails. Before this, the Chinese had taken great pride in their hair, dressing it elegantly. When they were forced to shave their heads, they left a tuft in the center of the head, in the style of their conquerors, letting it grow until it was a long tress

A traditional cemetery in Loktung, in the province of Kwangtung.

known as a *pen-ze;* this hung down at the back, or was concealed by knotting it under a hat.

The people who throng the streets of Chinese cities today gradually are acquiring new national characteristics which are the antithesis of the ideals and customs that prevailed for many thousand years. To outward appearances, they differ little from a Western crowd. The absence of pigtails is an indication of a complete change in the Chinese way of life and collective psychology.

Chinese people have thick black hair, expressive black eyes, and small noses. They are a handsome people. The old men have rather long and fine beards; beards grown by scholars, philosophers and patriarchs were never cut.

The streets in those Chinese cities which the Communists have more thoroughly organized have lost much of their former picturesque quality. Most people dress in a uniform way, mainly in overalls, or blue cotton garments, with jackets buttoning up to the neck. Men wear cloth caps and women go bareheaded, or wear scarves. Nevertheless, there are still to be seen, mingling with crowds of solemn Chinese workers, some wearing ornate costumes; these people usually belong to national minorities, who still prefer their traditional costumes.

Women's Feet

The practice of binding women's feet so that they would remain small is a feature uniquely Chinese. It is difficult to believe that Chinese women voluntarily underwent the considerable pain involved in halting the process of the natural growth of the feet, and accepted the almost crippling effect it had.

The small size of the foot was achieved after years of binding which began at an early age. The big toe was left free in its natural position, while the other toes were curved until they were hidden under the sole of the foot and held in place by tight bandages. Bound thus the foot's growth was extremely painful; it was deformed and became uniformly small. The result was that Chinese women moved with a hopping gait all their lives.

Fashion decreed that the deformation of the feet was a sign of distinction, and women, in the interests of beauty, submitted to the practice. Only peasant women, who had to walk and work the hard way, and

mountain people were not bound by the practice. If a girl rebelled against having her feet bound, she might be expelled from home; if not, her life at home would be made miserable.

THE EMPRESS'S FEET

The origin of the custom is unknown. According to some sources, it was invented by men, with the object of ensuring for themselves perpetual domestic fidelity by making it difficult for wives to move away from their homes. Others say it was invented to increase feminine grace and to teach women the virtue of discipline, by enduring pain, and the value of beauty. Some blame the custom on a legendary empress, who, having naturally small feet herself, decided to ensure their continuing beauty by tying them in tight bandanges so that they would not grow; thus she started a fashion that became a custom. But it is possible that the beautiful empress wished to transform a personal deformity into a desirable attribute.

The custom of binding women's feet lasted until the fall of the empire in 1912, when measures were taken by the republican government to stop it.

MEDICINE

ACCORDING TO LEGEND, THE FATHER of Chinese medicine was the Emperor Shen Nung, (c. 2838-2698 B.C.) who is believed to have had a transparent stomach; thus he was able to observe the workings of the digestive tract and write a thesis on the subject. The stethoscope is not used in Chinese medicine, which makes its diagnosis by feeling the pulse.

Hua T'o, a famous medical man, lived in the late 2nd century. He was very skillful at acupuncture, a method of puncturing the skin to relieve pain, but fell afoul of the Emperor Ts'ao Ts'ao (192-220 A.D.) who, disappointed by a course of treatment, sentenced Hua T'o to death. According to legend, Hua T'o presented his jailer with a book of prescriptions, which is still used today.

Quacks and Students

Until the Ch'ou dynasty China had no professional doctors in the Western meaning, and anyone from incompetent quacks to learned students of medicine could practice. Superstitions surrounding the dead prevented the

Funerary urns for preserving the ashes of the departed. The veneration of ancestral spirits is an important part of traditional Chinese religious practice. Formerly, most houses had a place set aside for the ancestral tablets, wooden panels inscribed with the name, dates and title of the deceased; they were not unlike Western tombstones.

carrying out of autopsies and operations, so that knowledge of anatomy was sketchy.

There were no guiding scientific principles in Chinese chemistry or physics. The basic theory of medicine was philosophic, deriving from a cosmic notion that the universe and the human body each was governed by the Yang, or male principle, which is light, active and represents heaven, and its balance with the Yin, the female principle, which is dark, passive and represents the earth.

The body was believed to be composed of five elements: water, wood, metal, soil and fire. These were associated with the planets, the climate, the colors and sounds, each of which were arbitrarily divided into five other different categories.

Astrology entered into medical deliberations and disease was sometimes diagnosed on the basis of a fancied movement of the planets.

Expertise was handed from father

the great forces that rule the world, *Yin* and *Yang*, which according to the *Nei Ching* acted both on the human body and on the universe, was another supposed cause of illness.

The object of acupuncture is to administer a shock to an organ which has atrophied. Puncture by silver needles was direct or indirect. The direct method was used in serious cases. When using the indirect method the body was divided into areas, one or more being punctured. Each area related to one of the five organs: the heart, kidneys, liver, lungs and spleen. These were considered storage organs. The viscera, which got rid of waste matter, included the stomach, intestines, gallbladder and bladder. Each organ was associated with a planet. There were 365 bones, one for each day of the year.

IN THE CASE OF A CORPSE

A body, after death, became untouchable, and autopsy led to popular resentment but this did not preclude post-mortem examination if foul play was suspected. Advice on the subject was given to magistrates in a book, *Lo Hsi Yuan Lu*, compiled during the latter Sung dynasty.

They were advised to establish, before death if possible, the exact number of wounds inflicted and the depth of each to avoid having to resort to dissection to learn the cause of death. If dissection were unavoidable, it had to be carried out with every precaution. The corpse had to be whole, not in a state of decomposition, and in view of the gravity of the inquest, the magistrate himself must preside. In spite of the rules laid down in *Lo Hsi Yuan Lu*, superstition persisted, and autopsy continued to be made difficult.

It was considered advisable to keep at hand earthenware bowls, onions, red pepper, salt, white plums, corn, and vinegar.

INVISIBLE WOUNDS

In the case of invisible wounds, vinegar and corn were sprinkled on the corpse, which was examined out-

to son, until during the Chou dynasty a medical school was set up by the emperor. This school awarded diplomas on the basis of available medical knowledge. Diplomas were given to doctors, surgeons and veterinary surgeons capable of dealing with 60 per cent of illnesses; it was considered that 50 per cent at least could be cured naturally, without recourse to medical attention.

In spite of these shortcomings, Chinese medicine had advantages. Sages and experienced doctors worked out, almost by instinct, methods of diagnosis; several treatments were sound; dieting was developed; and many diseases were cured with great effeciency.

The Blood and Medicine

The *Nei Ching*, an ancient treatise on physiology by an unknown hand, written probably in the 3rd century B.C., was the foundation of

Chinese medicine. This work reveals that the idea of the circulation of the blood was, at least, considered at an early date. It describes the functions of the heart.

Chinese medicinal preparations can be divided into three main groups: animal, vegetable, and mineral. The animal group comprised more than seventy basic substances, found in animals, fish, shell-fish, reptiles, insects, etc. The second group included more than 300 ingredients from plants. The mineral group included almost fifty substances, found in metals, minerals, and crystal.

ACUPUNCTURE

Acupuncture was practiced early in the history of Chinese medicine with needles made of flint. Acupuncture was thought to combat inertia on the part of one of the five main organs, besides disorders of the organ in question. Lack of equilibrium in its relationship with doors under an oil-cloth shade. Wounds, it was believed, would then appear.

If further difficulty in identifying wounds arose, white plums were added to the corn and vinegar. If the wounds still did not appear, red pepper, onion and salt were sprinkled onto the body

In cases where blows, real or simulated were suspected, an ointment was applied. This was made of several ingredients, including black plums, safflower, sapan wood, alum and boiling vinegar. If these were poured on to the body, it was believed that simulated blows would become apparent. Other ointments were used to find out if congealed blood was genuine or not.

SKELETONS AND RESUCITATION

If a skeleton was to be examined, a bright day had to be chosen. A trench for the skeleton five feet long, three feet wide, and two feet deep was dug, heated by burning coal and brushwood, and filled, first by sprinkling it with spirit and vinegar, and then, while vapor was still rising, with rushes and reeds. After two or three hours, the skeleton would be examined under a red, waterproof, canvas shade.

If the weather was rainy, the skeleton would be boiled in an earthenware basin with vinegar, salt and plums, and carefully washed. A method considered most effective, was to examine the skeleton under a yellow oil-cloth shade; this, it was thought, left no hidden wound undetected.

It was believed that there were ways of restoring a dead man to life. Traditionally, if a man had been hanged, it was thought possible to restore his life if death had occurred between dawn and dusk, but it was more difficult if death occurred at night. The mouth of the victim was covered by a hand for four hours, without interruption. If a little warmth remained below the heart, it was believed that the victim would revive. Another method was to take about a quarter ounce of goat's blood and rub it, mixed with wine, against the body.

Acrobatic jugglers give an open-air display of their skill before a packed audience. In accordance with Communist ideology, the present regime encourages the folk arts. Traditional pastimes and crafts of all kinds are sponsored by the state and special privileges are accorded to those who excel at them.

Chinese Herbs and Health

In China, as in all other countries, herbal, animal and mineral remedies for illness were developed by rural sages who treated the sick independently of academic medicine. At a certain stages in history these were absorbed into usage by physicians. The *Pen-Ts'ao Kang* (The Herbal Encyclopedia) of Li Shih-chen (1552-78) assembled some 1000 of such medicines which were part of the Chinese medical tradition going back to prehistoric times. The drugs included rhubarb, iron, camphor, aconite, castor oil and Indian hemp, all commonly used in the West and all first used in China.

The Chinese principle in using drugs was based on the classical Chinese medical aim which was to harmonize the dual forces of Yang and Yin; a drug was used to restore or preserve balance. The results achieved were impressive and, as elsewhere, the ancient rural traditions of herbal cures added much to medical science and achieved impressive results among the sick and poor.

CRAFTS

The Wall and the Secretive Craftsmen

The Great Wall of China is both a unique masterpiece of building and a symbol of ancient China's resolute isolation from the rest of the world. In the 3rd century B.C. it was created by Emperor Shih Huang-ti, who extended the already existing walls until they merged and became the Great Wall. The emperor designed it to defend his realm from barbarian invasions. In parts it is more than twenty centuries old. Within its confines the Chinese

sedulously developed their native crafts, of which it is a mammoth example. The secrets of their crafts were carefully preserved and protected. No foreigner was allowed to learn craft secrets. Finally, the Great Wall yielded before the onslaught of Genghis Khan and his armies of Mongols. But Chinese craftsmen still pursued their work in secrecy.

THE GREAT WALL

The wall stretches for 1500 miles from the Gulf of Chihli to Kansu province, over mountains and rivers, scaling inaccessible cliffs and crossing deep valleys; in places it is wide enough to serve as a road upon which an army can march. It is built of earth and stone, which in the eastern section was faced with brick. It has been modified and in places rebuilt, since it was first erected. Watch towers, ranging from thirty to forty feet high are placed on it at intervals of 200 yards with com-

plete forts built in at strategic points.

At least a million soldiers are said to have been garrisoned along the wall on the alert to stem Mongol invasions, which for sixteen centuries were successfully halted. After its strictly military use had come to an end following the ultimate and successful invasion of the Mongols, the Great Wall continued to enclose and protect Chinese culture from outside influences.

There are, as far as is known, no longer garrisons on the Great Wall today, and its interest lies in history and myth.

Writing with Reeds and Brushes

In China writing used to be done, and sometimes still is done, with a brush. According to tradition, the brush was invented by General Meng T'ien, who is renowned for having directed the building of the Great Wall in the reign of the Emperor

Shih Huang-ti (221-210 B.C.). Until recent times the writing brush was made of fox, beaver or rabbit hair. Before the brush was invented, Chinese calligraphers wrote with a rush or reed, the point of which was splayed out.

BAMBOO BOOKS

They dipped this in a black lacquer or varnish before painting with it on a tablet of bamboo. The *Bamboo Books* (299 B.C.) containing the annals of the state of Tsin and Wei are examples of this mode of writing.

Before the invention of black varnish the Chinese etched ideograms on bamboo with a stylus or sharpened, pointed stick.

INVENTION OF PAPER

Paper was invented in China in 105 B.C., as a result of the experiments of a craftsman named Ts'ai-Lun, who made it by a simple process. He pounded vegetable fibers to a pulp and then compressed them into sheets of paper.

OIL OF SESAME INK

Chinese ink is considered the best ink. It is made from lamp-black produced by a sooty flame of oil of sesame or turnip seeds. Solid ink was produced by burning resin, mixed with size or isinglass perfumed with a musk or camphor. Liquid ink was obtained by dissolving a piece of solid ink in a little water on a stone or marble slab.

SPECIAL INK FOR THE EMPEROR

In imperial times, the common colors used by their subjects were not good enough for emperors; they used a red ink made with vermilion, from an ore found in many provinces, especially Hunan and Kweichow.

There are different theories and dates about the origin of ink, but most scholars agree that it goes back to very ancient times. According to one tradition it originated in Korea, and was sent with other gifts from the king of that country to the emperor. The Chinese copied and refined it. Korean ink was made from lampblack obtained by burning seasoned pinewood; this was bound together with ash from burned antlers.

Having perfected an incomparable ink, the Chinese carefully guarded the secret of its manufacture for many centuries. Travelers and missionaries who later brought the for-

An old Chinese peddler carries his wares in the traditional manner.

mula back to Europe, spoke of mysterious compounds and ingredients which they could not obtain.

PAPER TREES AND PRECIOUS GARBAGE

Paper was made in early China either from the bark of the *cha* tree or the mulberry; or from the second layer of bark of the *fu-yung* tree, which is also called the paper-tree; or from the fibers of the second bark of the bamboo. The fine white paper obtained from bamboo was used for writing, printing and for the visiting cards which played a big part in Chinese social life.

Bamboo was the most important type of paper. It was manufactured in the southern regions of China, especially in the province of Fukien. Harvesting of bamboo on the mountains, was in June, when the early leaves began to grow. Pieces of the plant, five to six feet long, were cut, and soaked in a special hollow carved in the rocks. This artifical tank was filled with water brought in bamboo pipes from the mountain streams. Among the processes that followed was pressing the pulped bamboo into fine sheets, heating and drying them. In some provinces, no book made from bamboo paper was wasted; even if they were old, spoiled, or of no further use, such volumes were rescued and repulped after ink, drawings and markings were removed. In the north of China, paper was never considered mere garbage as in the southern Chinese provinces. Paper, to the northern Chinese, was precious.

The cleaning and repulping process was practiced rigorously. In the towns and villages of the north if a piece of paper was seen lying in a street, it would be taken to a factory to be made into new paper. This custom of reprocessing waste paper applied to both fine and coarse paper.

The coarsest paper was made from the bark of the *chu* tree. During the period of the T'ang dynasty a custom arose of burning offerings of "resuscitated" paper, instead of more expensive materials such as silks, as sacrifices to the dead. Funeral votive ornaments were specially manufactured with this second-hand paper.

In addition to those already mentioned, there were many other kinds of paper which differed according to methods of manufacture and to their purpose. This range included coarse, resistant paper for wrapping fruit; paper for screens for silk-

A Tibetan worshiper with a prayer wheel. Every time the wheel revolves the prayers inscribed on it are assumed to be sent to the deity.

Writing

The ancient system of Chinese writing is said to have been invented worm eggs, made from the bark of the mulberry tree; paper for lampshades and umbrellas; paper for windows and other types. Different provinces specialized in different types of paper manufacture.

by two legendary figures, Fu-hsi and Ts'ang-Chieh. As a result of this achievement, Heaven rained grain upon the peoples.

According to the legend, Ts'ang-Chieh thought of ideograms by observing the foot-prints birds make in the sand. This was said to have happened in about 3000 B.C. In Chinese writing, each character

have proliferated throughout history. A list of 3300 ideograms was compiled in the 2nd century B.C., while a later work, compiled toward the begininng of the Christian era, a period during which calligraphy flourished, comprised 7380 characters. The imperial dictionary of 1716 listed 40,000 ideograms.

It is calculated that 4000 of the characters in this dictionary are in current use and are necessary to read any kind of book, another 2000 are proper names and little-used technical terms; the other 34,000 are obsolete duplications of little value, which hardly anyone recognizes at first sight, and which are never used. In short, to be able to read every kind of book, one must know about 6000 characters.

PAGE OF CHINESE BOOK

The page of a Chinese book with its symmetrical arrangement resembles a chessboard, in which the tiny black characters are composed of several fine small lines which appear to have absolutely nothing in common with each other at first sight. Chinese writing has nothing in common with Latin, Russian or Arabic, but instead resembles Egyptian hieroglyphics, which, like Chinese characters, are pictures in a conventionalized form.

In the written language, ideograms do not correspond to a precise word but form only a generic idea, which is extremely difficult to translate precisely. Many characters are identical, but of different meaning. There is no punctuation, no capital letters, nor any arrangement in paragraphs. Understanding of Chinese, therefore, comes from practice, rather than learning rules. It is not a logical language, and reading it is almost impossible in the West, for all save a relatively few scholars who have given their lives to Chinese studies.

Weaving Fine Silk

According to legend, women, eager to exchange clothes made from skins for something lighter and more elegant, were responsible for the invention of silk.

was originally a picture of the object it denoted. Bronze vases, dating back to about 1500 B.C. carry symbols in the form of tiny figures; these give an idea of archaic ideograms describing sacred things, such as temples and sacrifices.

The ideogram is not limited to a pictorial representation of an object, but from quite early times they were used to depict abstract ideas. Today, however, when China is undergoing a technological revolution, and the whole structure of society is chang-

ing, problems of expressing the language in writing are increasingly apparent. For Chinese writing is, of its nature, unprecise and unfitted for scientific treatises and textbooks.

Modern scholars, for example, disagree widely on the meaning of many ancient phrases found on commemorative stones and in books on calligraphy. Even contemporary ideograms present problems.

Some Chinese attribute mysterious philosophical and magical origins to the ideographic symbols which

An empress, wife of the legendary Emperor Huang-ti, is mentioned as a patron of the rearing of silkworms. Silk, silkworms, mulberry trees and the art of weaving fine silk were brought to Italy from China, and then spread to the rest of Europe.

With the exception of the poorer peasants, who wore cotton, silk was worn by everyone. Certain provinces specialized in the manufacture of silk. The silk industry at Nanking for example, dates from very early times.

In 1368, at the beginning of the Ming dynasty, a Chinese craftsman wrote a treatise on silk and the care of silkworms. For centuries this was a standard book of reference for silk cultivators.

SILKWORMS

Parts of this work were quoted in an instructive and charming 18th century work by Leon d'Hervy. He wrote:

"Silkworms prefer quiet and cannot bear deafening noises; their houses, built of little boards, must be peaceful; they like warmth and suffer from damp. In a peaceful house, silkworms can escape from the shouts and cries of men; in a well-sealed house they can be sheltered from the sudden assaults of the south wind; the little boards protect them from exhalations and damp vapors rising from the ground. Let the house of the silkworms be placed far away from dungheaps and from everything that exudes offensive smells, such as stables and cowsheds. Be careful that no light penetrates the little windows during the night, nor flashes in suddenly. And extinguish during the rearing season, those paper wicks that give off such a bad smell."

"The worms do not like eating damp leaves; they do not like eating hot leaves; newly hatched worms cannot bear the smell of fried fish; do not beat on noisy instruments in

has given birth within the past month must undertake the rearing of silk-worms.

"Silk-worms will not take food from anyone who smells of wine; from birth they do not like smoke, they cannot bear the smell of burning skin, animal or human hair in their vicinity; they dislike the scent of musk or that given off by certain herbivorous animals; they do not like a window exposed to the wind to be opened during the day; worms shelter from the rays of the setting sun; they shelter from the keen strong wind when the temperature in the little house is high; they shelter from the heat when the temperature is fresh; and they do not gladly welcome dirty people."

Jade

Jade is hard stone, almost oily to the touch. It is plentiful in rivers near Suchow. It varies in color, ranging from green, greenish yellow, black and gray, and a mixture of black, white and gray. When jade is struck with a wooden hammer it gives a ringing sound. It is used to make dress ornaments, statuettes, pendants and buttons.

The Chinese believed that jade was pleasing to the gods and it was lavishly employed in imperial decorations. It was supposed to bring good

fortune, and was believed to be an elixir of youth.

Stones similar to jade are found in rivers in other parts of China. These are black or milk white in color and give off a metallic sound when struck.

There are also other Chinese stones from which percussion musical instruments are made. The most beautiful and melodious of these was called *ju*, but supplies of it are now exhausted.

Porcelain

Porcelain is said to have been made originally in the province of Kiangsi, where it is still an important industry. The early history of this art is uncertain. Some experts claim that it originated at the beginning of the 7th century A.D.

Kingtechen, a town in the province of Kiangsi, is famous for porcelain manufacture, and at one time it had more than 500 factories.

The method of manufacturing porcelain was kept such a close secret from foreigners that travelers were not permitted to stay overnight in Kingtechen.

INVISIBLE INSECTS

In a Chinese encyclopedic work in eight volumes, *The History of the Porcelains of the Imperial Factory of Kingtechen*, which was trans-

Women of the Miao, a national minority centered mainly in Kweichow, perform a traditional dance. The Miao, who are mainly farmers and craftsmen, have their own religious customs from which their dances have evolved. Dancing troupes from the national minorities are encouraged by the Chinese government, who look on dancing as a profitable group occupation; they are sent on tours of the large cities and even give performances abroad.

lated into French by Stanislaus Julien, there are essays and quotations from the chief works written on porcelain and the methods of firing it. The manufacture of porcelain has always been a difficult and delicate art, needing highly specialized training and study. Some of its secrets have been lost, for example, the art of painting fish, insects and other creatures or other animals inside vessels, which became visible only when the vessel was filled with liquid.

Lacquer

Like porcelain, lacquer is a typical product of China and finely exemplifies the skill of China's artisans. Lacquer is a varnish which on exposure to the air becomes a brilliant, shiny black. It is usually applied to tea caddies, delicate tables, screens and other small articles of furniture.

The town of Canton, where there are many factories, still specializes in this product, but the craftsmen of Nanking are considered the most skilled in the art.

Lacquer is a resin taken from a plant which grows in the provinces of Kiangsi, Chekiang and Honan in China, and also in parts of Japan. The Swedish naturalist, Carolus Linneaus (1710-1788), called the plant *Augia sinensis*.

CRAFTSMAN'S PATIENCE

From earliest times lacquer of various qualities was sent to Canton; the most highly valued was a light reddish brown in color, while others were of lighter shades. The whitish lacquers, like faintly tinted milk or mastic-gray, were not thought to be valuable.

After undergoing several complicated processes, the varnish is ready and is painted in thin layers on pieces of furniture.

Applying the design in color and gilding into lacquered surfaces is a work of infinite patience involving long and tedious processes. Working with lacquer is dangerous because the fumes may harm the craftsman's bronchial tubes.

Chinese Gardens

The Chinese are skillful gardeners, and are very fond of flowers. Flowers play a part in the life of every Chinese, giving aesthetic pleasure and having symbolic meaning.

Chinese gardeners, for many centuries, have used artificial heating to hasten the growth of fruit and vegetables and to grow them out of season. They have been able to modify the natural colors and shape of flowers to achieve more vivid floral effects. Dwarf varieties of plants are popular; giant species have been scaled down, and hedgerow flowers have been developed into exotic garden flowers. From China, methods of gardening and horticulture have been exported to the countries of Europe, together with a technical skill and delicacy in research that underlies the traditional artistic taste of a highly elegant type of craftsmanship.

Trees of peonies covered with large pink-red leaves, chrysanthemums, pink and blue hortensias, wisteria on its twisting stem, azaleas, and many other species grow throughout China.

In Chinese plays, when an emperor reads a proclamation to his people, it is written with a peony flower, as in the comedy *Chains of Love* by Chiao Meng-fu. In this play, one of the characters is a girl called Plum Flower or Peach Flower remarkable for her modesty, kindliness and virtue.

There are many poems and novels in which flowers are symbols and often form a basis for a framework of moral allegory.

Flowers composed into bouquets play a prominent part in festivals. The orchid, for instance, figures in several ancient plays. In other plays, young men and women meet and exchange flowers. In a Teheng drama, a mother conceives a child as soon as she catches sight of a special orchid, which is imbued with magical power.

The arrangement of flowers and their cultivation are perhaps the most characteristic of Chinese crafts. Chinese gardeners try to complement a beautiful landscape with magnificent flower gardens. Gardens are not symmetrically arranged; even the smallest traditional garden tries to give an impression of rugged mountain scenery and studied irregularity.

Rickshaws, Sedans and Carriages

A rickshaw is a light carriage with a hood, drawn on two wheels by a man trained to endure fatigue

Part of a courtyard in a temple in Peking, showing animal figures, which form an important and symbolic part of Chinese temple decorations.

in the more efficient form of the tricycle rickshaw.

BLUE LINING, BLACK CUSHIONS

In ancient China, the sedan chair was a common means of transport among the rich. In the past, the aristocracy and high officials regarded it as undignified to walk and so were carried everywhere in sedan chairs. Sedan chairs used by dignitaries were carried by two or three men, and were covered with green cloth. Apart from these, the nobility used a small horse-drawn carriage, similar to those used by poor people.

Some of these horse-drawn carriages were long and closed in front, with a door at the side; others were entirely open. All were lined in blue material and the seats were covered in black cushions. The driver, holding the reins, sat in front. Since those carriages had no springs, they were uncomfortable when the road was rough and travelers learned that discomfort could be lessened by sitting a long way behind the wheels, where there were fewer shocks. The back seats thus were more popular.

SEDAN ON A STICK

There were more modest sedan chairs which were supported by a pole passed through a ring on the cab, which resembled a cage. These were carried by two men who walked barefoot, lightly and swiftly.

These men were famous for their speed and the weight they could carry. This form of transport was particularly common in river ports.

An 18th-century chronicler, Du Halde, states that in the ports of the Min River on smooth flat roads, the Chinese hoisted a sail to their wagons and thus helped them to speed along like boats in a stiff breeze.

Chinese Pony Express

According to tradition, five thousand years ago China had a mail service covering the whole empire. This carried the emperor's edicts and the official gazette from Peking to the regional governments.

The system, in some parts of China, was similar to that used by the Pony Express of the old West in the U.S.A. Mailmen traveled on horseback to Tibet and Manchuria, and on foot to southern China. The job was strenuous; they covered over 200 *li* per day, that is, about sixty miles, and more if their messages

A peasant and a small girl contemplate the blossoms on a cherry tree. The contemplation of nature plays an important part in both Chinese art and philosophy, since it is believed that the study of beautiful landscapes, in particular mountain landscapes, generates a spirit of calm. Flowers are of similar importance and often have symbolic meanings when they appear in literature.

and to run quickly. The Communist government, for ideological reasons, prohibited these vehicles in 1949, but before that they were an integral feature of the Chinese scene.

At one time, rickshaws were to be seen in all large cities, lined up at railroad stations waiting for customers, like taxi cabs in European and American towns. Westerners compared rickshaw men to beasts of burden. An occupation so humble and tiring, it was thought, was unnecessary because in China there are many animals that could have been trained for transport purposes. It

should have been possible, it was said, to organize a less degrading form of transport. But in China manpower is cheap and easily obtained and the rickshaw man found his occupation profitable and did not consider it in any way degrading.

In appearance, almost all rickshaw men looked old; the work aged men prematurely. By nature the Chinese are docile and hardworking people with an innate kindness and desire to be useful to their neighbors. This attitude brought dignity to the humble occupation of pulling a rickshaw, which now survives only were urgent. They traveled quickly, changing horses often, using a series of runners each covering as little as three miles. There were many staging posts linking different parts of the country, all facilitating the distribution of information.

Messengers wore a special uniform, consisting of a wide-sleeved dark-blue silk coat, short trousers, and straw sandals.

They carried lanterns, which they kept alight as they sped through the night. Letters, journals, even parcels (parcels were very small) were carried on the mailman's back wrapped in a large kerchief. A bell worn at his neck tinkled and heralded the approach of the royal messenger.

There were separate organizations to take governmental and private mail. They offered the public prices based on distance, difficulty, and the value of the goods carried. As a useful security measure the recipient paid the postal fee, not the sender.

Marco Polo in his *Travels*, wrote: "Now you must know that from this

Members of a construction gang, resting from their work, are entertained by a local troupe of actors. Local drama, as distinct from the Chinese classical theater which centers on the great cities, is, like other folk arts, encouraged by the Communist regime. Traditional plays have been revived and revised to suit the needs both of modern taste and of political ideology.

city go forth many messengers to many provinces: the one goes to one province, the other to another, for it is laid down where each one shall go. Know, too, that when they set off from Comblau, these messengers find a post after traveling twenty-five miles along any road, and this post boasts a vast and beautiful mansion where lodge the messengers of the Great Sire." Marco Polo goes on to tell how these staging posts, situated at twenty-five mile intervals in every direction, each had hundreds of horses always at the ready for messengers as they arrived. In more sparsely populated areas they were further apart, sometimes as much as thirty or even forty miles.

TWO HUNDRED THOUSAND HORSES

In the whole empire, including every province, there were some 10,000 stages and 200,000 horses for the use of messengers. Foot messengers had their own posts at three-mile intervals between the horse stages.

These foot messengers carried "belts full of bells, which can be heard from afar. They run at full speed, as far as three miles, and the others at the end of the three miles hear these bells a long way off, and

being prepared run toward the messenger, and take whatever it is he is carrying, be it only a small letter. The next sets off at a run, covers three miles, just as the one before."

At the beginning of the 19th century, the Chinese postal service was remodeled on the Western pattern, with government control, revenue by means of stamps, and civil servants specially selected to control this service.

PASTIMES

Dice, Chess, Cockfights and Kites

THE CHINESE ARE INVETERATE GAMBLERS; their favorite game is cards. These are smaller in size and narrower than the Western type, and each pack contains more cards.

Dicing also is popular and the dice are marked like American dice.

Richer people played chess. Chinese chess boards unlike the Western kind are made up of squares in the same color divided by lines. There are popular variations on chess and checkers, and dominoes, too, is played. Chinese chess players are internationally famous in modern times.

Cock-fighting is a national sport, a taste common among Oriental peoples. Sometimes razor blades were strapped to the legs of the birds, which then were encouraged to fight to the death. Quails also were trained for fighting, and even crickets. The latter fought, wounding and disfiguring each other, on a special arena consisting of circular sieve on a table.

Betting was common at such fights; since this often led to public brawls it eventually brought official suppression of the sport, which, however, continued to be organized in secret.

CHINESE TOPS AND HUNTSMEN

Children amuse themselves more peaceably. Their favorite toys are tops and kites. Kites, though popular in America, have always been taken much more seriously in China. Chinese kites are most attractively made—indeed kite-making in China is an art form: the shapes vary, they have beautiful colors, and are painted with symbols and imaginative designs.

Hunting was a favorite pursuit of the upper classes, and extensive game reserves were set aside for hunting. Peasants were allowed to kill only those animals that damage crops because for them hunting was a necessity rather than a pleasure.

Birds and Pumpkins

In some provinces, fishermen train cormorants to catch fish. A ring is fixed round the bird's neck which prevents it from swallowing the fish completely. A catch lodged in its neck, the bird flies to its master's boat, where the fish is extracted. The cormorant is then returned to fishing.

Thousands of birds were used to fish in this way on the Imperial Canal of Peking and the nearby lake. The method is still practiced.

There was another ingenious way of catching fish, which consisted of fixing a white-topped table to a boat and tilting it so that the rays of the moon striking the surface made it glitter like a sheet of water. Fish were deceived into leaping on to the table and then they were caught in a net.

The pumpkin method of catching water-fowl was practiced on lakes. A hunter with a pumpkin over his head floated on the water toward birds and when he reached them he seized one by the legs and drew it under water. The whole process was

A classical Chinese drama being performed in Peking.

Pupils at a drama school receive an open-air lesson in the technique of make-up. In the traditional Chinese theater characters are distinguished by special make-up, symbolic colors and dress and false hair. Until 1949, female roles were always played by men, but in recent years Chinese drama has been much influenced by Western methods of staging, lighting and general production.

noiseless so that the other birds would not be frightened away. This method also is still practiced.

Gambling

The Chinese as has been noted, are inveterate gamblers and many are notoriously bad losers.

Mandarins in the 19th century were famous for wagering not only their houses, furniture and possessions, but even their wives. Wives were considered objects of property and at the free disposal of their husbands.

The Chinese did not gamble only at cards and dice. Litigation became a national sport, a game of chance played in the courts. People gambled by going to law with each other on trivial pretexts and often the result had serious, by Western standards, consequences. If a man lost a legal case, he might hang himself on his opponent's gate or in his garden, to bring the curse of Heaven on his opponent.

The unfortunate winner of the law-suit, besides being mortified at finding a corpse on his premises had to suffer the contempt of his fellow-citizens who considered him a criminal and provoker of the divine wrath.

STAKING THE LADY

No other country has had more riots, woundings and murders as a result of gambling. Laws against gambling quarrels were severe and they were carried into effect without discrimination. One famous case occurred in 1827, in Peking, when a prince was sentenced by order of Emperor Tao-Kuang (1821-1851).

The prince's name was Chang-Kang. He was young, handsome, educated and a favorite of his uncle, the emperor, who bestowed on him the privilege of walking along the *Sacred Way*, a road some twenty-five miles long, leading from the capital, Peking, to the imperial residence. It was sunk some three feet below ground level and had golden tracks for the emperor's carriage-wheels. Everyone, except those specially honored, were forbidden to use it, on pain of death.

But Prince Chang-Kang was a gambler and his insensate love of gaming was not disciplined by his love for his wife, the daughter of a mandarin. When she died, he took a young Mongolian girl as a concubine, dressing her elaborately in gold, pearls and other finery.

One day, Prince Chang-Kang gave a reception at one of his country villas, during which he was foolish enough to gamble with his friends, and despite his privileged position as *Walker of the Sacred Way* and his great wealth, he lost all—his money,

Actors of the Peking National Theater apply their make-up before a performance. In recent years Chinese theatrical companies have given successful performances all over Asia and in Europe, Canada and South America. Some traditional plays survive in their original form, but others have been considerably revised on religious, moral, nationalistic and political grounds.

horses, coaches, land, house and the jewels he had brought for his concubine. He would have staked the lady too, but his opponent sarcastically commented on his weakness which made him lose his temper. Seizing his dagger, he plunged it into his adversary's chest, killing him. The emperor wept, but justice was done and the prince was brought to trial, his face covered with a red veil, signifying that he had shed human blood.

In China executions took place once a year on a day set aside for the purpose. They were attended by great crowds who treated the affair as a public holiday.

On July 1, 1827, Prince Chang-Kang was taken to a garden containing tombstones; there, surrounded by the mandarins, the court and the emperor's family, he knelt before his father's grave. Priests recited prayers, and on completing them, they clapped hands and the bystanders burst into sobs of lamentation. After a few minutes a new signal ended this display of emotion and the President of the court read the sentence of the court and of the emperor. He then handed the prince a silken cord with a slip-knot, and the prince put this round his neck. Five executioners grasped each end and, in a silence broken only by the

beat of a drum, they pulled and the prince was strangled.

This was the normal form of execution for criminals of noble birth, and the story of the foolish Prince Chang-Kang is a cautionary tale on the evils of gambling which still is told to Chinese children.

Opium Smoking

Today the Chinese government is attempting to combat addiction to opium, and it is less widespread than formerly. Smoking-dens varied in type, some for the rich, others for the less wealthy. They were classed according to the number of lamps, servants and other amenities and provided everything needed by the addict, including pipes, bed and equipment for a modest price.

Opium smokers lie on wooden divans; between these are low rectangular tables holding pipes, boxes containing opium and metal lamps. These lamps are flat, with a wick soaked in sesame oil or soya oil projecting upward. The glass of the lamps is shaped like a truncated cone. The pipes, usually made of wood or ivory, though sometimes of bone, are about twenty inches long, closed at one end and open at the other. A flat earthenware or metal bowl with a small aperture is set about six or eight inches from the closed end.

THE OPIUM BOILS

The lamp is lit with a long stem, pointed at one end, spoonshaped at the other, and from the box one pellet of opium is removed. The opium is warmed by the lamp flame until it swells and hardens. It is rolled into a conical shape, and fitted into the hole in the bowl of the pipe. The smoker smokes the pipe, holding the bowl close to the wick of the lamp; the opium boils and the smoker inhales the smoke, exhaling through his nose.

Opium smoking causes great physical harm, and China was ravaged by it for centuries. The country had produced opium long before it began to be smoked. Opium poppies were cultivated for their decorative qualities, as early as the beginning of the 17th century. Before that, poppies had been imported for their medicinal qualities.

OPIUM GROWING

Poppies were sown in November, and the sap gathered in February and March, care being taken to see the soil was well turned, weeded and watered. Circular incisions were made in the capsule when the petals fell. This operation took place in the evening, and by morning the sap had exuded from the plant in black paste, which was collected and made into a cake.

To make it smokeable additional

treatment was required. It had to be boiled, dried over a fire, macerated, cooked again, strained and evaporated, using special instruments. Careful handling and constant attention were necessary.

Addiction to opium was deep-rooted among the Chinese in the 19th century, and traffic in opium involved British and French vested interests. During the second half of the 19th century, the famous Opium Wars were waged in order to assert the rights of these countries to import opium into China. Later, after conferences at Shanghai and at the

Young drama students in Peking practice during a music lesson. After 1949 the theater, which was then nearly bankrupt, came under state control and was granted substantial subsidies. In 1950 the Central Dramatic Institute was opened in Peking to provide a minimum of seven years' training for drama students from the age of eleven years. The Peking Drama School, opened in 1952, provides each graduate with a thorough grounding in sixty classical dramas.

A sacred figure in the temple of the Dalai Lama in Peking. The "Lord of Heaven", seated on a lion which serves as his throne, holds in his hands the symbols of his authority. The figure is ornamented with inlays of precious stones. Lamaism never achieved great success in China Proper, but it was encouraged by the imperial rulers as a useful link with the people of Mongolia and Tibet.

Hague, Europeans reduced their trade in opium. Subsequently, however, the weakening of central political authority and general unrest in the early years of the 20th century led to a spread in opium addiction throughout China.

Sports in China Today

During the 52 years since the establishment of the Chinese republic and since the Chinese Communist government was set up in 1949, sports in China have become Westernized.

Chinese now play football, basketball, volleyball and table-tennis. They excel at weight-lifting. They are good swimmers: Mao Tse-tung, Chairman of the Chinese Communist Party, for example, repeatedly swam the Yangtze while in his sixties to encourage the people to take up the sport.

FOOTBALL

Football is so popular that in Shanghai alone there are more than 3000 teams and 50,000 players.

The peasants of Kwangtung have organized their football teams into leagues or divisions, with twenty-eight in the A, or major, division and more than seventy in the B, or minor, division. There are also many teams for youths.

The leading football teams are Peking, Shanghai, Tientsin and the Army team which is known as the "August 1."

TABLE TENNIS

The Chinese have shown remarkable skill at table-tennis and in the World Table-Tennis Championships have held the World Men's Single title since 1959. Jung Kuo-tuan was champion in that year; and in 1961 and 1963 Chuang Tse-tung won the event. The women's world championship singles was won by Chiu Chung-hui in 1961.

WEIGHT LIFTING

As weight-lifters, the Chinese have raised themselves to the top level among the Communist countries which organize competitions among themselves. They have defeated Poland, the East German Socialist Republic and the U.S.S.R. The records they had achieved by 1962 are as follows:

Featherweights class	777 pounds
Lightweight class	854 pounds
Middleweight class	893 pounds
Light Heavyweight class	964 pounds
Heavyweight class	976 pounds

SWIMMING

Swimming is extremely popular and many public swimming pools have been built. In Shanghai alone, in 1961, 2,300,000 tickets for these pools were bought.

OTHER SPORTS

Athletics are enthusiastically encouraged by the Chinese Communist government. In factories and schools workers and pupils are organized into vast teams for the purpose of physical training.

The Westernizing of athletics is almost complete; it includes polo and mountaineering activities which in the West tend to be more specialized. But while the emphasis in China is on mass athletic activities, the individual sportsman is encouraged and, in the interests of national prestige, is elevated to the level of a folk hero.

FOOD AND DRINK

CHINA HAS MADE A CONSIDERABLE contribution in the field of culinary arts; Chinese cooking is noted by gourmets throughout the world for its pungent sauces, succulent meats and crisp, full-flavored vegetables.

"Chow Mein" and "Chop Suey"

Oddly enough, the two foods most prominently featured in Chinese restaurants in the United States and Europe—*Chow Mein* and *Chop Suey* —are not Chinese.

Chop Suey (which in the Cantonese dialect means "miscellaneous odds and ends") was probably introduced by the Chinese who emigrated to the United States to work on the railroads. These immigrants, unable to secure their traditional foods, would take whatever they could find and prepare it in a style vaguely reminiscent of their native land.

Chow Mein (fried noodles) bears no relation to the Chinese dish of fried noodles. It was probably so named because one component of this melange of Western ingredients is fried noodles, although, a completely different variety from those known in China.

The Art of Cooking

Since China was isolated from the Western world for so long, her cooking methods are unique and quite different from European customs. The most common ways of cooking are by the stir-fry method or by steaming. Stir-frying consists of constantly pushing food across the bottom of a *wok*, the chief Chinese cooking vessel. A wok is actually a round-bottomed pot shaped roughly like half a grapefruit. It can be as small as ten inches in diameter or as large as several feet across. By stir-frying, it is possible to cook foods very quickly. This is important in a country where fuel has always been scarce. Steaming is also a fuel-saver. A steamer may be composed of several bamboo segments that fit on top of each other in perforated layers; in this way it is possible to steam several separate foods at the same time. When placed over a vessel in which rice is cooking, an entire meal may be cooked with only a single heat source.

Cooking has always been considered a form of art in China. One ancient proverb states that to be well prepared a dish must smell appetizing as it is brought to the table; whet the appetite by its harmonious color combinations; sound pleasing as the food is being chewed; and taste delicious. Fine Chinese cooking still lives up to these standards.

THE CLEAVER

In the kitchen much of the work done by the cook requires precision and careful attention to detail. Since the Chinese do not use knives at the table, but only chopsticks, the cook must cut food into bite-size pieces, usually before cooking. Cutting is done with a razor-sharp cleaver. When properly used, Chinese cleavers are manipulated just as easily as conventional knives. It is very important for the ingredients in a dish to be cut into symmetrical shapes such as equal-size dice, shreds, squares or any combination of shapes the cook feels are best suited to the foods under preparation. This may be determined either by tradition or by the cook's good judgement.

Regional Variations

Cooking styles vary drastically from province to province. The country can be roughly divided into four gastronomical areas in order to explore these differences. The various styles or schools of cooking are actually named after the places of their origin. The most famous are

Cooks in a restaurant preparing typical Chinese food. Preparation of Chinese food is characterized by the precise and meticulous cutting of the food into small, even pieces. This is so that all the food will cook evenly and quickly, thus conserving fuel, and also because the Chinese do not use knives at the table, merely chopsticks.

offers an abundance of seafood and it is here that the famous Lobster Cantonese was perfected. Cantonese cuisine is distinguished for its roasted meats. Generally, in China ovens are a scarcity. But in the southeast oven cooking produces exquisite squabs, chickens and ducks. The poultry cavity is usually filled with a rich marinade. The bird is sewed securely and hung on racks in large ovens that resemble closets. In this manner the meat is basted from the inside and becomes very juicy and tender. The same unique oven is used for roasting whole pigs and many other types of meat including roast pork and spare-ribs which have been basted in a rich dark marinade made with soy sauce, honey and wine.

Traditional Foods

One method of preserving food that was developed in ancient China is still in use today. This is the process of drying foods. The variety of dried foods seems endless and among the most common are mushrooms, whole ducks which have been boned and pressed, shrimps, oysters, fish, sea cucumber and beancurd. There is also a vast assortment of dried herbs, roots and small creatures such as sea horses that are used medicinally.

DAIRY, RICE AND NOODLES

There has always been a scarcity of dairy products in China and as a result butter, cheese and milk are conspicuously absent from the Chinese diet.

Rice is the backbone of almost all Chinese meals. A peasant may have only a bowl of rice for dinner; a wealthy family may eat a 20-course banquet, but rice will be present all through the meal. There are two basic types of Chinese rice. Glutinous rice and a variety that closely resembles the kind of rice grown in the United States. Glutinous rice is used for making the shiny and translucent rice noodles. It is also used in a kind of flour frequently employed in making Chinese pastries and dumplings. The regular variety of rice, the kind most familiar to Westerners, is cooked by steaming so that it is fluffy, yet firm, and each grain of rice is separate. A bowl of rice is given to every diner and small pieces of fish, meat or vegetables are picked up with chopsticks and eaten, followed by a larger amount of rice. Rice is also used as a complete main dish when the cooked rice is mixed

Canton, Fukien, Honan, Shantung, Szechwan and Yangchow.

THE NORTHEAST

Northeastern China includes the Shantung and Honan schools. This cooking is light and delicate, characterized by the frequent use of scallions, leeks and garlic for flavoring. Probably the most famous creation to come from this region is Peking Duck. In this magnificent dish the duck is hung by its neck for several days to drain the excess fluids and to make the skin smooth and taut. Then it is marinated in wine before being slowly roasted to a deep golden color. Before serving, the entire duck is cut into pieces about two inches square. At the table these pieces of meat are eaten by wrapping them, together with a piece of scallion, inside a thin wheat pancake.

THE NORTHWEST

Poor soil and severe climate in the northwest of China have not per-

mitted the development of colorful cookery. Because of its great distance from the sea there is no seafood and even salt is almost unobtainable. As a result, vinegar is a principle seasoning and the food is not considered as palatable as other cuisines in the country.

THE SOUTHWEST

From the rich agricultural area of the southwest comes the spicy Szechwan school of cooking. Pork is quite popular and almost every preparation includes hot peppers and highly seasoned sauces. Moslems in Szechwan eat beef as their meat since they are forbidden pork in their diets.

THE SOUTHEAST

By far the most outstanding section for variety of foods and distinctive preparation is the southeastern region. Many of the great dishes of China originated in the Canton, Nanking, Yangchow and lesser schools of cooking in this area. Its long coastline with various combinations of meat, vegetables, eggs and seasonings.

In some regions, noodles are eaten in place of rice. One popular type of noodle is called *Lo Mein*. These noodles, made with flour and eggs, closely resemble spaghetti. Since the Italians brought some noodles back to Italy after visiting the Chinese Emperor Kublai Khan, in the 13th century, it is safe to assume that Italian spaghetti had its origins in China. *Lo Mein* noodles, however, are quite long. They are frequently served as part of a birthday celebration; they are called "Long Life Noodles" because the celebrant is supposed to eat his *Lo Mein* without breaking off any of the noodles, thus symbolically having promise of longevity.

A TEA LUNCH

The *Dim Sun* (Tea Lunch) is quite popular in Cantonese restaurants and consists of a great variety of delicate meat or fish-filled pastries. Diners choose their selections from the assortment of the day. It is served from 11 a.m. until about 2 p.m.

Most of the pastries and dumplings are steamed. However, some are fried or boiled; some are sweet, and most are savory or spicey. All are delicious.

SOUPS

Soups are popular throughout China. They include simple, clear chicken stock which may also provide the base for such delicacies as bird's-nest soup. These nests are made by a species of swallow that nests near the seacoast. The birds construct their nests by regurgitating a gelatinous substance which hardens with exposure to air. When used for soup these nests are carefully cleaned, soaked and simmered in broth. After cooking, the pieces of the nest resemble tiny translucent noodles and their flavor is very delicate. This is considered luxury food. The variety of soups is endless and range from gourmet delicacies such as this to hearty peasant soups which are thick and nourishing.

Beverages

Tea (from the Amoy dialect word T'e) was first described in a Chinese dictionary (c. 350 A.D.). Its early area of cultivation was in southwest China.

There are three basic types of tea: green tea, which is unfermented and mild; semi-fermented tea or oolong; and black or fermented tea which is actually roasted rather than fermented. A separate variety is scented tea which is usually made with dried flowers such as chrysanthemum, jasmine or rosebud petals added to green tea giving a perfumed quality to the brew. A cup of tea is offered a guest as soon as he arrives at a Chinese home. This is a never-overlooked symbol of good hospitality. With meals, tea is usually served last; although during a banquet various types of tea may be served between courses to help "change the taste". Tea is also used to help cool off during the summer, warm up during the winter and as home remedies for a variety of ailments.

WINE

Rice wine is the principal alcoholic beverage of China. Unlike Western custom, wine is never consumed alone but always accompanies a meal. Chinese rice wine is similar to sherry in flavor. It takes several years to make this wine. The longer the fermentation and storage, the more the wine is improved.

One custom concerning wine is quite practical. When a daughter is born her father prepares several barrels of wine. By the time she is ready to be married, the wine will also be ready for the wedding feast.

Su Tchwan is considered the finest kind of rice wine. It is pale yellow and may vary in strength.

Another kind of wine that is popular mainly in northern China, where it is made, is *Gaoling*. This is a strong white wine made from wheat.

TIBET

DESPITE ITS ABSORPTION INTO THE Chinese Communist Republic in 1951 and the violent suppression of Ti-

A family seated round a low table prepare small dumplings, or won-ton stuffed with meat. The most popular meats in China are pork, chicken and duck; beef, lamb and mutton are also sometimes eaten.

A Tibetan peasant in the traditional headdress of a horseman. Formerly, the social structure of Tibet was based on three main groups. The nomads, mainly engaged in stock rearing, traveled from place to place in groups, living in tents. The agricultural workers lived in closely organized villages ruled by elders or elected head-men. The upper classes lived mainly in the few cities.

betan individuality in 1959, Tibet still conjures up thoughts of monasteries, inaccessible buildings poised on soaring peaks, and of lamas absorbed in meditation. Tibetan lamas (Buddhist priests) were at one time the most powerful members of the community. Tibet was a theocracy—that is, a state ruled by priests. The priests headed the governing hierarchy. The lowest members of the hierarchy in the monasteries were neophytes, usually boys eight to ten years old. When they reached the age of fifteen, they moved up, provided they had the necessary intelligence, finally becoming lamas.

Life in a Lamasery

At one time, in the famous monastery of Tashi Lumpo, there were about 4000 monks under the direction of four lamas. Their duties were to pray and take part in the festivals which were organized to celebrate religious events.

All novices in the monasteries were under direct supervision of a novice master, a member of the community who had been chosen from among the best monks. In addition to maintaining discipline, distributing food and ensuring that ceremonies were properly carried out, this man had authority to punish.

In theory, Tibetans of the Yellow Hat sect, the reformed and ruling sect, were dedicated to the religious life: sworn to sobriety, they took an oath of chastity and lead an austere life. Under Chinese imperial protection, especially under the Mongol emperors, they became politically powerful. Anyone who opposed them, even when they had abused their power, was severely punished.

At the time of the Chinese Communist invasion, in 1951, there were more than 3000 monasteries. Life in these monasteries was divided between study, religious devotions and festivals, the last being held in spring and autumn.

At these festivals divinities from many sources, often originating in primitive times, were celebrated. Monks in masks and ancient costumes performed traditional dances, some known as "devil dances."

THE ELECTION OF A PRIOR

Every Tibetan monastery had at its head a prior, who was commonly designated with the title of "Living God." The election of the prior took place at a strange ceremony.

When a prior died, the lamas began to search for a boy in whose body the soul of the dead prior was believed to have been re-incarnated. When they believed they had found the right child, they brought him to the monastery. There, some days later, a macabre ceremony took place. The boy was placed on the dead prior's knees; the corpse, which had been preserved by the extremely cold, dry Tibetan air, was seated on a throne. A mantle of richly decorated silk was laid over the living boy and the cadaver; after prolonged prayers and complicated rites the mantle was removed. The priests then loudly proclaimed that the prior's virtues had been transfused into the child.

Students of the occult claim that the chosen boy quickly revealed a precocious knowledge of monastic ways and his duties as prior.

TRUMPETS IN THE VALLEYS

When the ceremony of electing the new prior was completed, the lamas proclaimed the result by blowing on long trumpets, the sound of which reached the most distant valleys. The people, mostly nomadic shepherds, on hearing the trumpets, hastened to the monastery to pay homage and publicly confess their sins. Then they joined in the festivities and celebrations.

Lamas lived solitary lives; they studied ancient practices and are said to have been deeply versed in mysterious occult sciences. Some, it was believed, had unearthly powers. Tales are told of lamas who became hermits, and exposed themselves naked in the freezing cold of high, remote places and came to no harm. A handful of snow was said to melt as soon as it touched their skin, because they could generate, at will, exceptionally strong body heat.

SURPLICE OF BONES

There were initiation ceremonies for novices in which frightening symbols were used. These were designed to inculcate a mystical attitude to life. The ceremonies ended in graveyards.

Tucci, a traveler in Tibet, gave the following account of the ceremonies: "During these rites a kind of surplice made of elaborately carved human bones is used.

"The large breast-plate is made of the bones of an arm and a leg, and has side-pieces, in the form of buckles, made from skulls; small bones, strung together like beads, join the sections of the garment. Images of ancient gods and symbols depicting phases of mystical exaltation are carved on the bigger bones.

"These grisly mantles are used in rituals in which even the most disciplined monks sometimes go mad; some die because of the ordeals they undergo. An aspirant, for example, must retire to a place where corpses are exposed bringing with him a flute made of a human tibia, a skull to use as a cup and a ritual drum made of two skulls over which strips of parchment are drawn tight. When he reaches the cemetery, the aspirant invokes the multitude of evil spirits of Tibetan mythology. To them he offers his body as sacrifice."

THE DALAI LAMA

The chief lama, called Dalai Lama, lived in a monastery on a mountain near Lhasa, capital of Tibet.

Despite the weird elements of magic that had been absorbed into Lamaism, the Grand Lama of Tibet received foreigners with great dignity, pomp and courtesy. He had the demeanor of a great U.S. president or European monarch, and lived in much richer and elaborate quarters. An English traveler, Samuel Turner, who led expeditions to Tibet in the second half of the 18th century, described the Dalai Lama's throne room and court as breath-takingly splendid.

Folk Religion

By introducing Buddhism to Tibet, India modified native beliefs and ceremonies; these originated in an ancient folk religion called *Bon*. This was based on animist beliefs and rites connected with birth, death and the forces of nature.

These pre-Buddhist customs have not been entirely extinguished; in part they were absorbed into Buddhism and in some regions, for example, remote eastern Tibet, *Bon* communities are still to be found.

These are only partly influenced by Buddhism. In their daily life many Tibetans came under the influence of astrological beliefs introduced from China.

COMPLETE BELIEF AND FATALISM

There is not one event or thought in Tibetan life which is not dominated by religion. Birth, death, sickness, thanksgiving for good harvest, marriage and journeys all are fraught with religious symbolism. Tibetans have complete faith in Divine Providence. This has engendered a fatalistic attitude.

They believe that they are protected or threatened by good and bad spirits, invisible but ever present. The good spirits are represented by two compassionate deities, who, if invoked in time of danger, will help them. But they must be invoked with a prayer fervently expressed in the correct formula and clearly spoken.

Traveling in Tibet was full of risks; it was important to choose wisely the day of departure and ascertain how the journey would finish. To know what would happen on the journey, the help of the *Ta*, was solicited. The *Ta*, a sort of benevolent witch, was a woman who could go into a trance in which she saw the past and future. If the forecast was bad, the travelers resorted to special ceremonies to placate evil spirits.

When mountain tracks (proper roads were not built in Tibet until after the Chinese invasion in 1951) were difficult, travelers did not halt to repair them, neither did the people of nearby villages; they murmured invocations to images of benevolent deities, which were carved on the nearby rocks, like wayside shrines in Europe.

MOUNTAIN CAIRNS

If an accident happened en route, it was not attributed to ill-will or neglect on the part of the gods. It was put down to the victim's faults in this or former lives.

A Tibetan traveler would occasionally stop on a high pass, take a stone and loudly shout "Lha ghiallo," ("long live the gods"); he then would throw the stone on to a heap made by earlier wayfarers. Around the top of a pole stuck in the cairn he would wrap a strip of colored cloth. A prayer was written on this piece of cloth and as it fluttered in the wind, the magic spell of the words was thought to waft through the air.

In this way the mountain gods were placated, and the traveler protected.

MAGIC SAFE CONDUCT

For every deity there was a special formula and the wrong formula would not produce the desired effect.

Malevolent powers were many and of different character; some were easily placated, others were haughtily dedicated to evil. The will of the former could be bent; if they were approached in the correct way they became docile. But the malevolence of the latter could be defeated only by a rite of exorcism which paralyzed them.

Influenced by Chinese medicine, illness was attributed to lack of balance in the five humors, which Tibetans believed regulated vital functions, or, more often, to the agression of evil powers. Evil powers were *lu*, dragons or serpents that stood guard at springs and other subterranean waters. At other times

A Chinese actor in the traditional costume of a warrior. In the Chinese classical theater costumes, both ornate and functional, masks and headdresses defined the social status and the character of the wearer, thus playing an important part in communicating the story to the audience. The military history of feudal times has inspired a great number of literary and theatrical works.

Tibetan children at school. Until Tibet was brought under Chinese Communist control in 1950 it was a theocracy, dominated by a priesthood which held all effective power. This led to abuses which had long been abolished in the more advanced countries of Asia and the West. Over the last few years the Chinese Communist government has legislated Tibet's former social structure out of existence. The country is an occupied zone and schools are now run on Marxist-Leninist principles and Tibet's former cultural identity is rapidly being absorbed into that of China.

they were *sadag*, spirits of the soil, but occupying a particular locality and, being jealous guardians of it, quick to take offense at intruders.

THE WITCH DOCTOR'S METHODS

Tibetans believed that many illnesses, especially nervous deseases such as epilepsy or insanity, were due to planetary influences. In this, again, they were akin to their Chinese neighbors. In such cases treatment was not entirely medical; exorcism was required. The exorciser invoked belligerent divinities of fearful aspect; these had many legs and arms. Gradually going into a trance, the exorciser became possessed by the powers he had invoked. He then drove out the demon and pinned it to the ground with a dagger. Thus he rendered it harmless.

In ancient times, it was thought possible, using the right occult physician, to have an illness transferred to an enemy. In more recent times, a likeness of the patient was made of butter and flour. After treatment, the effigy was burned. In more serious illnesses, complicated constructions of wood and colored threads were made; harmful spirits were trapped in these.

Death and Rebirth

Monks were called to a sick person's home where they read to him from sacred books. This reading was done by several monks speaking in chorus. The number of monks depended on the severity of the illness and the sick man's wealth; the reading lasted until the patient either was cured or died. In the latter case, effort was not thought wasted, for by virtue of the reading, the dead person would be reincarnated in good circumstances.

When hope of survival was relinquished, specially trained lamas carried out another ceremony to protect the dying man from rebirth. Tibetans believe life is nothing but sorrow. First the dying person must be made conscious so he will remember what he knows of life; then he must be prepared to avoid reincarnation to which unenlightened or unknowing people are condemned. A celebrated book, the *Bardotodol*, is read aloud to sharpen the sick man's awareness of his past. This is "the book of the intermediate stage between death and rebirth, that simply by hearing it read aloud leads to salvation."

REBIRTH IN HEAVEN OR HELL

The book expresses a common Tibetan belief. According to this belief, there is an intermediate state between life and rebirth which lasts for forty-nine days. During this time conciousness is detached from the body; it finds itself lost wandering on a plain where it is surrounded by ever interchanging lights, brilliant and multi-colored. Those who die in full knowledge of the hollowness of material life know how to dissolve their conscious being and their ephemeral personality in the dim, remote light of the Eternal Being. For others, life begins again; rebirth in paradise or hell, or in a new life will be the results according to the way they live.

FROM ALL TIME

The Tibetans believe that everything in life is pre-ordained; the destiny of a man is the sum total of his previous actions. Each human being personifies a spiritual "continuum" which has unfolded from all time. Men emerge from nothingness; one is what one had been; but one has freedom of will and can change one's destiny. Each one is a separate entity, but may be transformed into something different according to his adherence to religious teaching.

VERDICT OF THE STARS

When the forty-nine days of intermediate birth have passed, the conscious element of the dead person who was unable to understand the instructions that could have saved him is irresistibly attracted toward a new incarnation. Rebirth does not happen by chance.

The new life brings freedom of choice; but certain relationships are predetermined. For example, when young people marry it is not enough that they should love each other, or that the parents should agree; it is essential to have the opinion of the astrologer, so as to ensure that there is no insurmountable cosmic obstacle between the personalities of the betrothed. Consequently, in addition to the intervention of the gods, there is the additional vigilance of the astrologer to make Tibetans cautious in their way of life.

A MAN NEED NOT SUBMIT

In the past, life for the Tibetan oscillated between the present each had created and a fearful, anxious feeling of dependence on forces that any moment might overthrow and annihilate. However, faith in the power of the liturgies and in the magic rites substained the people. They were severely faithful to their cults.

These, as revealed by the ancient masters, were an affirmation of a power by which the human will, properly directed, could master everything. A man need not submit to cosmic laws; snatching their secrets he could dominate them or modify their apparent inviolability.

THE KINDLY PEOPLE

The Tibetans are a kindly people; an English traveler describes them: "Affectionate compassion and natural kindliness are typical virtues of these people. Without ever appearing servile, they always are well mannered and obliging; even Tibetans of high rank are never haughty; all are courteous and good-natured.

"The men like women, but are restrained in their passions; their behavior toward women is without a trace of boorishness or vulgar flattery. More than other Asiatic women, Tibetan women participate in society; they are supreme in the home and true companions to their husbands."

POLYANDRY

Polyandry was traditional in Tibet; a woman gave herself and her property to the brothers of a family The custom's origin is not clear; probably polyandry was adopted because the males greatly exceeded the females; women were relatively scarce, and one man could not aspire to the possession of a wife all to himself. It is possible, too, that custom was influenced by the poverty of a country that could not support an increase in population. Rich men, who could afford the luxury, had exclusive possession of a wife.

Marriage preliminaries were simple. A proposal was made to a girl and was announced by her family. Then came three days of dancing, music and singing. The engagement period ended, the marriage took place immediately. Husbands and wives were not allowed to separate, except by mutual consent. Cases of divorce were rare, perhaps because neither husband nor wife were free to contract a second marriage.

A woman had charge of her husband's earnings; all went into a common purse.

CORPSES ON DISPLAY

It was a Tibetan custom to pay tribute to the dead. Bodies of ruling lamas were displayed in specially made coffins, as sacred objects for public invocation and prayer. Bodies of lesser lamas were cremated and their ashes, contained in hollow metal idols, were put in special galleries dedicated to dead. Bodies of ordinary people were transported to the tops of mountains, or left in remote parts of the countryside. Some were thrown into rivers. Burial was rarely practiced, but a special day was set aside for honoring the dead.

SCARVES AND COMMERCE

Scarves are the most usual gift in Tibet, and exchanging them symbolizes love and affection.

Tibet had little industry; it was a country of busy traders. Gold dust, pearls, diamonds, corals, musk and woolen goods were sold to the Chinese; the Chinese sold Tibetans gold and silver brocades, silks, tobacco, porcelain and dried fruit. To Nepal, Tibet exported rock salt, gold dust and borax, receiving in exchange copper, rice and bales of cotton. No money was used, since the use of money was forbidden by the priests, and all dealings were by barter.

Food and Drink

Game provides the principal meat of the Tibetans. When an animal is killed it is first skinned, then hung by its feet in the cold air. This preser-

ves the meat and gives it an excellent flavor. Tibetan game, thus processed, is difficult to cut and must be divided along the grain of the fibers.

Here is a typical description of a Tibetan lunch: "They placed three small stools before us. Shortly afterward an official appeared with a white metal vessel, its surface embossed with yellow metal. This contained tea. The tea was different from that to which we were accustomed; it was a mixture of water and flour, butter, salt, and sun-dried tea with other rather bitter ingredients. The mixture had been cooked, all together, after being well pounded to make a thorough blend. Gladly we would have dispensed with swallowing the beverage; it looked revolting. But we deemed it prudent to suppress signs of our repugnance. We also ate cooked rice."

A woman pottery seller in Lhasa, Tibet. Lhasa is the main trade center of Tibet, the chief articles of commerce being craft products such as pottery, rugs and articles of gold and silver, and commodities such as grain, tea, spices, drugs and salt. There are a number of important annual fairs at which large markets are held, notably the fifteen-day New Year Festival.

A li vase of reddish clay decorated with blue-black whorls, dating from around the 2nd millenium B.C., preserved in the Cernuschi Museum, Paris. The earliest remains of Neolithic pottery found in China date from not later than 3000 B.C. and consist of funerary urns and pottery for general use. They appear to have been made by hand, although a slow potter's wheel may have been employed in some cases. Designs were applied in red, black, purple or white pigments before firing.

AN ANCIENT CIVILIZATION

THE CHINESE IS THE OLDEST CONTINuous civilization in the world, its history stretching back for more than 4000 years. But the first true historic records are those of the Bronze Age culture of the Shang that flourished from around 1766 B.C. to around 1123 B.C.

The Chinese civilization developed in an area that was largely cut off from the rest of the world. To the east stretched the Pacific, a barrier until modern times; Japan and Korea, China's neighbors to the east, drew their civilization from China. In the west, huge mountains and deserts isolated East Asia. To the north were inhospitable territories reaching to the Arctic, while in the south were jungles inhabited in early times by backward peoples. Because of its geographical situation, the Chinese called their land "the Central Country" or Chung-kuo, which often in the West is translated as "the Middle Kingdom." It is still the Chinese name for China.

For centuries, their neighbors were at a lower cultural level than themselves and as a result, the Chinese believed that their land was the center of civilization. They looked down on all non-Chinese people, including Westerners; when they first came into contact with Europeans they regarded them as barbarians. This attitude was unaffected by technical developments in the West.

The Chinese still regard themselves as the world's most civilized people, and are determined, now that they are establishing an industrialized state under the Communist regime, to win a dominating position in Asia. They regard leadership as theirs by right, as China is the cultural center of the area, and because their land contains nearly a quarter of the world's people.

The Periods of Chinese History

As elsewhere in the world, there were the Paleolithic, or Stone Age, the most ancient human culture, which extended for 500,000 to 1,500,000 years, and Neolithic Ages, 10,000 B.C. to 3000 B.C. in China; these are known by their archaeological remains.

The Shang dynasty, a Bronze Age culture, dates from about 1766 B.C. to around 1123 B.C.

There followed the Feudal Age, covered by the Western Chou period from around 1122 B.C. to 771 B.C. and the Eastern Chou period from 771 B.C. to 222 B.C.

During the latter period there were two subdivisions: the "Spring and Autumn" period, from 770 B.C. to 475 B.C., named after a famous historical work, and the "Warring States" period, from 475 B.C. to 221 B.C., named after a similar book. Confucius, the philosopher whose work has dominated Chinese culture, is traditionally believed to have lived at the end of the "Spring and Autumn" period.

The Feudal Age ended when China was united under the First Chinese Empire. This was accomplished under the short-lived Ch'in dynasty (221 B.C.-206 B.C.). The Ch'in was succeeded by the Han dynasty (202 B.C.-220 A.D.), whose rule covers a period comparable to that covered by the Roman Empire in Europe.

Disintegration and Refounding of the Empire

After the fall of the last Han emperor, the country was divided for more than 300 years, from 220 A.D. to 589 A.D., a time known as the period of the Six Dynasties. China was reunited under a dynasty with only two rulers, the Sui dynasty (589-618). The Sui was succeeded by the T'ang dynasty, which lasted from 618 to 907.

The decline of the T'ang dynasty plunged China into a short period of disunity, known as the period of the

A painting on plaster showing the Buddha in meditation, preserved in the Museum of Oriental Art, Rome. Chinese painting is executed in watercolors, in opaque or semi-transparent washes, using either vegetable or mineral pigments. Figures are outlined in ink and glue is used as a binding medium. The introduction of Buddhism from India around the 1st century A.D. brought an Indian influence to Chinese art.

Five Dynasties and the Ten Kingdoms (907-960). Unity was restored by the Sung dynasty which lasted from 960 to 1279.

The end of the Sung overlaps the beginning of the first foreign empire in China, that of the Mongols. Known as the Yuan, established in 1280, it lasted to 1368. The most famous Mongol Chinese emperor was Kublai Khan, Marco Polo's employer.

The alien Yuan rulers were overthrown by a native Chinese dynasty, the Ming, which reigned from 1368 to 1644. The Ming, in turn, succumbed to another foreign dynasty, the Manchus from the north. The Manchus, known in China as the Ch'ing dynasty, ruled from 1644 to 1912, when the last Chinese empire fell.

A revolt in 1911 put an end to Manchu rule in the following year. In 1912, the Republic of China replaced the empire. In 1949, this republic, long dominated by Chiang Kai-shek, was expelled from the mainland of China by the Communists led by Mao Tse-tung. The Communist People's Republic of China has, since 1949, ruled the mainland from its capital, Peking.

TWELVE ERAS OF HISTORY

China's history can be divided into:
1. The Shang dynasty, c. 1766 B.C.-c. 1123 B.C.
2. The Feudal Age or Chou period, c. 1122 B.C.-222 B.C.
3. The First Empire, made up of the Ch'in dynasty, 221 B.C.-206 B.C., and the Han dynasty, 202 B.C.-220 A.D.
4. The Six Dynasties period, 220 A.D.-589 A.D.
5. The Second Empire, made up of the Sui dynasty, 589-618, and the T'ang dynasty, 618-907
6. The Period of the Five Dynasties and the Ten Kingdoms, 907-960
7. The Sung dynasty, 960-1279
8. The Yuan (Mongol) dynasty, 1280-1368
9. The Ming dynasty, 1368-1644
10. The Ch'ing (Manchu) dynasty, 1644-1912
11. The Republic of China, 1912-49
12. The People's Republic of China (Communist China), 1949-present

A painting of the legendary Emperor Yu, who is traditionally supposed to have lived at the end of the 23rd century B.C. It is recounted that during his life, with the help of an expert on agriculture called Chi, Yu was able to educate the Han people in the reclamation of agricultural land from floods, thus making possible resettlement on the banks of the Yellow River.

RECENT DISCOVERIES AND RESEARCH have shown that the plains of northern China were one of the most ancient centers of human settlement. At Choukoutien, near Peking, skulls and bones of the *Sinanthropus pekinensis* were found; this "Peking Man" is considered to be one of the most interesting predecessors of *homo sapiens*. The remains are dated by anthropologists at about 400,000 B.C.

During the Paleolithic Age, between 20,000 B.C. and 10,000 B.C., men settled in the same region and developed a society of hunters and fishermen. These ancient peoples, anthropologists believe, are the ancestors of the present-day Chinese.

Neolithic Remains

There is, however, a distinct gap between these Paleolithic peoples and the late Neolithic civilization which flourished in northern China somewhat before 2000 B.C. One culture of this age is known as the Yangshao culture. Bows and arrows were used and, as various excavations in Paoki, in Shensi, have shown, millet, and later rice, were grown and pigs, dogs, oxen and sheep were reared. Round and square mud huts were built, grouped together in villages surrounded by moats; and the art of pottery-making was highly developed. Society was organized in matriarchal clans (clans ruled by women) and production and consumption were probably organized along lines of primitive collectivism.

In the Lungshan culture of the same period, men used stone scythes, made pottery on wheels and cultivated different types of plants. This development of agriculture meant that men, as opposed to women, played an increasingly vital role in the life of society. With improved techniques, production began to exceed consumption. Society became patriarchal and gradually tribal; showed signs of division into different social classes, one of the highest being priests.

Early Legends

As with all ancient civilizations, the beginnings of China's history are known only through legends. These, despite their fabulous character and the successive additions and transformations which they have undergone, reflect with a degree of faithfulness the phases, problems and society of China's earliest civilization.

The earliest legends of historic interest concern Huang-ti, the Yellow Emperor. He is said to have lived at the beginning of the 3rd millennium B.C. and to have defeated rival tribes. His wife is credited with having introduced silk-weaving.

THREE WISE EMPERORS

The middle of the 3rd millennium is said to be the era of Yao, Shun and Yu, three emperors subsequently quoted as sages. Each chose his successor because of his suitability, passing over his less worthy son. They are said to have laid the foundations for ancient Chinese society, organizing the system of land ownership and dictating the moral rules on which society was based. They are also credited with having been the first Chinese rulers to bring nature under man's control; and Yu himself is said to have organized the strengthening of the river banks in northern China. He worked for some years at the head of an army of laborers.

According to legends, Yu was the founder of the Hsia dynasty. One source states that this dynasty ruled from 2205 B.C. to 1766 B.C., while another dates it from 1944 B.C. to 1523 B.C. Under the Hsia rulers, agriculture and craftmanship progressed, a class system emerged, more property was privately owned and various great families rose to power.

This dynasty was overthrown by a revolt against a depraved ruler, and the Shang dynasty was founded by a man called T'ang. The Shang dynasty is the earliest period of Chinese history with documentation.

THE SHANG DYNASTY

THE SHANG DYNASTY IS THOUGHT to have lasted from 1766 B.C. to 1123 B.C., or, in the view of some experts, from 1523 B.C. to 1027 B.C.

During the reign of the Shang, some fine bronze work was produced. The dynasty is credited with the development of writing and improvement of weapons; during this period a ruling class emerged.

These developments took place in the provinces of Hopeh and Honan, where the Shang capital, Yin (near the modern town of An-yang) was built in the 14th century.

Shang society was agricultural, its main crops being millet and wheat. Silk production and animal-rearing were also highly advanced.

THREAT OF THE YELLOW RIVER

One of the main problems faced by this and later dynasties was that of controlling the rivers, and stopping the frequent floods which caused loss of life and crops. The Yellow River, as always in China's history, was a serious threat in this respect.

Under the Shang, astronomy was studied, and calendars were made regulating the dates of religious festivals and agricultural events, such as sowing and harvests.

Shang society was made up of three classes: at the top of the scale were the aristocrats in their palaces;

The remains of a circular pit-dwelling of the Neolithic Age, dating from about 5000-4000 B.C., uncovered at Pan-p'o-tsun. Thirty dwellings of this kind were discovered here, proving that the semi-nomadic people of the period often settled in fairly large communities. The holes for pillars to support the roof and the recess for the cooking fire can be clearly seen in this illustration.

then, a long way down, the land-workers or peasants; and at the bottom, were the slaves, who lived in crude pit dwellings.

The aristocracy were the warriors and priests and the Shang emperors could command an army of 5000 men.

The gods worshiped by the Shang were nature deities and their own ancestors. Human sacrifice was frequent.

The emperor headed the religion, and also had supreme political power.

The most famous of the Shang emperors, was Pan Keng, who reigned in the 14th century B.C. and founded the capital, Yin.

The dynasty fell as a result of unrest on its frontiers. The Shang had tried unsuccessfully to bring these regions under Chinese domination, but they remained independent and warlike.

THE CHOU DYNASTY

AFTER THE SHANG CAME THE CHOU dynasty, which reigned from 1122 or 1027 B.C. until 222 B.C., thus making it the longest dynasty in Chinese history.

The Chou were at first strong and efficient rulers; later, however, there were periods of as long as a century, during which their power was seriously curtailed.

During this time, Chinese society changed from its primitive form to the basic form it retained for centuries. The code of behavior, which had a profound effect on Chinese society, originated in this period, and governed the ethical and political life of the Chinese in a unique way.

Chronicles written about this period by followers of the Chinese philosopher, Confucius, call it a Golden Age. So great was their praise of it, that it is difficult to determine what really happened.

A CORRUPT TYRANT

Nevertheless, there are two important Chinese classics, the *Document of History* and the *Book of Odes*, which help to provide a picture of Chou society and history. Archaeology has supplied additional material, so that an almost complete picture can be obtained.

The Chou came originally from the valley of the Wei River, and from the middle of the valley of the Yellow River, in what is now Shensi. They had therefore come into contact with the nomad " barbarians " of the west and north, who lived by herding sheep.

As the Chou rose to power, the Shang power was declining, and the last Shang emperor, a corrupt tyrant, did much to hasten this decline. He was defeated by the leader of the Chou, Wu Wang, at the Battle of Muyeh (1122 B.C.).

The Western Chou Period

The victor, Wu Wang, was helped throughout his reign by the Duke of Chou, his brother. When Wu Wang died, the duke continued to serve his nephew.

They organized their kingdom into states, rather like the states of medieval Europe. That is, a feudal system was instituted. The rulers of the states were the emperor's vassals, and were obliged to pay him tributes and provide him with an army in time of war. Within their own states, however, they had absolute power over the peasants.

The exact number of these states, covering most of the North China Plain, is unknown.

Until 771 B.C. the Chou state retained this form. Because of the location of its capital in western China, the period up to 771 is called the Western Chou period.

THE PEASANTS' BURDEN

Under the Chou, agricultural methods were improved, and a standard was reached far higher than that attained by the Shang. Because of their improved techniques, farmers in the Chou period were able to produce more than ever before, and could maintain a supply large enough to cover their own needs and pay the necessary tributes to their overlords.

Nevertheless, the peasants were burdened with having to fight for their overlords when required, and were also forced to provide labor for public works. Some of these, particularly the control of the waters

A ritual mask of the Chou dynasty (1122-222 B.C.), preserved in the Musée Guimet, Paris. It was during this period that iron began to be used in place of bronze, the first lacquer-work was produced and the crossbow made its appearance as a military weapon.

A bronze ritual vase dating from the 10th-9th century B.C., now in the National Museum of Oriental Art, Rome. Bronze-casting in China began around 1500 B.C., and the Bronze Age is generally considered to have ended around 300 B.C. Most remains of the artistic products of the Chinese Bronze Age are ritual vessels, of which the one illustrated is an example. Such vessels were used to hold offerings to ancestors or were presented by a ruler to his vassals.

of the Yellow River, were of direct benefit to the peasants, but many were only for the enjoyment of their overlord.

The peasants lived in villages, and together, farmed the land leased to them, provided their own farm implements, and took turns farming each part of their land, so that each family would benefit from the more fertile land. The best fields, however, all belonged to the overlord; the peasants cultivated them for him and gave him all the produce.

Besides the peasants, who had some freedom, there were some slaves who were the direct property of the lords.

SPREAD OF CHOU POWER

The organization of the Chou state was much more advanced than those surrounding it, and because of its social and political superiority, the Chou gradually spread eastward and southward. The states on its borders became buffer states, coming partly under Chinese influence, though not wholly part of Chou society.

The advances made in agriculture meant that the Chou could cultivate the newly won territory, much of which had not been farmed before.

Chinese civilization spread outward from the center of the Chou Empire, the capital of which was Ch'ang-an, now known as Sian.

Great developments were made in literature and technology. Chinese civilization at this time began to take a definite and individual shape.

Chou religion was derived from that of the Shang, the worship of nature gods being combined with magic. The emperor was high priest of this religion, and was believed to be able to control the elements and communicate with the gods.

After the 10th century B.C., however, the structure of Chou society began to decay with the barbarians to the west beginning to attack the frontier. Since society was delicately balanced, any weakening of the power

of the emperor, such as that caused by the barbarian attacks, brought about a strenghtening of the power of his vassals.

THE LAST EMPEROR

The overlords of the feudal states, therefore, became virtually independent. Hsuan Wang, who ruled at the beginning of the 8th century, was the last emperor to retain effective control of his empire.

The barbarian attacks increased, until eventually, in 771, the Ch'uan Jung reached the capital and destroyed it. The emperor, P'ing Wang, fled to Loyang, where he established a new capital. This new capital was situated in Honan, fur-

ther to the east, where it was hoped that a new, smaller, but stronger, empire could be founded. The period that followed this move to the east is called the Eastern Chou Period.

The Eastern Chou Period

The Eastern Chou Period lasted from 771 B.C. until 222 B.C. It was not, however, a period in which the Chou dynasty flourished. In fact, the power of the emperors sank to a nominal overlordship, their sole function being that of religious leaders.

The real power was in the hands of the state rulers. Their independence was complete, and some states became very powerful. During the

Above left: *Confucius (551-479 B.C.), the most important Chinese philosopher. Confucius, a native of the state of Lu, advocated the reduction of taxes, the introduction of less severe punishments and the solution of disputes by peaceful means. His insistence on the duties of the subjects toward the state and of children toward their parents established an ethical code which was to have an immense formative effect on Chinese thought and behavior throughout history.*

Above right: *Emperor Shih Huang-ti (221-207 B.C.), the founder of the Ch'in dynasty. Shih Huang-ti is known as "the First Emperor," since he established a firm, centralized government and limited the power of the feudal aristocracy. It was during his reign, in 213 B.C., that there occurred the "Burning of Books," after he issued a decree that all books containing ideas inimical to the state should be destroyed.*

7th century several of these powerful states emerged, notably the state of Chin in the province of Shansi, Ch'i in Shantung, Ch'in in Shensi, Sung in the central plain of the Yellow River and Ch'u in the plain of the Yangtze.

The "Spring and Autumn" Period

This period takes its name from the *Spring and Autumn Annals* which describe the period between 770 B.C. and 475 B.C.

The period is characterized by the rise and fall of several different states. The state of Ch'i, for instance, rose to power in the middle of the 7th century. Its main rival at this time was the state of Ch'u, but under its ruler, Huan, helped by his minister, Kuan Chung, the state of Ch'i gained the support of the others against its rival.

The position was extremely unstable, however, and by the end of the century it was reversed, and another state had become prominent. Between the 6th and 5th centuries new powers emerged, particularly the state of Wu at the mouth of the Yangtze, and the state of Yueh in the present province of Chekiang.

The political situation was further complicated by the introduction of iron. By the 6th century, this metal was commonly used for weapons and agricultural implements. Iron farm implements made possible the cultivation of the Yangtze valley, and this new farm land was fiercely sought after by different states.

The feudal system of land ownership began to break up. Land was bought and sold, and this altered the situation of the peasants considerably. A class of landowners grew up which was not composed of feudal lords. Some of these were small farmers, but many owned large tracts of land.

THREE-CORNERED STRUGGLE

The feudal lords, encouraged by the increased production brought about by the introduction of iron tools, tried to increase their revenue by demanding a larger share of the harvests in tribute.

A series of three-cornered struggles ensued. The conflicting interests were those of the peasants, many of whom were now landowners, the new class of wealthy landowners, and the feudal lords.

Feudal estates began to disappear, and were replaced by privately owned lands. A last blow fell when, early in the 6th century, a new system of taxes was introduced. Taxes were now based on the area of land owned, a system which replaced feudal tributes.

The "Warring States" Period

The "Warring States" period, (475 B.C.-221 B.C.) saw the further disintegration of feudal society.

As its name implies, this was a time when the states were in a continual state of conflict. Fighting took place both in the heart of the empire and in the border regions.

Foremost in the struggle were the states of Yen, in the province of Hopeh, Chao in Hopeh and Shansi Ch'i in northern Shantung, Lu in southern Shantung, Ch'in in western Shensi, Wei in the central valley of the Yellow River, Sh'u in the central valley of the Yangtze, Yueh at the mouth of the Yangtze, and the new state of Shu in Szechwan.

END OF FEUDAL BONDAGE

Many changes were taking place, which affected the structure of Chinese society. The village was no longer the basic unit of agricultural production. Bondage to feudal overlords disappeared, as the power of private landlords grew. Instead of living and working on the estates of the overlords as before, the peasants either owned their land themselves, or rented it from landlords.

As agricultural techniques improved, more manpower was available for working on flood control, and for cultivating and settling the regions on the frontiers, which were being seized from the nomads.

TAXATION AND ARMIES

The breakdown of the feudal system meant that a new kind of government was needed. Feudal society tended to break up into small independent units, which were self-supporting. Now, however, a strong central government was necessary to unite the old states with the newly colonized frontier lands.

Since the feudal overlords were disappearing, a central government was needed to take over responsibility for the control of the rivers. A bureaucracy was necessary to collect taxes, and an army was needed to defend the borders.

Gradually, the necessary centralized government took shape, as one state emerged from the warring states as the supreme power.

THE RISE OF CH'IN

Between 256 B.C. and 221 B.C., the state of Ch'in, in the extreme west of China, rose to power by defeating the armies of the other states.

Many factors contributed to this success. The state of Ch'in had become increasingly prosperous, due partly to the improved techniques of working in iron, and partly to the building of one of China's most important waterways, which was a canal in the Wei river valley, in Shensi, in the middle of the 4th century.

The Minister Shang Yang had introduced important reforms in the middle of the 4th century, which had made Ch'in economically and politically stable. He abolished the feudal system of land ownership, and encouraged the settling of frontier regions. He set up a centralized bureaucracy, and made each village responsible for collecting taxes and administering justice. He instituted military training for the whole population.

These reforms made Ch'in a strong and stable state. Because of this, in the second half of the 3rd century, the prince of the state of Ch'in was able to defeat his rivals and found a united China. He became known to history as Shih Huang-ti, the "First Emperor."

Confucius and the "Hundred Schools"

The reforms which brought Shih Huang-ti to power, gave China new unity and stability. This stability continued until the middle of the 19th century, although it was sometimes shaken by events such as barbarian invasions.

This stability was reinforced by the formulation of a philosophy which governed official life for centuries. During the "Spring and Autumn" period many different schools of thought emerged, partly because of the tensions and uncertainties of society at that time.

In fact, this period is known as the period of the "Hundred Schools." As in ancient Greece, political changes caused philosophers to devote much of their attention to the

A detail from an illustration showing scenes of rural life under the Han dynasty.

problems of political theory.

The most important of these philosophers was called by the Chinese " Master K'ung," *K'ung-fu-tzu* or, as he is known in the West, Confucius (551-479 B.C.).

CONFUCIUS' TEACHING

Confucius' primary concern was to devise a method of government based on correct behavior. He went back to principles of early Chinese society, and stated that it was necessary to maintain a stable society, with every member playing his proper part to maintain order. To do so, nature must be subjected to man's needs, and the welfare of the community should be a primary concern of the government.

Confucius was not deeply concerned about religion; he condemned superstition, and believed that man himself should strive to improve his own situation, rather than rely on the gods.

The virtues he praised were those that helped the ruler and the people to live together in harmony. These virtues were moderation, the acceptance of one's place in society, respect for the elders of the family, trust in the ruler, and for the ruler himself, he advocated a benevolent attitude to his people. The ruler should use persuasion when governing his people and not harsh laws and violence.

Returning to the values of an earlier age, Confucius believed that the older members of the family should direct family affairs. He praised the social order of the period of the legends and that of the Western Chou. His teaching was, therefore, distinctly conservative.

On the other hand, it introduced new values of wisdom and moderation to contemporary society, which had been for a long time governed by violent and capricious rulers.

Mencius and Confucianism

Confucius formulated a series of principles for good government. Mencius (c. 372-c. 289 B.C.), a follower of Confucius, revised these, forming them into a more general political theory.

This process was carried a stage further by Tung Chung-shu (179-104 B.C.), who developed the basic philosophy into a precisely ordered code of behavior for the bureaucracy. In subsequent centuries Confucius' theories of government were developed and elaborated still more, until they became rigid, thus encouraging a policy of conservatism in Chinese government.

Confucianism, therefore, became the basis of Chinese political theory. It was not, however, the only school of philosophy to have an effect on Chinese politics.

A view of a section of the Great Wall of China, which extends from Kansu to the Yellow Sea. Besides providing a definite northern boundary for China in the 3rd century B.C., its forts and garrisons provided an important defensive system against the attacks of nomadic tribes. The Emperor Shih Huang-ti, among his other great construction works, rebuilt the Great Wall as a defense against the Hsiung Nu invaders from the north.

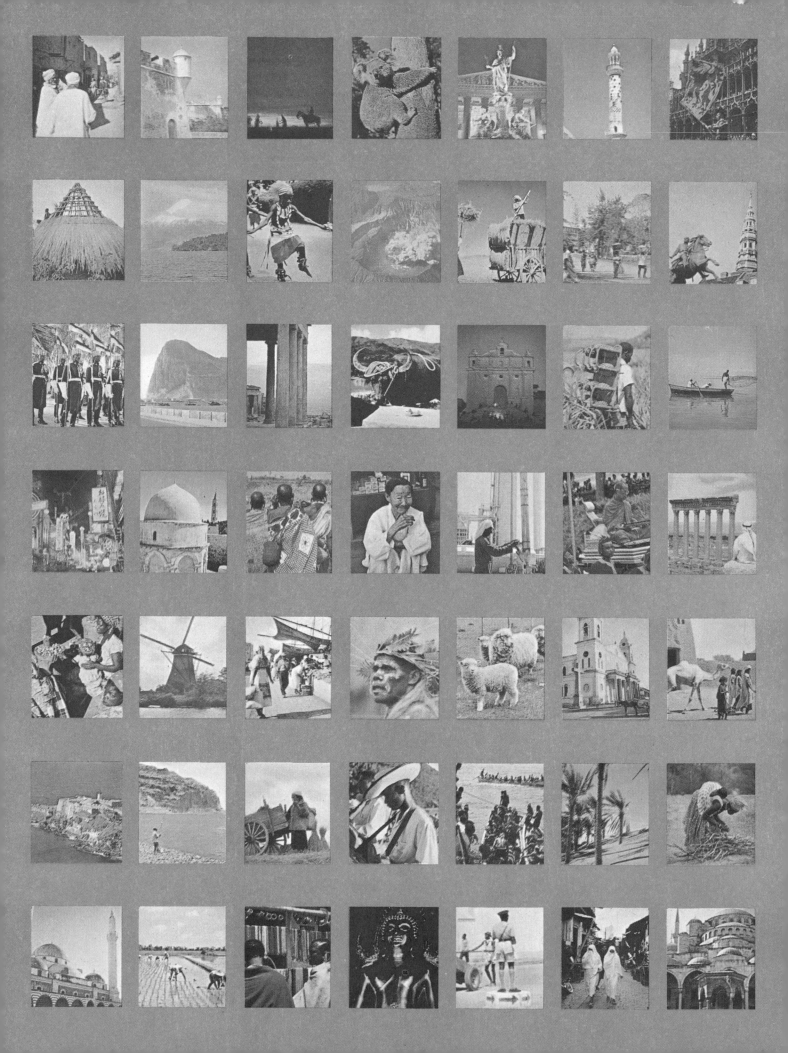